Science as Thinking

The Constants and Variables of Inquiry Teaching, Grades 5–10

Wendy Ward Hoffer

Illustrated by Diana Froley de Forest

HEINEMANN
Portsmouth, NH

Heinemann
361 Hanover Street
Portsmouth, NH 03801–3912
www.heinemann.com

Offices and agents throughout the world

Library of Congress Cataloging-in-Publication Data
Hoffer, Wendy Ward.
Science as thinking : the constants and variables of inquiry teaching, grades 5–10 / Wendy Ward Hoffer ; illustrated by Diana Froley de Forest.
p. cm.
Includes bibliographical references and index.
ISBN-13: 978-0-325-02577-3
ISBN-10: 0-325-02577-0
1. Science—Study and teaching (Middle school). 2. Science—Study and teaching (Secondary). 3. Inquiry-based learning. I. Title.

Q181.H74 2009
372.35—dc22 2008048263

Editor: Robin Manning Najar
Production: Vicki Kasabian
Cover design: Shawn Girsberger
Cover photograph: © iStockphoto.com/Tom Mounsey
Illustrations: Diana Froley de Forest
Typesetter: Eric Rosenbloom, Kirby Mountain Composition
Manufacturing: Steve Bernier

Printed in the United States of America on acid-free paper
18 17 16 15 14 VP 3 4 5 6 7

For my dad,
Dr. John Fawcett Ward,
my first science teacher.

We are what we think.
All that we are arises from our thoughts.
With our thoughts we make the world.

—The Dhammapada

Contents

Preface

Faith is the cornerstone of this book. What is the place of faith in science education? Simply this—when we believe in the unique potential of each of the student scientists in our classes, we dedicate our teaching efforts to drawing forth their brilliance. With faith that every learner can think like a scientist, that every student *is* a scientist, we can find the energy and motivation to develop exemplary learning experiences for all.

Acknowledgments

I gratefully acknowledge all those whose faith in my work brought this book into being. While it is not possible in the confines of these pages to name each, the following deserve special recognition:

For teaching me what I have come to know about learning, I am grateful to every student I have had the privilege to teach, as well as to each teacher I know.

For providing me with an intellectual home and community, I would like to thank the entire staff of the Public Education & Business Coalition, past and present. For her vision in launching the PEBC Science Institute, and her tangible support of this book, I am grateful to Suzanne Plaut. For his excellent science teaching and partnership co-facilitating the PEBC Science Institute, I am thankful for Jeff Cazier. For their support and vision, I appreciate Judy Hendricks, Moker Klaus-Quinlan, Ellin Oliver Keene, and Rosann Ward.

For working with me throughout the process of developing this book, offering their insights and editing, I would like to thank Beth Dorman, Liza Eaton, and John Ward. For sharing their classrooms and students' work with me, I am indebted to teachers and families at Denver East High School, John Dewey Middle School, Kunsmiller Middle School, The Odyssey School, and The Rocky Mountain School of Expeditionary Learning. For being willing to pick up her artist's pen again, I am grateful to my lifelong friend Diana Froley de Forest. For their work wrestling my writing into a real book, I am grateful to Robin Najar, Vicki Kasabian, and all of the folks at Heinemann.

For his patience with and support of this project, I am grateful to my husband, Jeremy. For reminding me that there are few things more urgent than wonder, I appreciate my children.

Introduction

What Is Above the Sky?

"What is above the sky?"

"How come thunder makes that sound?"

"Where do we go when we sleep?"

"Why do bugs die?"

"Am I going to die? Are you?"

Last summer, my four-year-old drove us crazy with questions. And for each answer we offered, she came up with another question:

"What are those pipes?"

"Chimneys."

"What for?"

"For the smoke from the oil refinery."

"What is that?"

"That's where they make crude oil into something we can use in our cars."

"Why?"

"Because when it comes out of the ground, it is not ready to use."

"Why?"

"It needs to be cleaned and changed—refined—before we put it in our cars."

"What for?"

"Cars are powered by combustion engines."

"What's that?"

"A motor that burns gas to make energy to make it go."

"No kidding." She was finally satisfied. I was relieved.

Driven by the curiosity natural to all children, my daughter inquires constantly in an effort to understand. Whether posing questions, experimenting with materials, trying out new behavior, testing my patience, or formulating mud pies in the sandbox, she is making meaning of the world based on her experience.

Inquiry, then, is nothing new to any of us. Students and teachers alike, we each began life with the same drive to comprehend. Sometimes years in classrooms feed the fire of children's curiosity; in other instances, schooling dims that flame. Our challenge as teachers is to enliven our students' lives with experiences that will awaken the scientist innate in each of them in order to spawn lasting understanding. How?

Seeds

I started my career as a terrible teacher. My first semester in the classroom, we studied plants because I love photosynthesis and was sure my middle school students would similarly marvel at nature's miracle. They threw paper airplanes at me. I spent every night wringing my hands, racking my brain, worrying that the kids would not have enough to do to fill the length of the next day's science class. I photocopied all kinds of worksheets—fill in the blanks, crosswords, word searches, coloring tasks—anything I could find vaguely related to botany that would keep them in their seats. Not one seventh grader was enraptured by my science class.

Hoping to pique my students' interest, I decided to risk giving them the freedom to conduct a lab; we spent the two weeks before Thanksgiving break painstakingly preparing for a monumental investigation on optimal conditions for seed germination. My students set up their experiments and left their planted seeds in the classroom over the holidays. We came back from break to find that not one scarlet runner bean had sprouted: the building's heating system had broken down, and the temperature in our classroom had been below freezing for four days.

In retrospect, the seed lab catastrophe was a metaphor for everything that went on in my classroom that fall. Hard as I was working to set things up and keep everyone going, nothing was happening. I would walk into the room and teach my heart out every day, only to return the next to find my students more rambunctious and my resolve withering. By December, I could look back and count up the long list of readings, activities, worksheets, and lecture notes on the number of topics we had covered. But what did my students really understand about any of it? What did they care? I had to be honest with myself: I had no idea.

Time

It was time to stop and think. As we embarked on our next unit—the solar system—I was determined to refine my teaching in ways that would require the students to do more of the thinking and talking in class. Influenced by exemplary colleagues, I puzzled to design a culminating task for this unit that would be a true demonstration of students' understanding. I knew that worksheets and tests requiring the memorization of isolated facts were not taking us where I wanted to go. I scavenged to find what we could, or should, be doing instead.

One essential concept I wanted all to comprehend was the astronomical meaning of our units of time: a day, a month, and a year. "If my students really understood the idea of where a day, month, and year came from, what would they be able to do?" I asked myself. With this question in mind, I decided to brush aside the travel brochures to the solar system project I had initially planned. Instead, I asked learners to work in small groups to make calendars for different planets, based on that planet and its moon(s)'s rotation and revolution rates. I had no clue where this would take us.

What seemed like a good idea at the time turned out to be excruciatingly difficult conceptually and mathematically for my students. Identifying the correct data, accurately lining up the necessary ratios, then completing the calculations with precision took several students to the end of their rope. I ended up teaching a lot more math than I had anticipated. Their work produced unruly results: A day longer than a year? Three days every two years? Can these be right? How do we draw that? Students were forced to test their understanding of the units—day, month, and year—and then struggle through the task of creating calendars to represent the realities of their calculations. Smoke was coming out of everyone's ears. Everyone's.

As overwhelmingly difficult and ridiculous as this project was for many of my students, at last I felt like I was doing something right. Students were thinking, puzzling, talking with one another about their work. Students cared. Students tried. Students learned.

While none of us will likely ever need a calendar for Jupiter, the process of its creation was engaging and evocative for my once-disinterested students; in working on this project, learners did attain my stated understanding goals—comprehending the astronomical meaning of our units of time. The final products, their planet calendars, were marvelous representations of scientific understanding, as well as of a great many other things students learned along the way about math, cooperation, art, and relativity.

In the years since, I have worked backward from that "aha" moment, deconstructing the many facets of curriculum and instruction integral to engaging students in science inquiry which culminates in understanding. Throughout my years in the classroom, I puzzled to devise interesting scientific thinking opportunities for my students. In my current work as a teacher educator and staff developer, I am inspired by hundreds of teachers similarly motivated to examine and revise their practice.

This book is a collection of experiences and ideas—mine and others'—which I hope will be helpful to you on this same path, ready to reflect deeply about inquiry, about teaching science to promote thinking in service to understanding.

Why Read This Book?

Based on a "minimal set of criteria," 93 percent of American adults are scientifically illiterate. These were the findings of Jon Miller of Northern Illinois University in 1992. He defined scientific literacy as possessing basic vocabulary of scientific and technical terms, understanding the process and methods of science, and understanding the impact of science and technology on society (Williams 1992).

The 2006 Program for International Student Assessment compared fifteen-year-olds from thirty countries; America's students ranked twenty-first in science and twenty-fifth in math (National Center for Educational Statistics 2008). Simultaneously, the decrease in graduates from American high schools pursuing graduate work and careers in science and engineering suggests that there is vast room for improvement in science education in America (Matthews 2007).

We Need Science

Beyond the goal of raising test scores and sparking engineering careers, science's wonder and explaining power have the potential to delight and inspire people of all ages. As professor Brian Greene explained in a *New York Times* article, "We must embark on a cultural shift that places science in its rightful place alongside music, art, and literature as an indispensable part of what makes life worth living" (Greene 2008). Science, understood, offers us a sense of meaning and perspective.

In addition to science's aesthetic value, science is an integral part of our lives: the tools and comforts we enjoy, the food we eat, the health care we rely on all are products of science.

Perhaps more pressing, science has the problem-solving power to preserve life as we know it. At present, humans face unprecedented environmental, health, and social problems—global warming, the AIDS pandemic, nuclear waste disposal issues, unmet energy needs—that must be solved in the near future. While we could argue about the severity of these situations, the causes, or where to place blame, we can agree that our students deserve to marvel at, understand, and be empowered to help preserve the world in which we live.

We Need Scientists

Youth today can and must develop a sense of competence as scientists. Science itself does not explain the world, solve problems, or cure disease; it is the great minds of *scientists* that accomplish these feats. Learners in our classrooms must develop a sense of themselves as competent scientific thinkers capable of understanding complex scientific dilemmas, formulating opinions, and solving problems. We teachers can look within our classrooms, within our curricula, and within ourselves to find the means to create greater opportunities for scientific thinking by our students.

Book Structure

In this book, we explore "inquiry" linked to "big ideas" as a means to enhance students' thinking and understanding in the context of any instructional strategy. We examine the workshop model, dissect the classroom culture and the carefully crafted tasks we can all create to ensure that our students are learning. Through a variety of examples, I offer the means to transform commonplace curricula into exemplary learning opportunities for all of the young scientists in our care.

This book is organized into two sections: constants and variables. You may elect to read straight through, or to duck in and out of chapters that apply to your current needs. My hope is that you will take the time to go through at least the first five chapters, the constants, sequentially since they lay important groundwork for the variables section.

Constants

The constants section represents important mainstays in any science classroom, regardless of the specific content or learning task. In this section, I explore five questions: What is inquiry? What are we teaching? How are we teaching? Who are we teaching? How will we know when they know? The answers are bundled into five chapters that investigate information integral to teaching science for understanding.

- Inquiry
- Big Ideas
- Workshop
- Assessment
- Culture

Variables

The second section, variables, surveys instructional staples common to many science classes and offers specific strategies for improving each in order to deepen classroom opportunities for student thinking and learning. These chapters delve into:

- Labs
- Demonstrations
- Lectures
- Discussion
- Reading
- Projects
- Activities
- Fieldwork

Format

Within both sections, each chapter shares a common format, and most include the following:

- Think Tank questions inviting you to reflect on your current practice,
- a typical teaching scenario presenting an instructional staple,
- reflection questions based on that scenario,
- a case for modifying the typical scenario to engage students more deeply as thinkers,
- strategies for refining the chapter's featured teaching practice,
- planning questions to help you put the theory presented into practice,
- sample responses to the planning questions,
- model implementation of the suggested planning steps, and
- sample rubrics.

"If We Knew Better, We Would Do Better"

The vignettes found in this book are composite tales of teachers just like you and me striving, as we all are, to create optimal learning opportunities for young people.

A few years ago, Danise Korb (a veteran science teacher who benefited from the coaching and staff development work of my colleague Moker Klaus-Quinlan) explained how involvement with the Public Education & Business Coalition (PEBC) had positively impacted her teaching practice. She, like all teachers, always wanted to do the very best for her students—but had often felt isolated in her own classroom, not knowing how to improve or where to go for support. "If we teachers *knew* better, we would *do* better," she explained, grateful for her opportunity to begin to "know better."

Danise's comment inspired me to create one special exemplar, Ms. Knewbetter Dobetter, who represents the aspiring teacher in each of us. In the closing sections of these chapters, Ms. Dobetter (a composite character) models for us her thinking, planning, and teaching as she strives to improve her practice. For the purpose of this book, Ms. Dobetter teaches all grade levels and strands of science, though this aspect of her character is purely fictional.

Who Should Read This Book

As a teacher, teacher educator, and staff developer with the PEBC, I work with a broad range of teachers: beginning to veteran, primary level to high school advanced placement, urban to rural, those who rely entirely on textbooks or kits to those who never open them . . . the variety is perfuse. Whether visiting classrooms, coaching teachers individually, conducting onsite staff development workshops, or presenting teacher Science Institutes, I am always struck by the dedication and commitment of the educators I meet. I learn from every one of them. My hope is that teachers from the same diversity of settings and approaches will each find something of value in this book.

The science content and sample lessons shared here are drawn from a breadth of classroom experiences and teacher conversations, and designed to address the needs and interests of teachers working with students in grades five through ten. I trust that as you read you will be able to extrapolate from these composite models to imagine how the ideas and strategies presented here could be applied in your own unique situation, whatever grade level and scientific discipline you teach.

In some ways, teaching is like sowing seeds. We plant experiences, and learning sprouts from them. Under optimal conditions understanding blossoms. I offer this book as a gardener's guide, full of strategies for maximizing the results of your hard labor.

I am sure that you are doing so many things well already. As you read, consider how you can build on what you *already* know and do to take students to new heights in inquiry, thinking, and understanding. My hope is that this book will give you a few more ideas and insights, inspiring you to create for your students richer, deeper opportunities to experience science as thinking.

Constants

Are your students thinking like scientists today? This is the measure of your teaching.

The five chapters in this section present key means to enhance learners' scientific thinking opportunities. Just as the five fingers of your hand collaborate continuously, these five constants—inquiry, big ideas, workshop, assessment, and culture—can work in concert to create a context where student scientists thrive.

What is inquiry? In Chapter 1, "Inquiry," I begin by explaining this familiar term as defined by the National Research Council. I discuss how inquiry can promote thinking, then offer various ways we can weave inquiry into students' everyday learning experiences, whether they are conducting an in-depth investigation or engaging in other important science work.

What are we teaching? In Chapter 2, "Big Ideas," I explain the value of connecting content learning to overarching themes that intersect all the disciplines of science. These big ideas can help us as teachers to hone our instruction around central and important concepts, as well as assist students in making connections between discrete units of study within their growing body of scientific knowledge.

How are we teaching? In Chapter 3, "Workshop," I present the workshop model as a structure for designing classroom instruction around significant blocks of independent work time. Starting with a minilesson to set the stage, students can then, with guidance and support, engage in working and thinking as scientists for the majority of the class time. A workshop closes with time for sharing and reflection.

How will we know when they know? In Chapter 4, "Assessment," I describe the importance of assessment *for* learning. To this end, we as teachers need to clarify understanding goals and learning targets at the outset of an instructional sequence, then check for students' understanding before, during, and after learning activities. I offer a variety of assessment ideas and suggest strategies for rubric making, tracking student progress, and grading.

Who are we teaching? In Chapter 5, "Culture," I discuss the essential elements of classroom community and positive peer culture that catalyze students' science learning. I describe ways that classroom norms, the physical setting, the structure of learning activities, and feedback systems can all work symbiotically to create a productive culture of thinking and understanding.

Each chapter offers thinking points and thorough planning questions. The planning questions from all five chapters are not meant to be worked on all at once; that could be overwhelming. Rather, each set offers you a different angle from which to examine and refine your teaching.

These five constants lay the groundwork for the second section of the book, variables. In those later chapters, you will see many more examples of how the constants interweave to support student thinking.

CHAPTER 1

Inquiry

Inquiry is scientific thinking. Students learn science content as well as the nature of science through cognitive experience with the essential features of inquiry.

Think Tank

- Why is inquiry-based instruction important?
- Why should students inquire?
- How do my own experiences of inquiry as a learner affect my teaching?
- How does my understanding of inquiry inform my teaching?

Step with me into a middle school classroom to see an all-too-typical example of "inquiry" being implemented. Keep your eyes and ears open to see to what extent students are thinking like scientists.

"Inquiry into Electricity," a photocopied handout, waits in front of each learner. The tables are ready with tubs of brightly colored wires, shiny new batteries, and a collection of flashlight bulbs. Mrs. Duke gets started:

"Don't touch anything," she begins emphatically. "Today, we are going to do an 'inquiry' lab on electricity. Who would like to read the introduction to us?" A tall boy with a confident voice begins reading aloud from the handout. The text explains how electrical circuits work. As he reads, Mrs. Duke records selected words on the board:

circuit   current   parallel   resistance   series

	Circuit 1	Circuit 2	Circuit 3	Circuit 4	Circuit 5	Circuit 6
Did the bulb light up?						
Was it bright or dim?						

FIG. 1.1 *Data Table*

When he's done, the teacher instructs the class to complete Section A of the "lab worksheet" by going back through the text and finding the meanings of the terms on the board.

Mrs. Duke invites students finished copying definitions to move on to Section B, replicating six different circuits sketched on the handout, and recording observations in a data table something like Figure 1.1.

Learners cooperate to connect the supplies in ways that duplicate the circuits shown: one battery with one bulb, then two batteries in series with one bulb attached, next two batteries in parallel with one bulb, next two batteries with two bulbs in series, and so on. Mrs. Duke bops from group to group troubleshooting faulty circuits and correcting confusion about the difference between series and parallel, a common mistake. Students remain in their seats, engaged in the hands-on task, working together:

"Which number are we on?"

"Three."

"Okay, bright or dim?"

The atmosphere is calm and productive. The students are busy, their teacher relaxed.

With five minutes left to the bell, Mrs. Duke stops the class and tells learners their homework: "Complete the analysis questions on the back of the lab worksheet."

1. What is a circuit?
2. What is resistance?
3. What is the difference between parallel and series?
4. In your investigation, which circuit produced the brightest bulb?
5. In your investigation, which circuit produced the dimmest bulb?

Students calmly sort the materials back into the tubs on their tables, click their binders shut, and wait for the bell. Mrs. Duke smiles as the group files out.

Reflection

In what ways did the students' tasks mirror the work of professional scientists?

What kinds of thinking were students asked to do during this science class?

What would you predict that learners came to understand through this experience?

The above example illustrates how far science teaching has come, and yet how far we still have to go. Many schools and curricula have transitioned from a "sit and get" instructional format to embrace more hands-on learning experiences like this where students grasp materials, assemble models, and record their own authentic (yet predictable) data.

But the *next* step we need to make in science curriculum development and science teaching is to move from hands-on to *minds*-on. The learners described above—while calm, engaged, and busy—were only reading for definitions, following directions, replicating models, and recording data. They were not invited to experience the essence of inquiry; they were not asked to think as scientists. Below, I elaborate on what such thinking entails.

Elusive Inquiry

We are heading into murky waters here. Students love kinesthetic tasks. In my own early teaching, I was prone to mistake *engagement* for *learning*. For example, when my class studied the rainforest, we constructed a three-dimensional, twelve-cubic-foot life model of a jungle out of craft paper in the back corner of my room. Cutting, taping, coloring—students were in heaven. Maybe they were learning a few things, but it wasn't *science*. I somehow made the mistake of thinking open-ended and active meant "inquiry."

In some classrooms I visit as a staff developer, I see teachers at the opposite end of the spectrum, relying on kits and texts that march through procedural tasks like the "Inquiry into Electricity" described above without engaging in any higher-order thinking—questioning, reasoning, or synthesizing.

What, then, is inquiry-based instruction? It is *not* chaos. It is *not* a curriculum. It is a *stance*.

To design for student inquiry, teachers must ask students to engage with science content in the same way that professional scientists think about and come to understand the world.

As described by a high school student in Figure 1.2, scientists wonder, question, reason, infer, justify, and explain. The student scientists in our classes can—and deserve—to do the same.

Creating an inquiry-based classroom starts simply with believing in students' ability to think well. Regardless of the time, texts, resources, or materials available, skilled teachers can engage students' good minds daily, whether through long-term investigations or simple conversations.

Experience with Inquiry

"Talk about a time when you *felt* like a scientist." I often ask this at the beginning of a science staff development workshop. Teachers share all kinds of examples:

> "I experimented and came up with the best possible recipe for red velvet cake for my sister's wedding."
>
> "As a kid, playing in the stream behind my house, blocking and controlling the flow of water."
>
> "Working with my mother to research the best treatment for her cancer."
>
> "Figuring out how to get rid of the gophers digging up our school's soccer field without killing them."

Scientists are the modern day explores of our world. They probe the far reaches of human understanding. They commit themselves to understand how and why our world works the way it does. Their life's work help us move into the future. Scientists have a natural inquizitive personality, they do not just memorise facts but they think why. When they want to know something, they work their very hardest to find out the answer. They push through all drawbacks to find the right answer. They stop at nothing to teach others what they know. All of these things is what it mean to be a scientist.

FIG. 1.2 *Student Perspective: What does it mean to think like a scientist?*

FIG. 1.3 *A high school student's depiction of a scientist*

I am always surprised how very few teachers, in response to this question, tend to describe classroom experiences or even those that took place in an academic context. Most people seem to think of themselves as scientists when they are figuring something out for themselves. Others think of scientists as a small, elite, stereotypical group, as depicted by the high school artist of Figure 1.3. Unfortunately, few of the many teachers I've met jump to share a memory of "being a scientist" from their years as a student.

Aristotle never copied definitions from a glossary. Galileo never filled out a worksheet. Einstein did not develop the theory of relativity by following directions. Sure, each of these great scientists began life acquiring a certain knowledge base, but their most important work is the result of wondering, reasoning, and imagining. These thinking skills, combined with their content knowledge, equipped them to make monumental discoveries.

Great discoveries begin with small ones. When we organize our classrooms to create opportunities for students to experience the latter, it is more likely that they will believe in their ability to pursue the former.

Inquiry Defined

Over the past twenty years, leading science educators have worked hard to develop documents describing what science is important to know and how we should best teach that content. Across all of the efforts of the National Science Foundation, National Research Council, and the American Association for the Advancement of Science, "inquiry" came out on top. Inquiry, these astute organizations agree, is the most important aspect of science we ought to teach.

In defining student inquiry, the National Research Council offers the following:

> Inquiry is a multifaceted activity that involves making observations; posing questions; examining books and other sources of information to see what is already known; planning investigations; reviewing what is already known in light of experimental evidence; using tools to gather, analyze, and interpret data; proposing answers, explanations, and predictions; and communicating results. Inquiry requires identification of assumptions, use of critical and logical thinking, and consideration of alternative explanations. (National Research Council 1996, 23)

More, then, than *doing* what scientists *do*, inquiry involves *thinking* as scientists *think*.

Inquiry-based instruction does not mean pandemonium—students running helter-skelter between the aquarium and the autoclave with no sense of order or direction. It does not mean sacrificing content for process.

Imagine the work of Thomas Edison painstakingly tinkering toward the first light bulb or Marie Curie carefully cataloguing the qualities of radioactive substances; professional scientists require freedom within structure. Similarly, as teachers designing for student inquiry, it is our duty to scaffold engaging, structured real-world science experiences, rich with opportunities for learners to think deeply about science as scientists.

Inquiry Alive

Watching eighth grader Taylor Jones work would convince anyone of the virtues of an inquiry-based classroom. As a teacher, I asked my students to build mousetrap cars. They wrestled to figure out how to transfer the potential energy of the trap into the kinetic energy of forward motion, how to attach wheels to reduce friction, and how to keep things going in a straight line. Everyone marveled at Taylor's creation: CD wheels propelled by a mousetrap arm that had been extended a full eight inches with a chopstick to create more forward motion from the string tied between the chopstick and wrapped around the vehicle's thin axle. It went furthest of all. We all cheered at his innovation and insight, noticing that he found and extended the limits of the mousetrap's power with that chopstick. Classmates were spurred on to revise their designs.

Why Inquiry?

The seminal volume *Science for All Americans* illuminates the importance of scientific literacy for all. The authors stress the importance of both the teaching and learning processes mirroring the process of scientific inquiry. In the chapter "Effective Learning and Teaching," the authors advise,

> Do not separate knowing from finding out. . . . Science teaching that attempts to impart to students the accumulated knowledge of a field leads to very little understanding and certainly not to the development of intellectual independence and facility. (American Association for the Advancement of Science 1990, 202–203)

Science teaching and learning, then, must include the excitement and wonder, the stresses and struggles experienced by professional scientists in their work. Picture a cluster of hushed learners hunched over a single ant watching to see which of their food offerings she will choose. Imagine a gaggle of anxious adolescents awaiting the outcome of their fifth trial building a toothpick suspension bridge that will hold the contents of their coin purses.

When we teach science through student inquiry, we prepare learners to understand not only science *content* but also science as a distinct way of *knowing*—one that expands from curiosity, requires active engagement, relies on evidence, and takes place in a community of discovery.

Inquiry Culminates in Understanding

In his chapter, "What Is Understanding?," David Perkins (1998) names understanding (as distinguished from knowledge and skill) as a unique goal of teaching: "In a phrase, understanding is the ability to think and act flexibly with what one knows. To put it another way, 'an understanding of a topic is a flexible performance capability' with an emphasis on flexibility" (40). In other words, when we truly understand something, we can demonstrate that understanding in a variety of ways and under a range of conditions.

The goal of inquiry-based instruction is for learners to develop their understanding of science content, as well as the ways in which scientists think about and understand the world. This means that in addition to students being able to recall knowledge and replicate skills, they will also (and more importantly) be able to demonstrate understanding by transferring that knowledge and those work habits to new, related problems and questions.

For example, if students truly understand the effects of gravity on Earth, they will be able to make reliable predictions about the behavior of certain toys aboard the space shuttle in freefall orbit above the Earth, as NASA invites learners to do through the slightly dated curriculum "Toys in Space."

Teaching inquiry-based science for understanding is like building a trellis for a runner bean plant: the culminating product of each task or investigation in an inquiry-based science class—whether a written reflection, graphic lab reports, or a three-dimensional model—demonstrates students' individual understanding, their ability to transfer and apply what they know to a new context. In other words, students would be unable to complete these culminating tasks if they did not grasp the key concepts. For example, Taylor's insight (see sidebar above)—finding and overcoming a system's weakness by lengthening the mousetrap's arm—is an essential engineering skill that he taught the class, one that could be transferred to a variety of related problems.

Inquiry-based instruction does allow students opportunities to ask many questions, to engage in hands-on experiences, and to veer (on occasion) from the curriculum map—echoing the sorts of approaches actual scientists use (see Figure 1.4). At the same time, teachers can design, define, and assess the learning goal of each experience.

Teaching for Inquiry

I don't know where you went to school, but my own memories of learning science in elementary, middle, and high school include a lot of rote memorization of important facts: the equation for photosynthesis, the rock cycle, the chambers of the heart. Much as I enjoyed the classes, I remember very little inquiring, creating, or designing. I knew I was learning about the content of science, but I did not feel like a scientist.

For those of you who, like me, did not learn science in an inquiry-based environment, implementation of inquiry as a teacher becomes all the more challenging. In order to develop our vision, we must dissect inquiry into its component parts, its essential features, presented in the following section. Inquiry changes our job as the science teacher.

Teachers I know working to promote student inquiry in their classrooms find that their role changes from that of police officer or accountant to one of ally and coach. When students are truly engaged in thinking about what they are learning, we do not need to bait them with points or chase them back to work with threats of going late to lunch. We have the opportunity instead to serve as a resource, consulting with learners about their growing understandings. What a relief!

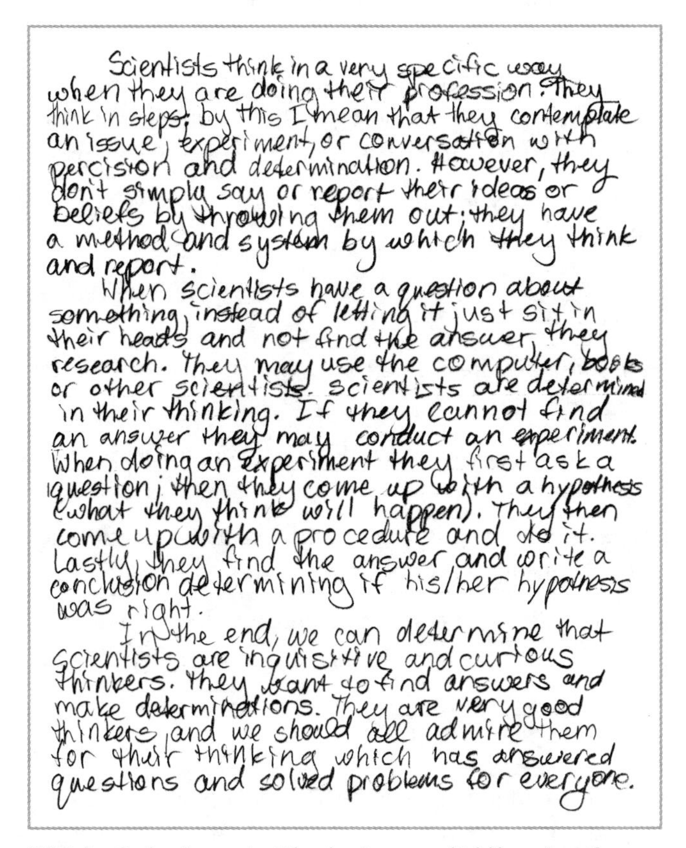

Scientists think in a very specific way when they are doing their profession. They think in steps; by this I mean that they contemplate an issue, experiment, or conversation with percision and determination. However, they don't simply say or report their ideas or beliefs by throwing them out; they have a method and system by which they think and report.

When scientists have a question about something, instead of letting it just sit in their heads and not find the answer, they research. They may use the computer, books or other scientists. scientists are determined in their thinking. If they cannot find an answer they may conduct an experiment. When doing an experiment they first ask a question; then they come up with a hypothesis (what they think will happen). They then come up with a procedure and do it. Lastly, they find the answer and write a conclusion determining if his/her hypothesis was right.

In the end, we can determine that scientists are inquisitive and curious thinkers. They want to find answers and make determinations. They are very good thinkers and we should all admire them for their thinking which has answered questions and solved problems for everyone.

FIG. 1.4 *Student Perspective: What does it mean to think like a scientist?*

After an initial investment of time and energy revising curricula and training students to become more independent, learners in inquiry-based classrooms are highly motivated; thinking and learning are raised to new heights.

Inquiry Is Higher-Order Thinking

Benjamin Bloom's taxonomy of learning behaviors distinguishes higher-order thinking from less complex mental tasks. As we look at a summary of Bloom's work in Figure 1.5, we see many of the kinds of thinking professional scientists do—demonstrate, analyze, design, hypothesize, invent, develop, judge, justify—situated toward the top (higher-order thinking) end of the chart.

Evaluation	Critique, Judge, Justify, Recommend
Synthesis	Create, Design, Develop, Hypothesize, Invent
Analysis	Analyze, Categorize, Compare, Contrast, Separate
Application	Apply, Compute, Construct, Demonstrate, Solve, Use
Comprehension	Describe, Explain, Illustrate, Paraphrase, Summarize
Knowledge	Define, Label, List, Name, State, Write

FIG. 1.5 *Bloom's Taxonomy (adapted from the work of Benjamin Bloom)*

These higher-order thinking skills are important in every content area. For science learners, they map closely to the Essential Features of Inquiry presented by the National Research Council. Look at the verbs:

- *engaging with scientifically oriented questions* involves creating, hypothesizing, and inventing;
- *giving priority to evidence* requires comparing, contrasting, and categorizing;
- *developing explanations based on evidence* entails analysis, invention, and justification;
- *connecting explanations to scientific knowledge* involves analysis and judgment;
- *communicating and justifying* requires creativity, development of ideas, and justification.

As we work with these essential features to develop students' capacity for inquiry, we have ample opportunities to promote higher-order thinking.

School-based science inquiry should be a vision, not a guilt trip. Not every activity can be a titillating scientific zenith; throughout the course of a day, a week, or a year, our classes will reflect different facets and levels of inquiry. Yet when we believe students can and should think like scientists, inquiry methods can guide us to create increasing opportunities for learners to do so, even in small ways, within the work we are doing in class each day.

Essential Features of Inquiry

Instructional strategies that encourage and support students' thinking foster ideal conditions for inquiry.

To help us get a better sense of what students may be doing and thinking about in an inquiry-based classroom, the National Research Council (2000) presents five Essential Features of Inquiry:

- engaging in scientifically oriented questions;
- giving priority to evidence in responding to questions;
- formulating explanations;
- connecting explanations to scientific knowledge; and
- communicating and justifying explanations.

These features offer us a useful starting point in our thinking about and planning for student inquiry. Though each is valuable and important, we need not address them all at once. For example, when conducting a lab to investigate the effect of stimulants on brine shrimp, you might select one of the features of inquiry to teach explicitly through that learning experience, allowing yourself to guide the students more closely through the other features at another time.

Inquiry-based instruction can include a broad range of instructional methodologies adjusted to suit the content and context; later in this chapter, I offer you specific ideas for engaging students in each of these features.

Developing Student Self-Direction

The National Research Council (NRC) developed a table (Figure 1.6) demonstrating how a student's experience of each of the features of inquiry can vary along a continuum from more to less teacher direction and less to more student self-direction. In presenting this chart, the NRC is careful not to pass judgment on either end of the continuum but instead to acknowledge that our lessons and units range in the number of inquiry features they incorporate, and the extent to which each feature allows for student self-direction.

Later in this chapter, I elaborate on each of these five features individually. For now, let us consider an approach to teaching all: In most classes, it is not appropriate to give students complete ownership of each of these inquiry features within every learning sequence, especially early in the year. Yet the more scaffolding and then autonomy we can offer our students in each of the areas described above, the more learners will experience inquiry firsthand and develop their capacity to reason as scientists.

Essential Features	Variations			
1. Learner engages in scientifically oriented questions.	Learner poses a question.	Learner selects among questions, poses new questions.	Learner sharpens or clarifies question provided by teacher, materials, or other source.	Learner engages in question provided by teacher, materials, or other source.
2. Learner gives priority to evidence in responding to questions.	Learner determines what constitutes evidence and collects it.	Learner directed to collect certain data.	Learner given data and asked to analyze.	Learner given data and told how to analyze.
3. Learner formulates explanations from evidence.	Learner formulates explanation after summarizing evidence.	Learner guided in process of formulating explanations from evidence.	Learner given possible ways to use evidence to formulate explanation.	Learner provided with evidence and how to use evidence to formulate explanation.
4. Learner connects explanations to scientific knowledge.	Learner independently examines other resources and forms the links to explanations.	Learner directed toward areas and sources of scientific knowledge.	Learner given possible connections.	
5. Learner communicates and justifies explanations.	Learner forms reasonable and logical argument to communicate explanations.	Learner coached in development of communication.	Learner provided broad guidelines to sharpen communication.	Learner given steps and procedures for communication.
	More ← Amount of Learner Self-Direction → Less Less ← Amount of Direction from Teacher or Materials → More			

FIG. 1.6 *Essential Features of Classroom Inquiry and Their Variations*

While there is a time and place for the range of student self-direction, our goal as teachers training young scientists is that step by step, over the course of a school year, we coach our students in the thinking skills necessary to work independently toward the left hand column of the chart.

The Need for Guided Inquiry

In my naiveté as a new teacher, I asked my students to design their own sundials. I thought it would be really clever of me to supply cardboard, scissors, and an open door to the playground, then leave the whole project open-ended. It was ridiculous. Picture fast-moving seventh-grade boys, asphalt, and sharp objects. What I did not realize at the time was that self-directed does not mean letting kids start alone from scratch with no support. My dear students needed some guidance, some prompting, some background knowledge, and some baby steps to get them on their way. Wouldn't you go running with scissors if asked to create an accurate sundial from scratch?

We must train and guide our student scientists, gradually releasing to them the responsibility for doing the majority of the wondering, thinking, talking, inferring, doing, and presenting in our classrooms. Creating opportunities for students to experience the elements of inquiry needs to be a step-by-step process, taking these elements one at a time.

In Chapter 3, I describe the workshop model as a useful structure for planning instruction that supports students taking ownership of their own learning. By teaching targeted minilessons and offering students ample supported work time, teachers can introduce and invite students to practice the essential features of inquiry one by one. By apprenticing our students as scientists in this way, we train them in the habits of mind required for success in this field.

Our vision could—and should—be that by the end of our year with them, students have progressed not only in their capacity to conduct scientific inquiries independently, but more importantly to think as scientists more proficiently. Using the workshop model, we can slowly scaffold students understanding of and capacity to inquire independently, feature by feature.

Incremental Inquiry

Sometimes all five of the essential features described above can be nicely encompassed within a project, lab, or task. But when they can't, we can still seek opportunities to weave the thinking behind each of these inquiry features into our everyday teaching. Let us look at each of the five features more closely and consider the small ways we can invite our students, on a regular basis, to think like scientists.

Learner Engages in Scientifically Oriented Questions

My friend Josh once called to ask an urgent question. Something was bothering him: "You know, at night, when you turn off the light, and a room goes dark, where does all the light go?" What an excellent science question! We all are asking questions all the time, I love to remind students.

Our classes can start with similarly compelling questions: Instead of the dry title "Electromagnetic Spectrum," why not call the unit, "Where Do Rainbows Come From?" Instead of "Cells," why not ask, "How Do Organisms Work?" "Vectors," could be retitled, "Why Do We Go Where We Go?"

Questioning like this mirrors the work of professional scientists: they pose a question and gather data to formulate an answer. Even when the content of our curriculum is prescribed, we can find opportunities to invite scientific questioning and thinking.

According to research by Pearson and Gallagher (1983), questioning is one of seven specific comprehension strategies competent learners use to make meaning of new information across the curriculum. Questioning, explicitly practiced, can significantly boost students' understanding of science—or any other—content.

In Figure 1.7, I offer some specific suggestions for bringing scientifically oriented questions to life in your classroom.

Learner Gives Priority to Evidence in Responding to Questions

After realizing that an eerie silence had fallen over our small house, I went in search of my young daughter, whom I found in the hallway clutching a crayon looking guiltily at the wall she had just covered with scribble. Stupidly, I asked her, "What is going on here?" She looked up and explained with a very serious face, "A duck did it." I could not help but burst out laughing.

I tell this story to remind us that we all already know what it means to give priority to evidence. Science is not based on belief or hearsay; it is based on facts. The fact is no crayon-toting duck could have gotten into our house. Ducks can't carry crayons—besides, the doors were locked. Much as she would have liked me to believe her claim, all of the evidence suggested that my daughter was the mural artist.

Science as a way of knowing differs distinctly from belief. Professional scientists support their theories with evidence; their methods of data collection and interpretation are subject to the review of peers. Similarly, we can guide our students to understand how accurate data can be gathered and used to answer questions, how data can be analyzed and assessed, as well as possible pitfalls of working with data.

Figure 1.8 suggests a variety of ways for students to practice giving priority to evidence.

Suggestion	Example
When starting a new unit or project, invite students to pose their own questions about the topic at hand.	When introducing the topic of tectonic plates, ask "Have you ever experienced an earthquake?"
Reframe labs and other activities as scientific problems or questions.	Rather than telling students they are to study the effect of density on buoyancy, we can begin with an open-ended question: "What does it take to float?"
Sort questions into categories—those that are scientifically oriented and those that are better addressed from another vantage point—philosophy, for example. Science answers many "how" questions, but not as many of the "whys."	"How do you stay in your seat when a roller coaster turns upside down?" can be answered by explaining the principles of physics; meanwhile, the question "Why do we have gravity?" calls for an explanation of the principles behind our universe's very nature, an explanation that science may not entirely be able to offer.
Post and refer back to students' questions and discuss which were answered and how. Develop strategies for answering the rest. Keep the questions alive.	A chart on the wall in the classroom can be a storage place for questions. Answered ones can be checked off; new ones can be added.
Invite new questions based on new knowledge.	After a learning experience, in addition to asking students what they now understand, offer time for them to think about what new questions they have.
Believe that it is okay not to know all the answers. Resist the temptation to explain away students' questions.	A student asks, "What is a quark?" Rather than giving a quick response, perhaps return the question with, "What a great question! I am curious to know what a quark is, too. How do you think we could find out?"

FIG. 1.7 *Learner Engages in Scientifically Oriented Questions*

Learner Formulates Explanations from Evidence

After a long day of picking mice skulls and bones out of a mass of regurgitated owl food, a group of students continued to insist that owls eat worms. Their teacher asked repeatedly for their evidence supporting this notion. Although they had none, they were reluctant to let go of the misconception (perhaps reinforced by childhood literature) that the owls who produced those pellets had eaten worms.

These students were relying not on evidence, but on their own preconceptions. As most students, these learners needed support in understanding that scientists develop explanations based on evidence—what they or colleagues have observed. Sometimes the evidence seems to point towards a clear explanation; at other times the data is inconclusive, and more research is required. This is not a setback but a part of the scientific process.

Students need not wait for a lab investigation to learn to infer explanations from evidence. They can practice formulating explanations based on evidence in many ways. See Figure 1.9 for ideas.

Learner Connects Explanations to Scientific Knowledge

Were dinosaurs warm- or cold-blooded? For many years paleontologists speculated about this question. Evidence suggests that dinosaur bones grew at nearly the same rate as those of modern mammals, indicating to some scientists that dinosaurs were warm-blooded. Meanwhile, fossil evidence suggests that dinosaurs did *not* have respiratory turbinates, a structure found in all warm-blooded animals to help us retain moisture while breathing; based on this evidence, a paleontologist would infer that dinosaurs were cold-blooded. These two inconclusive pieces of evidence and the explanations drawn from them demonstrate how scientists strive to connect what they learn to what is already known in an effort to make meaning, even when the facts are not conclusive.

Suggestion	Example
Discuss how data drives our decision making every day.	Talk about whether the stoplight is red or green, what time the clock says, what is in the refrigerator, and how all of these observations affect our decisions.
Explore data collection methods; discuss the importance of accuracy and honesty in news reports and scientific studies.	What evidence do we have about the health effects of cell phone use, and how does that compare to people's fears of brain tumors?
Investigate the need for constants and variables in an experiment to ensure reliable results.	Discuss an unreliable experiment with too many variables.
Invite students to examine a range of authentic data displays with an eye out for bias.	Talk about how data presented in promotional materials may not tell the whole story.
Examine data sets gleaned from your class's work, and look for anomalies.	After students work in small groups to complete an experiment, post each group's data and analyze class trends.

FIG. 1.8 *Learner Gives Priority to Evidence in Responding to Questions*

Suggestion	Example
When presenting new information, explicitly describe the evidence and then the explanation scientists offer. Train students to look for these two parts to any scientific theory.	Claim: The Earth is turning on its axis. Evidence: Throughout the night, the stars appear to move across the sky.
Rather than offering an explanation, give students just the evidence and allow them opportunities to share their own explanations.	When any student offers a conjecture, ask "How do you know?" "Are you sure?" "Why?"
Leave students room for uncertainty.	Challenge uncertain claims with, "What other information would you like to have to give you confidence in this conclusion?"
Review historical instances where scientists drew different explanations from the same evidence.	A good example would be the geocentric versus the heliocentric theory controversy.
Teach students to read and analyze data that presents itself in their daily lives.	Look at cereal box nutrition panels, graphs and charts from newspapers and magazines, and statistics given in advertisements. What does this data tell us?

FIG. 1.9 *Learner Formulates Explanations from Evidence*

All great science stands on the shoulders of previous discoverers' work. Most doctoral dissertations begin, for example, with a review of related research and current findings in the field. Similarly, students can be encouraged to see the relationship between their new learning and what they and other scientists already know. So in addition to using observational data and other evidence to draw conclusions, young scientists can begin to connect their own explanations to their prior knowledge—as well as to explanations offered by others.

In Figure 1.10, I offer some ideas to get you started thinking about how to help learners connect explanations to scientific knowledge in your classes.

Learner Communicates and Justifies Explanations

Unlike Galileo who suffered long for his efforts to communicate the truth as he knew it, scientists today are expected to share what they know with the world. Professional scientists do not work in isolation but report their learning to audiences including peers, funders, consumers, politicians, and citizens of all ages. Sometimes scientists must explain their work in simpler terms for the layperson, while other researchers must utilize the special vocabulary required to demonstrate their knowledge to colleagues in the field.

Similarly, student scientists can develop the skills of sharing their understanding in a variety of formats with a broad range of audiences. Figure 1.11 offers some specific ideas to help get you thinking.

Inquiry Every Day

Inquiry can be the oxygen giving life to students' learning experiences in science each day. We need to plan our teaching to ensure that students regularly engage in such opportunities to think as scientists.

Suggestion	Example
Elicit students' background knowledge before delving into a new topic.	Ask students to "Write down everything you already know about the lymphatic system."
Discuss current events, and how new information relates to what is already known.	How does new data collected by the Phoenix Mars Lander fit with what scientists believed about Mars in the past?
Explain the importance of replicating an experiment to prove its accuracy.	Talk about why the FDA requires pharmaceutical companies to perform complex trials before a drug can be approved.
Introduce students to the "big ideas" (see Chapter 2) and invite them to connect new learning to one or more big idea.	Introduce the big idea "energy" to help students relate what you are learning about the greenhouse effect to their prior knowledge about thermodynamics.
Discuss the relevance of new science learning to students' life experiences.	How do you experience Newton's Laws every day?

FIG. 1.10 *Learner Connects Explanations to Scientific Knowledge*

In the above descriptions, I suggested small steps to offer students experience with each of the essential features of classroom inquiry, regardless of the task or content of the unit. Every time we invite students to think along these lines, we can draw the parallel for them between their own work and that of professional scientists. When we weave these features into all of the learning experiences in our science classes—rather than waiting until the science fair—we seed the atmosphere with inquiry, a key step in training students to think like scientists.

Suggestion	Example
Invite students to present their understandings in a range of genres.	Writing, drawing, and graphing; on paper, posters, through oral presentations, via electronic media . . .
Look together at the work of professional scientists for exemplars of each presentation format; discuss what quality looks like.	Get a hold of actual documents—posters, papers, PowerPoint slide shows—and, better yet, the scientists who created them. Use these resources to develop a rubric with your class.
Gather unique audiences for your students' work.	Students could share their learning with students of other ages, parents, administrators, experts in the field, local political figures, stakeholders concerned about an issue, veterans, or any other special interest group concerned about the topic at hand.
Create opportunities for students to participate in peer review, allowing learners to give one another feedback on the process and products of their inquiries and to build stronger understandings from each other's ideas.	When students are done or nearly done with a project, create time for them to share their work in small groups; structure means for peers to offer constructive criticism to one another; allow time for learners to integrate that feedback into their final products.

FIG. 1.11 *Learner Communicates and Justifies Explanations*

The most important question we need to ask each day is whether our lessons are getting students thinking as scientists about important science content. If the kids are thinking, we are doing it right.

Roadblocks

Two big challenges face teachers striving to create a more inquiry-based classroom:

- releasing absolute control, and
- resisting the temptation to rescue students.

One must be willing, as a teacher, to begin to experiment with these two distinct but related issues in order to embrace inquiry-based instruction and hand over the thinking and learning to the students.

Releasing Control

Anyone who has ever been a parent or known a toddler has some experience watching a child learn how to eat. It is not pretty. When my son first took possession of his own spoon, it was a painful process to observe. The mess was abundant: the floor, the table, the shirt, the ceiling—splattered with yogurt, peas, or whatever else I had foolishly laid before him. Ugly as the scene was, I knew, as do all parents, that the kid needed to learn to feed himself. And, the only way for him to learn was through experience.

Let's face it: many of us go into teaching because we are control freaks. We love to hold the spoon. We love to be in charge. We love to be on the stage . . . but when it comes to inquiry, it is time to let the students be the scientists rather than ask them to watch and listen to *us* be scientists.

Now learning through inquiry does not mean turning the entire curriculum over to students, relinquishing all control and responsibility. Instead, inquiry requires us as teachers to continue to be in charge of the content of the course, the structure of the course, and the learning outcomes. Many teachers wrestle to find the delicate balance between structure and open-endedness.

Inquiry-based instruction, though, leaves room for students to be in the driver's seat some of the time. They need to practice thinking like scientists. We need to be willing to hand over the wheel, as appropriate, through a process of "gradual release of responsibility," which I discuss in Chapter 3. This can be scary, yet when we offer students the support they need, coupled with appropriate high expectations for their performance, they amaze us. My son will someday feed himself and walk away with a clean shirt.

Resisting Rescue

I learned to drive on our stick shift Volkswagen Rabbit, which was particularly hard for me to get into gear. Fed up as my dad became with my use of what he called "kangaroo fuel" (gas that allegedly caused the car to hop all over the parking lot) as I struggled to learn to use the clutch, he did not hop out and ask me to relinquish the driver's seat. He knew I just had to keep trying. The tendency to rescue is a close cousin to the need for control.

Similarly, when we hand the reins over to our students, it may take some extra time to get where we are going. We may be tempted to swoop in and tell them when they've missed the mark, correct their procedures, and fix up their work to ensure that they arrive at right answers. What would this behavior on our part really tell them about our level of trust and confidence in their abilities? If students are truly to master the skills of inquiry, we must coach and train them as much as possible in advance, then resist the temptation to rescue them if they take a wrong turn along the way. Living through and learning from their errors will ultimately teach them much more than if we as teachers pad the way, ensuring a safe landing.

It is difficult to let go in this way; we love our kids and want them to succeed. Yet when we truly place the responsibility for success squarely on their shoulders, only then will they taste the true victory of self-sufficiency.

Implementing Inquiry

Whatever the content or learning activity, we can always deepen opportunities for student thinking, for student inquiry. That is why this is the first chapter in the constants section: we must teach science not only *through* inquiry but also *as* inquiry. In other words, we use inquiry methods, as well as emphasize these as the very nature of scientific thinking itself.

Here are some planning questions designed to get you thinking about how to keep the spotlight on inquiry when planning or revising a learning experience.

Implementing Inquiry: Teacher Planning Questions

What are the learning goals of this task?

What has to happen? (What control will I retain over the lesson content and process?)

What scientific thinking will students practice during this task?

Which of the essential features of inquiry (question, evidence, explanation, connections, communication) will my students experience through this task?

For each feature, where do I envision my students on the continuum of self-direction?

Which features will I directly teach? What will that instruction and scaffolding look like?

How will I assess learners' understanding of and skill with each inquiry feature?

Dobetter Inquiry

In each chapter of this book, you will read an example of Ms. Dobetter, a fictional composite teacher, answering planning questions like these as she begins to plan or revise her instruction.

Right now, she is working on designing a series of lessons for her ninth-grade physics students around an engineering project—building the tallest possible towers out of a limited supply of newspaper and tape. While this task could be completed by much younger students, Ms. Dobetter is working to develop it in a way that will promote serious scientific thinking. Let's listen in on her planning and teaching.

What are the learning goals of this task?

Through this project, I want students to learn about both the process and content of science: processwise, I want them to experience and understand trial and error, refining their thinking based on experimental data. From a content perspective, my learning goals include students understanding the basic principles of structural engineering, which are principles of physics: mass, force, load, and inertia.

You know, I did this project with my classes last year, and they really liked it, but I don't think I expected enough of them in terms of thinking like scientists. They were just making towers. It was fun, but I think I missed an opportunity to be more scientific.

What has to happen? (What control will I retain over the lesson content and process?)

Well, I would like everyone to build a tower—more than one, actually, probably three or four different revisions of a tower. And I would like them to document their thinking as they work. This is the tricky thing. Everyone wants to tape things together, but they are also going to need to stop and record what they are doing and thinking in their science notebooks.

What scientific thinking will students practice during this task?

Students will be gathering a lot of data—evidence—firsthand of what works and does not work. They will be thinking about what that evidence means to them in terms of how to refine their towers, make them taller, or more stable. So I guess that will be considered explaining, developing explanations for new designs based on evidence from their previous trials.

Which of the essential features of inquiry (question, evidence, explanation, connections, communication) will my students experience through this task?

It seems like this task would lend itself best to this idea of evidence and explanations. I will allow students some time to mess about with the materials, but pretty quickly I want them to be thinking and planning and reasoning as they design these towers.

For each feature, where do I envision my students on the continuum of self-direction?

At this age, I think students are ready to figure out for themselves what kinds of evidence would be valuable and how to interpret or explain that evidence. I will need to do some modeling, but I think that the kids will have a good sense of what the variables are and how to approach this problem as scientists.

Which features will I directly teach? What will that instruction and scaffolding look like?

I will need to work with students on the evidence. Initially, I want to brainstorm with them what kinds of documentation, design sketches, measurements, data, and so forth they could include in their notebooks.

In terms of the explanations, I will need to slow down to the point of really thinking and recording what they are doing next, not just throwing things together. I think I will have them keep two-column notes in their journals: What I Am Doing / What I Am Thinking. Then, I probably need to provide some specific reflection questions to scaffold their thinking after each trial. Something like the following:

- What were the strengths of this design? How do you know?
- What were the weaknesses? How do you know?
- What ideas do you have for revision?
- Why do you think those ideas will work?

In this way, I will really force them to stop and think about what they did and saw before rushing into another trial.

How will I assess learners' understanding of and skill with each inquiry feature?

I will have students do a final write-up after they have finished their trials. This would be a formal assessment of their communication skills, as well as their thinking processes. In the past, I have used a more traditional lab report format, but this year I revised that to include one section for each feature of inquiry: question, evidence, explanation, connections to science. The communication feature is implied. In the evidence section, I will need to have students write more of the plans and procedures.

Outdoing Dubai

Online, Ms. Dobetter found a recent, short *New York Times* article about Burj Dubai, the world's tallest building to date. Copies of the article wait on the students' lab tables as they enter the room. Some students start reading right away; others wait to be asked, but after a few minutes of silence, Ms. Dobetter asks all to turn and talk to a partner about the article: "What does it make you wonder about?"

Calling all back from their individual conversations, Ms. Dobetter asks students to share their initial questions based on the article, then asks, "What do you think it takes to make the world's tallest building?"

"Money."

"Only money?" she probes.

"Materials, workers."

"How do you know it's not going to fall down?" she asks.

"You need an architect, someone to design it."

"Yes," Ms. Dobetter affirms. "Almost every building you have ever been in started as a design on a piece of paper. But how do architects, designers, and structural engineers know what keeps a building up?" She turns her palms toward the ceiling and glances at the fluorescent bulbs buzzing above their heads.

"I guess they just keep trying new things, learning from other places what works."

"Mmmhm. So, want to try?" She asks, grabbing from her desk three copies of yesterday's paper she picked up from the newsstand. "We are going to do some building this week, an experiment, to see just how tall of a tower you can build with only three"—she holds them up to illustrate—"sheets of newspaper, and 30 cm"—she reaches for a meter stick—"of tape."

"How tall do you think it could be?" Ms. Dobetter records learners' predictions on the board, and then describes how they will work in pairs and have numerous chances to try and retry the task, recording all of their work in their science notebooks.

"But before you can design a good tower, I would like you to get some sense of the materials." She quickly passes around newspaper and tape and allows about ten minutes for some open exploration.

Calling the reluctant builders back together, she asks, "So, what do you think we will need to document as we work? Thinking like scientists, what is the most important evidence you will be looking for to assess your design and find ways to improve?"

"How long it stood."

"How tall it is."

"I also think the design is a kind of evidence, what you did, so you know how you can change it."

"I think so, too," said Ms. Dobetter. She goes to the white board and draws a two-column chart. "This is how I want you to document your efforts in your notebooks," she explains. "On the left hand side, write down everything you are doing—all of your data, evidence of how you set up your tower. This will include a sketch, measurements, everything you think that is important to record in order for someone else to come along and build the same tower as you did." She writes *Doing* in block letters at the top of that column. "On the right, while or after you build your tower, I want you to write down what you are *thinking* about what you did. Maybe you have a new idea about how to use the tape, or notice a classmate trying something that makes sense to you that you want to remember." She writes *Thinking* on top of that side of the T-chart.

"If your tower falls, write the data about that on the left. 'Tower buckled at second joint and slowly bowed down,'" she jots on the board by way of example. "Then, on the right you are going to write what you are *thinking*. Why did it do that? What is your explanation?" Ms. Dobetter restates the primary importance of this step—documenting and thinking about what you are doing or have done.

"What questions do you have?" Learners are curious about materials, where they are allowed to work, how they will be choosing teams, and whether now they can use the restroom. Once these are cleared up, Ms. Dobetter asks students to pull out their science notebooks; set up their page with the date, title, and two columns; and to get started with their designs.

She works the room, encouraging thoughtful ideas and high quality documentation, prodding the minds of students—"Have you thought about other shapes? Why do you think that will be best?" To a team who says the task is too hard, Ms. Dobetter asks, "What makes it seem so hard?" and listens attentively, problem solving by breaking the job of designing a tower into smaller steps.

Before the end of class, Ms. Dobetter invites all teams to complete their designs by tomorrow so that they can begin building. At the bell, students are still comparing ideas on folding versus rolling the newspaper for maximum strength.

The next day, Ms. Dobetter is ready to share an example with her students. She herself did a first trial of the tower experiment the night before and recorded her planning, thinking, and observations in her own science journal. She flicks on the document camera and shares her work, inviting students to critique the quality of her documentation. They point out measurements she missed and other information they would like to see added, and ask her to tell more in the right hand column about what she thinks happened. Happily, she asks students to apply this same level of scrutiny to their own draft tower plans before sharing them with her.

As teams are ready, she looks over their notebooks, and (if all looks good) hands over the materials and an opportunity to get started. As students work, she visits with teams, checks their documentation, and asks questions to promote thinking. After the first tower topples, she flashes a short list of questions onto the overhead and asks the builders to complete this reflection in their notebooks before starting a new design.

- What were the strengths of this design? How do you know?
- What were the weaknesses? How do you know?
- What ideas do you have for revision?
- Why do you think those ideas will work?

Students repeat this cycle of planning, building, and reflecting. On the third day, before work time, Ms. Dobetter introduces some vocabulary she has heard students using and clarifies the science definition of each term: mass, force, load, and inertia. She encourages students to use these science words from now on when documenting what they are doing and thinking.

After a week of work, students' designs are becoming increasingly refined. Ms. Dobetter applauds the students' good thinking and explains their homework: "Based on your work in your notebook, write up a formal report of this investigation. It needs to include the question or challenge, a description of what you did, what you observed, and what you learned." She refers students to their last write-up task to clarify her expectations, emphasizing that she is more concerned about the thinking than the formatting.

So What?

In this example, Ms. Dobetter took a typical task—building newspaper towers—and built around it a structure for and expectations of scientific thinking. Engaged in this task, students had the opportunity to get their hands busy as well as keep their minds involved in inquiry.

To hold inquiry constant in our classrooms does not mean doing a lab every day. It does not mean throwing the doors open for students to pursue independent studies week in and week out. It does not mean following a prescribed course of instruction. To hold inquiry constant, we only need to shift gears. Instead of planning a lesson by considering what students will be *doing* during class, we need instead to focus on what they will be *thinking and learning*. If we change nothing else about our curriculum but simply stand vigilant to identify and maximize opportunities for scientific thinking in our classes, we will transform the classroom experience of our student scientists.

Figure 1.12 offers you an opportunity to consider where you are in inviting your students to experience these five essential features of inquiry. With a trusted peer, take some time to fill in the middle column of the chart, each documenting all of the work you are already doing now to support students in thinking like scientists. Discuss your areas of strengths with your colleague, and listen to what she is doing well. Then, in the final column, consider the suggestions from this chapter as well as your own insight; think about some new ideas you could implement to increase students' thinking opportunities.

Essential Features	What am I doing already?	What more could I do?
1. Learner engages in scientifically oriented questions.		
2. Learner gives priority to evidence in responding to questions.		
3. Learner formulates explanations from evidence.		
4. Learner connects explanations to scientific knowledge.		
5. Learner communicates and justifies explanations.		

FIG. 1.12 *Planning for the Essential Features of Classroom Inquiry*

"Yah, but . . ."

- *"Who has time for all this inquiry? We have a rigorous curriculum we need to cover, a lot of content."*

Amid all of the pressures for coverage, inquiry *can* feel like one more thing. But the good news is, it need not be. By tweaking the work we are already doing in our classes, science thinking skills can walk hand in hand with content learning. Naturally, this will take some planning, and it cannot happen all at once, but begin. Try one day at a time to look for opportunities for learners to think as scientists a little more. As you set up for your next lab, start by eliciting scientifically oriented questions; close by asking students what further questions they still have about their findings. It will take just a few minutes. See where this effort leads you.

- *"There is just no way I can answer all of their questions."*

Do you have to? Inquiry, to me, is more about asking than knowing, more about being curious than being right. Let them ask. Teach them how scientists find answers. Allow students to walk away still wondering about something. What better gift could you give?

- *"For some activities, in chemistry especially, it would be totally dangerous to hand the materials over to the students!"*

Be safe! Not every learning experience needs to be in the students' control. In Chapter 7, I offer guidelines for making demonstrations highly engaging learning opportunities.

Yet if we offer students appropriate background knowledge and support, it is possible for them to design safe chemistry experiments. We are each the experts on our content and our own students and need to make wise choices about what learners are ready to handle. Still, I encourage you to trust your students—little by little, give them some opportunities to be in control. You may be surprised by how well they manage themselves.

- *"Isn't it kind of fake, to pretend to let students draw their own conclusions on something when we already know what the right answer is?"*

I don't know. The other day, my preschooler was messing about with blue and yellow paint, and all of a sudden I heard him shouting, "It's green! I made green! Green!" Of course, by looking at the world around him, he could easily have inferred that he was not the first person to make green. But this time *he* made green. *His own* green. He did not care what anyone else had ever made.

I did not tell him to make green, keeping the recipe secret, and waiting with a crooked eyebrow for him to guess right. I let him mess about. When we open the door to discoveries, we have to do just that—be open, rather than play a game of "guess what is in my head." And then, students can surprise themselves and us with what they find and figure out.

Can you remember a time when you had that opportunity? How did you feel?

Inquiry is the cornerstone of thoughtful science instruction. In the next chapter, we will discuss *what* we might inquire about: big ideas.

CHAPTER 2

Big Ideas

Students understand and retain science learning when it is connected to overarching big ideas that permeate the distinct disciplines of science.

Think Tank

- How do I select the content I teach?
- How do I select what content I don't teach?
- What do I hope students will understand and remember?

When I was a student teacher, my mentor was amazingly organized and prepared. She had been teaching the same courses for as long as anyone could remember and kept master copies of labs, task sheets, notes, and project handouts organized by unit in color-coded binders on bookcases behind her tidy desk. In a file cabinet, she stored extra copies of each, knowing that they could be used again the next year.

Before leaving my student teaching internship, I asked my mentor's permission to leaf through her files and take one copy of everything. I neatly filed her generous gifts in color-coded folders of my own.

In the weeks before taking on my first teaching job, I gathered other resources as well. I painstakingly researched the appropriate content for my science courses: I located the state's latest Science Content Standards, noting their differences from the National Science Education Standards I had studied in graduate school. I searched the school to gather resources; some texts came with multimedia kits, videos, CDs, and catalogues of supplies supporting the content of the course. Then I drummed up a copy of our state's new standardized testing guide—complete with sample questions as well as a demonstration packet and scoring rubric.

When it came time for me to forge all of this material into syllabi and units, I was lost. All I had was a collection—an enormous collection—of stuff about science. What was I supposed to do with it? The district's benchmarks listed all kinds of topics, but what were the students really supposed to learn about each? What was important? How was I supposed to know?

Reflection

With resources in abundance, why was I confused?

What would you say to the young, overwhelmed teacher described above?

What else did I need?

My personal experience described above parallels that of many new teachers I meet. The resources, choices, and the vastness of science itself can overwhelm us. We struggle to know where to put the emphasis, and what to leave behind. In this chapter, I offer the "big ideas of science" as a useful filter to assist us in streamlining course designs for maximum student understanding.

The big ideas of science are overarching themes that permeate all of the discrete science content strands; when studying science with these ideas in mind, learners develop a framework supporting their growing understanding of the field of science as a whole. Furthermore, content becomes more accessible.

Pack Light

Sometimes curriculum planning reminds me of packing for a trip. I usually start getting ready to travel by pulling out everything I would *love* to take—fresh clothes for every day, a swimsuit, cozy sweaters, extra socks, a well-stocked toiletry kit, hardcover books, my laptop, and a variety of shoes—and tossing it all onto the bed. Next I pull out my compact suitcase and petite carry-on and realize that the stuff on my bed is never going to fit.

The vetting begins: I have to set some priorities. I have to ask myself why I am going on this trip after all: Am I really going to get to swim? Am I going to have time to work? Which of these shoes could I live without? Ultimately, a lot gets left on the bed.

Similarly, when planning a science course, the desk is piled high with possible ingredients, material to "cover": standards, topics, books, activities, investigations, resources, field trips, and connections. This is a very nice way to start, with everything out there to sort and sift through. Yet as teachers we need to set our own priorities: What are the must-haves that we need to put in our carry-on bags, without which all would be lost? And what are the other important ingredients to pack in our suitcases?

These questions are easier to answer when we consider the imperative of Grant Wiggins and Jay McTighe (2005) to begin with the end in mind. In *Understanding by Design,* these authors discuss two major pitfalls, or "twin sins," observable in many schools and classrooms: activity-based teaching and coverage-based teaching. Neither approach necessarily culminates in understanding. Conversely, according to Tomlinson and McTighe (2006), instruction designed around broad, enduring understandings has the power to

- engage and motivate learners,
- connect to learners' life experiences in relevant ways,
- offer differentiated entry points, and
- allow teacher flexibility in how learning goals are accomplished.

In this chapter, I will introduce worthy, overarching science learning goals—big ideas—that can be supported through all ranges of content studies. The second section of this book, Variables, will assist you in constructing learning experiences that will lead learners to that understanding. Once we have that vision of where we are going in a science course, we can efficiently flip through a stack of resources and identify which will help our students to achieve those learning goals, and which are just dead weight.

So where *are* we going?

Standards and Benchmarks

The standards movement represents an effort to streamline the content areas and clarify important learning targets. The Science Content Standards articulated by the National Research Council in the *National Science Education Standards* (1996) suggest that we teach

- unifying concepts and processes in science,
- science as inquiry,
- physical science,
- life science,
- Earth and space science,
- science and technology,
- science in personal and social perspectives, and
- history and nature of science. (104)

Alongside these broad standards, the American Association for the Advancement of Science, in Project 2061, goes further to articulate the benchmarks of science literacy in a volume by that same name. Further, they give us the *Atlas of Science Literacy*, a fascinating book which maps the connections between the benchmarks over the years of a student's science learning from K–12, demonstrating how early science education lays the foundation for future studies. On the one hand, these documents can serve as tremendous resources for curriculum planning; on the other, they can bury us in minutiae. There is just so much to learn.

I do not offer the big ideas as a replacement for standards but as a tool for sifting and sorting them. When we can contextualize standards and benchmarks within a framework of big ideas and offer that organization to our students with great transparency, we promptly increase the efficacy of our instruction. In this way, we make what we are studying important and meaningful to our potentially skeptical adolescent audience.

Breadth Versus Depth

Science learning in the United States has been characterized by the trite expression, "a mile wide and an inch deep." In other words, we are expected to skim the surface of a great many topics but take the time to delve into none. A quick glance at a typical middle school science textbook will support this criticism: numerous topics are presented in pithy, three to five page chapters, each offering only a superficial exposé of the facts. This approach is like going on a road trip yet never being able to get out of the car—we have no time to go inside the Carlsbad Caverns, we'll just drive past and say we saw them. This fast-paced survey approach offers students a mere tour of the landscape of science, without allowing them the essential time to understand its geology or to appreciate all of the work of the thousands of scientists that led to our current understanding. No wonder some kids act bored and unmotivated!

To stop and explore one topic in depth at the middle or high school level is a rare luxury, yet some science teachers are strong proponents of this teaching style: a colleague explained that through his students' work studying telescopes, they would study light, lenses, the solar system, and the nature of science. This effort toward depth often results in an integrated approach, drawing several standards or topics together within a single study. The debate over breadth versus depth highlights some dilemmas for today's science teachers: what to cover, how to cover it, what to leave out, and how to justify that.

The Vastness of Science

This dilemma between pursuing breadth or depth grows more vexing as the quantity of known scientific information continues to expand. When our grandparents were in school, the volumes of scientific knowledge recorded were considerable. But that knowledge is infinitesimal compared to all that has now been documented in so many fields of science. College major choices once included biology, chemistry, or physics; now those interested in pursuing a degree in science can choose from such specialized undergraduate majors as neurobiology or tropical oceanography. A few generations back, reasonable teachers could expect their students to truly master the content of science by the time they graduated from university. Today, this is not so. With the advent of technology as a research assistant, as well as the Internet as a tool for information sharing, the breadth of known science (as well as our access to that research) is overwhelming.

Given this exponential growth of scientific knowledge, we cannot expect our students to understand every concept and remember every fact. Yet we teachers often feel that we are expected to strive for this unattainable goal: states, districts, and schools are responding to the explosion of available knowledge by thickening textbooks and lengthening tests, expecting students to simply learn more content. This strategy will soon prove unsustainable.

While the amount of information has grown, the big ideas underlying science are constant and can serve as our foundation. Our students are best served by building, through their science learning experiences, a framework for understanding the growing field. They may never have time to delve into the details of every topic, but with the big ideas as a filing system in their minds, they will be equipped to more easily connect new learning to their existing background knowledge. In other words, we explore important content studies in order to make meaning of the field of science as a whole, rather than simply one corner or another of the universe.

Big Ideas as a Framework for Understanding

Given the vastness of science and the limits of instructional time, we must prioritize our content. By placing an emphasis on big ideas rather than discrete topics, by focusing on content that supports understanding of these important, transferable overarching themes, we feed two or more birds with one piece of bread.

For example, rather than studying the carbon cycle simply as the interesting phenomenon that it is, we can use learning about the carbon cycle to illustrate the bigger idea of cycles as a common "pattern of change" in the natural world. This big idea, Patterns of Change, is an example of an enduring, universal theme that is illustrated in all the discrete content areas—biology, chemistry, geology, physics, and so forth—of science.

Students who master basic content in the context of big ideas are prepared to synthesize new knowledge in meaningful ways, continually deepening their understanding of the field of science. The big ideas are not a curriculum unto themselves; yet when saturating our courses with big ideas, we invite students to forge essential connections, making their science learning more meaningful.

When I taught middle school, I found that the big ideas served as an excellent tool for streamlining my curriculum toward deeper student understanding. Chemical bonding, for example, I placed into the context of the big idea "Energy." When looking at atomic bonds through this lens, students could connect their knowledge of the details of these scientific processes with other important topics, including food webs, magnetism, and photosynthesis. When we invite these sorts of connections in the context of big ideas, we encouraged students to synthesize a range of content learning experiences in service to worthy understanding goals. Big ideas and content objectives enjoy a symbiotic relationship, each one helping learners to understand the other.

While they may not be able to "cover" all of the chapters in their thick textbook, teachers working with big ideas offer learners a strong grasp of what science is about. Prioritizing big ideas often implies making some changes to your course content in order to hone a focus. If you elect to focus on one big idea, "Stability," while studying the ozone layer in the context of a meteorology course, you are obliged to then sort all of the available learning material and activities to determine which will best serve the goal of understanding the big idea. Learning activities about the ozone layer's composition, threats, and self-corrective capacity will need to take precedence over other possible material about its discovery or dimensions. Keeping a big idea in the viewfinder means being willing to crop the frame, tighten the focus, and leave out some topics in order to do important learning well.

Whose Big Ideas?

Several notable groups have worked to assemble their own versions of science's big ideas. In 1990, the National Center for Improving Science Education presented the following themes: cause and effect, change and conservation, diversity and variation, energy and matter, evolution and equilibrium, models and theories, probability and prediction, structure and function, systems and interactions, and time and scale (Bybee et al. 1990). Quite a long list!

Also in 1990 the American Association for the Advancement of Science presented their own short and sweet set, the Common Science Themes: systems, models, constancy and change, scale and structure. Then in 1996, as part of the *National Science Education Standards,* the National Research Council presented their own version—the "Unifying Concepts and Processes": systems, order, and organization; evidence, models, and explanation; change, constancy, and measurement; evolution and equilibrium; and form and function. Their five concepts are actually each a collection of two or three, bringing us up to a total of thirteen ideas here to work with. For me, this is too much!

But California, to my mind, seems to have gotten their list just right. The themes they developed are broad enough to offer numerous examples from each content strand, yet sufficiently distinct to allow one to achieve a focus. As a teacher, I found this list an excellent resource in curriculum planning. The 1990 *Science Framework for California Public Schools* presents a very sensible set of "Major Themes of Science":

- energy,
- evolution,
- patterns of change,
- scale and structure,
- stability, and
- systems and interactions. (California Science Curriculum Framework and Criteria Committee 1990, 27)

But the good news is this—it does not matter whose list you choose, or even if you decide to develop your own. The point is simply to choose something important to hang each unit on, something bigger than volcanos or microscopes or Newton's laws. We should be able to say to our students, "Volcanos are important in and of themselves, yet through studying volcanos we can deepen our understanding of an even bigger idea . . ." (what do you think it could be?).

You are right! You have a lot of choices! You could study volcanos to understand energy: how the heat energy of the magma is transformed into the energy of motion. Or you could study volcanos as an example of evolution: how our landscape changes over time because of certain forces of geology. Or is that a better example for patterns of change? Or maybe they are really about stability, about how pressure beneath and within the Earth affects the apparent stability of its surface. My point is simply that when taking this approach of teaching for understanding big ideas, if the connection works for you and you can make the connection clear to the students, it works. You get to decide which big idea suits each unit best.

	Definition	Earth and Space Sciences Examples	Physical Sciences Examples	Life Sciences Examples
Energy	Forces underlie all systems and interactions.	• Convection currents within the Earth • Gravity	• The ability to do work • Chemical bonds	• Photosynthesis • Respiration • Decomposition
Evolution	Patterns and processes create change over time.	• Plate tectonics • Star life cycles	• Time and direction in a reaction	• Comparative anatomy • Taxonomy
Patterns of Change	Trends, cycles, and irregular patterns of the past help us predict the future.	• Seasons • Tides • Rock and mineral cycles	• Chain reaction • Radioactive decay	• Life cycles • Biochemical cycles • Food webs
Scale and Structure	Structure relates to function; there is a hierarchy, properties at each level.	• Phases of the moon • Mountain building • Erosion	• Structure of matter • Properties of matter	• Cell biology • Physiology
Stability	Constancy is a result of equilibrium.	• Planetary motion • Renewable energy	• Equilibrium • Balanced forces	• Homeostasis • Symbiosis • Ecology
Systems and Interactions	Components and relationships between them, their input and output, and the feedback within a system.	• Solar system • Water cycle • Weather	• Chemical reactions • Inertia • Harmonic motion	• Organisms • Conservation biology • Environmental science

FIG. 2.1 *Big Ideas with Definitions and Examples (adapted from California Science Curriculum Framework and Criteria Committee 1990)*

To help you play matchmaker between your content and some big ideas, let's take some time to understand California's big ideas. Figure 2.1 offers definitions and examples illuminating each big idea in more depth.

Once you decide on an idea, tailoring your instruction in service to both the content objectives and big idea will streamline your unit planning. After you choose, look back over all of your teaching materials and decide which learning activities will truly support students' thinking and understanding about the topic and its relationship to the big idea. Be willing to let go of materials that do not serve this purpose.

Putting the Big Ideas to Work

The lists of standards and benchmarks you are expected to address within the course of a year may be lengthy enough that this new list of big ideas presents an unwelcomed imposition. Yet, these big ideas are not content goals in and of themselves, but rather lenses through which the ever-growing lists of content objectives can be refined. When adopted as a tool, big ideas guide our planning to help us to make the standards meaningful; big ideas encourage us to make best use of students' learning time by focusing our content learning toward important, broad understandings. The big ideas can be useful to teachers and schools in many ways:

- as a lens, ensuring that discrete studies connect to broader principles;
- as a planning tool, encouraging you to touch on a range of important science themes throughout the year; and
- as a schoolwide framework, offering students and teachers a common language and organizational system for science content knowledge.

Big Ideas as a Lens

The big ideas can help contextualize the studies you have planned within a broader framework, as can be seen in Figure 2.2. As described above, rather than simply teaching about volcanos, your learners can use the study of volcanos to support their growing understanding of energy, a central concept cutting across all disciplines of science.

When you select one big idea as the lens, or viewpoint, through which a topic is examined, that determines certain areas of focus within the study of that topic. If you are looking at volcanos through the lens of energy, for example, your unit may include tasks exploring temperature and pressure as related to volcanos. If, instead, you elect to focus on scale and structure through the study of volcanos, you might spend more time

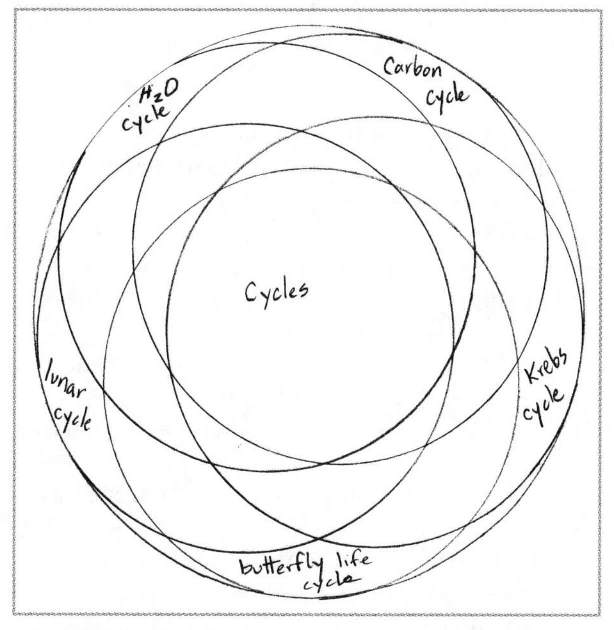

FIG. 2.2 *Related Topics Studied as Examples of a Big Idea—Cycles—Deepen Students' Understanding of Each*

discussing volcanos' formation and composition. Either way, you are still studying volcanos. This big idea simply serves to narrow the scope and create a loftier aim than studying volcanos for volcanos' sake.

With the big idea as a lens, you can hone your planning to support your students in connecting their learning about the specific subject or benchmark to a worthy, overarching, and enduring understanding goal. In other words, when the unit is done, students ought to be able not only to explain a volcano but also to identify important relationships between, say, volcanos and the water cycle as illustrations of the big idea of energy.

When our attention is focused on the big idea, we can sort through familiar curriculum materials and select those best suited to our learning outcomes. If we are looking through the lens of systems and interaction, for example, we may decide that creating a Venn diagram contrasting the structures of plant and animal cells will promote deeper understanding than a task like coloring diagrams of the two cell types. In this way, planning through the big idea perspective focuses us on the thinking and learning that is most essential.

Big Ideas as a Planning Tool

While all of these big ideas are equally important, a wise teacher may decide that touching on just a few of them throughout the year would make the most sense. Rather than trying to weave all six into every unit, which could result in confusion, you might look through the topics in your course and assign one big idea to each unit, addressing as many of the ideas as will sensibly connect. In this way, you ensure that each segment of instruction ties to one of these broader principles, continually inviting students to make connections between new information and their background knowledge from other science learning experiences.

For example, in an anatomy and physiology course, one big idea might be paired with each body system as illustrated in Figure 2.3.

As the teacher of this course progresses through these units, she will use the content of each to illuminate the important big idea. While studying the musculo-skeletal system, she could take the time to describe the associated big idea in detail, inviting students to connect the content of this unit example to their related science back-

Body System	Big Idea	Content Links to Big Idea
Circulatory	Stability	diffusion, osmosis, blood pressure
Digestive	Energy	cellular respiration
Endocrine	Patterns of Change	adolescence development, aging
Integumentary	Stability	temperature regulation, excretion
Musculo-Skeletal	Scale and Structure	structure and function
Nervous	Systems and Interactions	reflex arc, sensory organs
Reproductive	Evolution	meiosis, genetics

FIG. 2.3 *Sample Human Anatomy Curriculum Linked to Big Ideas*

ground knowledge about scale and structure. To take another example: while studying the circulatory system through the lens of stability, students can be encouraged to make connections to their studies of ecosystems. In this way, regardless of the course or content, students are continually deepening their understanding of these overarching topics and the interconnectedness of science's disciplines. This assists learners to develop confidence and competence as scientific thinkers, and to believe in their own capacity to making meaning throughout all of their future science studies.

No harm is done by repeating an idea more than once in a year's sequence, or electing to leave one out. Simply using these big ideas as a framework throughout our studies will guide students to connect their new knowledge with past and future science learning.

When matching big ideas to course content, you may also find holes or weaknesses in your curriculum and decide that some overarching adjustments need to take place to ensure that a course serves the broader goal of supporting science understanding, rather than simply surveying a discrete body of knowledge.

Big Ideas as a Schoolwide Framework

As a staff developer working with teachers and science departments to organize curriculum, I have found the big ideas a tremendous resource. The big ideas are *not* a curriculum in and of themselves; they invite us to refine course content for maximum student learning. When adopted as a common language throughout a school, these big ideas can serve as a filing system in students' minds as they navigate the myriad concepts and content areas of science over the years.

Some departments elect to "assign" a single big idea to each course or grade level, while others simply encourage teachers to shop for the appropriate big idea to accompany each unit. You can imagine, though, the power of these ideas being reinforced and emphasized time and again in different contexts over the course of a student's science career. Over the years, each learner will develop a strong framework into which lifelong scientific learning can be integrated.

When working with your science department members to connect big ideas with your curriculum, consider several matters.

- What are the main units or topics you explore in each of your courses?
- Which content standards are addressed?
- Which big idea best connects to each?
- Look at Figure 2.4. Where on this matrix would you place each of the topics you listed and why?

To tie the big ideas to an existing curriculum, you can start with an empty matrix like Figure 2.4. Teachers can examine the content of their courses and identify which topics belong where. Often discussion and debate ensues, and some disagreements may not be easily resolved. As described above, any connection between a science topic and a big idea can work if it makes sense to you; matching them up is simply a decision about what can be best supported through the learning process. Nonetheless, to take a stand and argue for a link between a big idea and a science topic is a useful exercise.

With the big idea at the center of your unit planning, you can begin to sift and sort through resources and materials, as one sorts belongings before packing for a trip. Examining each learning task, you can ask yourself, "Will this help my students understand the content within the context of the big idea?" This is an opportunity to recycle

	Earth and Space Sciences	Physical Sciences: Chemistry and Physics	Life Sciences
Energy			
Evolution			
Patterns of Change			
Scale and Structure			
Stability			
Systems and Interactions			

FIG. 2.4 *A Matrix of Big Ideas of Science and Content Strands*

some old material, and to develop new. The following planning questions can help you think through integrating a big idea into an instructional unit:

Streamlining Curriculum with Big Ideas: Teacher Planning Questions

What are the learning goals of this unit?

Which big idea could this topic best illuminate? Why?

What important content from this unit will support understanding of the big idea?

In what ways can I tailor my instruction and learning tasks to ensure that the big idea is conveyed clearly?

How will I assess students' ability to transfer their understanding of the big idea?

Dobetter Planning with Big Ideas

Ms. Dobetter is ready to give these questions a try as she plans her sixth-grade unit on light. In the past, she has always rushed through this unit jumping from activity to activity, all fun stuff, but this year she hopes to do a better job of targeting and achieving clear learning goals linked to a specific big idea.

What are the learning goals of this unit?

Light. We usually study the wave and particle natures of light, the visible and electromagnetic spectrums, the speed of light, reflection, refraction, lenses, and mirrors. We have a lot of great kits full of activities about light, but in the past this unit has been like a buffet of appetizers—a lot of quickie activities, but with no real main course.

Which big idea could this topic best illuminate? Why?

I think energy would be a natural. I could see going with "systems and interactions," or even "patterns of change" if we were planning to focus on the lenses and mirrors and all. I think the big idea of energy best connects to the very nature of light, which ought to be our focus.

What important content will support understanding of the big idea?

I want students to understand that light can act as both a wave and a particle, that the white light we can see is made up of all the colors of the visible spectrum, and that light energy comes from many sources and is used for a variety of purposes. I think all of these topics relate specifically to light, and connect well to the big idea of energy. I would like to put the focus here for this unit, rather than getting distracted building periscopes.

In what ways can I tailor my instruction and learning tasks to ensure that the big idea is conveyed clearly?

I think I need to look back over all of the light-related activities we have and really find those that pertain to light as energy. There are just so many things we can do and have done; yet I don't think they all served the purpose of understanding. I think I will need to cut back a lot on coverage, and dive deep into a few important tasks. We should do the prism investigation, talk about wave and particle theory, and talk about light in the context of students' lives. The sun prints and flashlight tag in the gym may have to go.

How will you assess students' ability to transfer their understanding of the big idea?

I think our final unit assessment will be open-ended, asking students to explain whether light is a wave or a particle and why, and then asking them to describe how light illuminates energy as a big idea.

Our next unit will actually be on sound, so I am thinking perhaps we will keep this big idea going as a bridge between the two. We can do a lot of work comparing and contrasting light and sound to support students synthesizing this information.

Energy

When the students enter class, it says *Energy* on the whiteboard. Ms. Dobetter made a decision to start here, rather than with *Light*. This way, she frontloads the big idea.

"What do you think 'energy' means? Why do you think scientists might be interested in energy?" She asks the class to write silently about these two questions. Learners have a lot of ideas, including textbook definitions—"Energy is the capacity to do work," and its corollary, "If we don't have any energy, we can't do anything." Now that she has primed the pump of students' thinking, Ms. Dobetter sets up a Give One–Get One (see Chapter 4) brainstorming activity, inviting learners to come up with as many examples of energy as they can. When the class is done sharing, the list reads "music, heat, light, food, bounce, the sun, gravity, sound, electricity, pushing, pulling, static, magnetism, and cars." Ms. Dobetter ends class by clarifying which of their ideas are and are *not* examples of energy by further exploring each and explaining energy's definition. She knows they will have to talk about this some more.

The next day, Ms. Dobetter is ready to link the big idea to the content: she starts class by distributing prisms and invites students to spend fifteen minutes trying them out in the sunny windows, recording what they notice and wonder. After gathering their observations, Ms. Dobetter asks the learners if they saw any evidence of energy. Students talk about heat and about rainbows. She pauses to introduce a vocabulary word, "spectrum."

Over the next few days Ms. Dobetter guides her students in investigating the nature of light based on their observations of how prisms function. Through this task, she introduces them to important unit vocabulary—wavelength, frequency, intensity, and more. In this way, students enter the unit by observing light's energy and how it plays with a prism.

After learners draw some general conclusions from their work splitting light into its component parts, Ms. Dobetter explains that the exploratory nature of their investigations with the prisms match the research of early scientists into the nature of light. Ms. Dobetter produces copies of original observations and analysis by two important scientists, Robert Hooke (wave theory) and Isaac Newton (particle theory), and works with students to make meaning of these texts (see Chapter 10 on reading for ideas about how). In class, they replicate some of the demonstrations they read about to further illustrate light's nature as a form of energy.

As a final unit task, Ms. Dobetter invites students to relate their understanding of light to their daily lives. They brainstorm sources and uses of light, and divide into small groups to research many of those: the sun, compact fluorescent bulbs, photovoltaic cells, television screens, solar water heating, and so forth. Each team is charged to teach the class about how their particular source or use of light involves energy transformation.

Each of these three major tasks—the prism investigation, the Hooke and Newton studies, and the light research—takes about a week of carefully planned workshop model instruction (see Chapter 3). With this much time devoted to these major projects, very little is left for many of the fun, quick activities Ms. Dobetter had done with students in the past—lens experiments, scientific notation, and the speed of light, sun prints, and more are left out. Some optics topics do come up during their research presentations, yet her class does not "cover" everything to do with light, as they had in the past.

Just as Ms. Dobetter is starting to get nervous about her departure from the survey approach to curriculum, students are completing their unit assessment. She is delighted by their explanations of light's wave and particle natures, and sees from reading students' work that most do understand light as a model of energy. They draw parallels between light and ocean waves, electrical current, and even weather patterns. Many cite examples from classmates' research as evidence, and others reach back to their work with prisms to support explanations. In all, students convey a great intensity of understanding of light as a means of moving energy from one place to another very quickly.

So What?

Big ideas lighten the load. Rather than being the straw that breaks the camel's back, big ideas have the potential to be the ergonomic saddle that allows the camel to sensibly distribute a load. As demonstrated by Ms. Dobetter in the example above, big ideas can help a busy teacher to focus instruction on understanding goals that really matter in terms of students' lifelong experiences as science learners. When we take the time to organize our courses and curriculum around big ideas, we hone our ability to teach toward worthy understandings.

"Yah, but . . ."

- *"Aren't the standards enough?"*

That is the problem: the standards are more than enough. They are so broad that we can never do them all justice. So, the big ideas help us to tighten our focus and teach important standards-based content while illuminating an overarching idea that our students can carry with them for life.

- *"Are you kidding me? Who has time to go back and rework their entire curriculum?"*

No one has that kind of time! And don't feel pressured to make a sweeping change. Try slowly, one task or unit at a time. Test out a big idea. See how it fits. Test ways to bring it to life. Discuss it with your students. Revise. Each time you take steps toward integrating big ideas, you become more familiar with this process. You may also find yourself motivated by the elegance and efficacy of this approach. Take your time.

- *"I don't think California has it right at all. I found another list of big ideas that makes much more sense."*

Fantastic! If you have found a list that works for you, by all means use that set! Just double check that the ideas are truly big—overarching, thematic, cutting across all of the many disciplines of science. If the ideas you are working with do that, you are on your way to expanding your students' ability to make important science connections.

Now that we have explored inquiry as an approach to science teaching, and the value of selecting content that supports students' understanding of a big idea, let us look at how we can use the workshop model to train students to become self-reliant scientists.

CHAPTER 3

Workshop

When teachers use the workshop model to structure instruction, students engage, experience success, and develop independence as scientific thinkers and learners.

Think Tank

- How do students spend their time in my classes?
- How do I ensure that students are thinking and learning in science class?
- What evidence do I gather to assess students' understanding?
- How do I use that evidence to adjust my instruction?

A tray of materials waits on each table. "Okay, guys, take your seats. Today we are going to do the salt crystal activity on page 124. Everyone is going to need their books. After you do the activity, answer the questions at the bottom of the page. You can work in pairs if you want. Then answer the questions on notebook paper; that is your ticket out the door."

Some students dig textbooks out of their backpacks; others try to cozy up to neighbors whose books are open. The teacher returns to his desk and starts recording attendance, which is due in the computer within the first ten minutes of class. "Miller!?" He calls out. "Is he here today?" A few pupils share that they think he is absent today. "Dominguez?"

"Here." The teacher finishes at his desk, then strolls up and down the rows checking on the students' progress.

"Stephan, where is your book? Myra, read the directions. That is way too much salt . . . Tom, what are you supposed to be doing?" A few more comments to the working teens, then he walks to the light switches and flicks them off. "People, it is way too loud in here!" The class simmers down; most are following the directions in the book to create a salt solution, some with more precision than others. The teacher resumes his tour of the class, pausing to praise Melissa and Anthony for their accurate measurements. Sage spills Vance's solution, and the two get into an argument, which the teacher diffuses. They all work together to clean up the wet mess.

With ten minutes left in the period, most teams are done mixing solutions and have begun to chat. Their teacher reminds them that they need to tidy up the materials and store their work on the back counter, and that the written answers to the questions are their "ticket out the door." Students rip paper out of their binders and start to write one-word answers in response to the book's questions about their predictions. The teacher seizes the opportunity to talk with Olivia about missing homework assignments, and how those are bringing down her grade. The bell rings. The teacher shouts, "Questions!" then stands at the door gathering a mass of papers as the students push past him.

Exhausted, he straightens the sheets into a pile quickly as the next class shuffles in the door. He has just enough time to refill the salt supply on each table before the next bell rings.

Reflection

In this class, what structures were in place to support student learning?

What was the teacher's role during work time?

How will the teacher know what his students understand?

Why Workshops Work

If we look at the hidden curriculum behind the day's activity described above, a student might describe science as "following directions," and summarize her learning with the monosyllabic answers recorded on torn-out notebook paper. Undoubtedly, there is a time and a place for simply following directions; that is how the astronauts aboard Apollo 13 saved their own lives. Yet if our curriculum relies solely on procedural tasks—following steps, copying definitions, replicating models—rather than conceptual ones, we are missing a golden opportunity to steep our students in the thinking of science. How can we best train our students as scientific thinkers?

Years ago, Donald Graves introduced the workshop model as a means to train learners to become self-sufficient in the craft of writing (1983). Providing a gradual release of responsibility (Pearson and Gallagher 1983) and sufficient scaffolding (Wood, Bruner, and Ross 1976), workshop model instruction fosters independence by giving students training and support, then affording them ample time to work and think. After a short "minilesson," students spent the majority of time in a workshop model classroom talking, thinking, and working.

A version of the workshop model can be implemented in science classes as well to apprentice our students as scientists. By empowering learners as thinkers and workers, workshop model instruction promotes student engagement and content understanding.

The workshop model reduces the amount of time teachers spend talking and explaining to the whole group, and increases the amount of time students confer individually with their teacher. Workshops promote student ownership of the process and product, and thereby place the responsibility for learning in the students' laps. The workshop model allows for an ongoing cycle of assessment to guide daily instruction; workshop model instruction creates time for both students and teachers to think about what they are learning, why their learning is important, and how it fits with what they already know. Workshops work.

Workshop Structure

Whether during literacy classes or science, the rhythm of a workshop remains the same.

- *Before* work time we must set a purpose linked to a big idea, engage the students, break the task into doable steps, and then model the inquiry skills students need to succeed.
- *During* work time learners practice, with support, and teachers confer with them about their learning.
- *After* work time, students share, reflect on, and receive feedback about their thinking and products.

In this way, each segment of instruction—whether contained in a class period or an entire unit of study—has a clear beginning, middle, and end. Throughout the chapters of this book, you will see various versions of the workshop model demonstrated, but the phases remain the same. Ideally workshops include before, during, and after phases within each lesson, each day, each project, each unit, and even each year.

Gradual Release of Responsibility

The Gradual Release of Responsibility model designed by Pearson and Gallagher (1983) helps us to think about the transition between wholly teacher-led modeling or instruction and students' sustained independent work. For many learners, there are important middle steps between these two—shared practice and guided practice.

Shared practice of a thinking skill takes place when the teacher continues to lead the group but invites students to think and work with her through a task. For example, rather than simply explaining the meaning of a graph of Arctic and Antarctic ice measurements taken over the past one hundred years, a teacher could invite students to use their background knowledge and discuss together as a class their explanations based on that evidence. With the teacher still in the lead, learners think and talk together, practicing their inferring skills and experiencing firsthand one of the essential features of inquiry.

The next step in the Gradual Release of Responsibility as described by its authors is guided practice. During guided practice, students take on more of the responsibility for thinking and talking, although the teacher remains intimately involved. During this stage, we may have students discussing the graphs in their table groups, guided by a series of questions: For a few minutes, groups may be asked to discuss what trends they notice, then called to turn back to the whole group and share their thinking. Next, back in their groups, students could discuss possible explanations for those trends, then again come back together with the whole group to share. At this stage, their teacher is still monitoring the groups' progress and thinking, though learners are increasingly independent.

These two stages, shared practice and guided practice, prepare students for the ultimate goal of gradual release: focused, successful independent thinking.

Before

Before we ask students to work independently, we need to frame the day's work. This includes

- setting a *purpose,*
- *engaging* learners in thinking about the task,
- *scaffolding* the task by breaking the learning activity into smaller steps, and
- *modeling* the thinking required to complete the work.

This chunk of instruction before work time is often referred to as the "minilesson." By the end of the minilesson, students should know what they are learning and how they are going to go about that learning; they should feel empowered and motivated to get started. Below, I elaborate on important ways to set the stage for students' success during work time.

Set the Purpose

Sometimes I hear students entering class ask, "What are we *doing* today?" Teachers usually respond with a description of the task: "some reading," "a lab," and so forth. These answers tend to satisfy students' curiosity and many learners may be willing to give the job their best effort. It is curious to me that I never hear students ask, "What are we *learning* today?"

As a staff developer visiting classrooms, I sometimes ask individual learners that question, "What are you learning right now?" I am amazed by how often this query stumps even the most engaged students. We owe it to them to set a clear purpose—share the day's learning goals and connections to a big idea, not just the task description—with them. Instead of hearing students answer with, "We are doing this lab," it is always delightful to hear one say, "We are learning about specific heat, an example of the big idea 'energy.'" This is the difference between students understanding the task versus the learning goal.

This purpose could be presented in writing, aloud, or in some other mode of communication. I have found that highlighting the purpose of the day's work goes a long way toward getting students' minds on the task before them.

Engage

For years, my students challenged me daily with adolescent questions—"Who cares?" "When will I ever use this?" "Why do we have to learn this?" While annoying in the moment, these questions were actually important to my development as a teacher. I decided that if on a given day or for a given activity I could not answer those questions reasonably, I should either rethink what I was asking learners to learn or perhaps even toss out the task. But once I began to think about my content and learning activities more carefully, it was not too much of a stretch for me to come up with an answer to explain the value of just about anything I had planned.

After setting the purpose or learning goal for any given lesson, and contextualizing that learning within the frame of a big idea, I would head my students off at the pass by answering their questions before they asked.

"Why do we need to know about plate tectonics?" I told them the true story of my childhood experiences with earthquakes in Los Angeles.

"Who cares about the endocrine system?" I related honest tales of a relative's struggle with thyroid problems.

"What is so important about the electromagnetic spectrum?" I shared the story of a neighborhood business's debate about the placement of a cell phone tower.

"How am I going to use this stuff about acids and bases?" We discussed cooking, digestion, and stain removal.

And so on. I admit, sometimes I would embellish the truth or spin tales for the sake of my listeners, but the premise always remains true: this stuff matters. Sharing stories about each topic's real life relevance creates an opportunity for my classes to get to know me as a person, not just a cog in their educational system.

Once we get talking, students are often ready with stories of their own; elicit their background knowledge, brainstorm their questions, invite their connections and predictions about the content at hand. In addition to open discussion and sharing, Figure

Quick Write	Give everyone a half-sheet of paper. Pose a thinking question or two: What do you know about meiosis? How would you explain the difference between meiosis and mitosis? Though "quick," give students plenty of time to write—three to five minutes to start. If you give only one minute, you will likely receive very brief responses. By progressively lengthening the quick write time, expecting sustained attention and thoughtful responses, you strengthen students' capacity to respond thoughtfully in writing as scientists. No need to worry about spelling or grammar; focus instead on getting the thinking down.
Quick Draw	Like a quick write, but instead of asking learners to use narrative, invite them to draw and label a picture or diagram. For example, "Sketch and label a picture that shows what you know about ionic bonding."
Think-Pair-Share	Again, open with a question. Invite silent time for thinking: "What would you look for in a quality conclusion to a science investigation?" Ask students to raise their thumbs or otherwise signal when they have thought through their own answers. Then invite students to turn to a partner, share their own thinking, and next listen to their peers. Since you have given everyone a chance to think, share, and listen, you can then feel free as the teacher to call randomly on anyone in the room to share an idea—their own or their partner's—with the whole class.

FIG. 3.1 *Structures to Engage Thinkers*

3.1 offers some other concrete strategies and structures for getting students engaged in thinking about the topic at hand.

Scaffold

Once students are engaged, we are ready to set them on the right track in their thinking and working. We can do this by breaking the day's work into bite-sized chunks, perhaps including some of the distinct features of inquiry.

Every class includes learners of diverse interests and abilities. We have all met seventh graders ready for college, and tenth graders who cannot read. To best meet the needs of all of our students and their range of abilities, it is helpful to break tasks (whether simple or long-range) down into smaller steps and provide checkpoints along the way to ensure that all are on the right track. Some students may not necessarily need this sort of support, but we are unlikely to hinder their progress by showing them the steps.

For example, the other day my four-year-old created a hair salon in her bedroom. Essentially this meant pulling out every toy and doll and stuffed pet and accessory in the house and arranging them all just-so around a pint-sized chair. We played hairdresser for several days, and finally I decided it was time to clean up her room. So I said, "Clean up your room," and walked away. I came back, and it was still a hair salon. Recognizing my folly, I got more involved. "Remember where the stuffed animals go? Put them all in the bin." I put Ella the baby doll away. "Now let's pick up all the jewelry and put it back in the box." I leaned over and grabbed a handful of plastic accessories and one crown. And pretty soon, we had her room back together.

Your students' work is obviously more complex than tidying a child's bedroom, but the same principles apply. This is scaffolding: selecting discrete tasks essential to the completion of the whole, and providing targeted instruction and support for students completing each. We need to explain the steps, then take those steps one by one together with them.

Model

Once the task has been broken down into bite-sized pieces, we ideally will model small chunks of thinking each step of the way. Whether asking students to read a chapter, conduct an experiment, create a physical representation, or design an investigation, we need to first show—not just tell—them what we mean.

Does this suggest giving students the answers? No, we need only demonstrate the habits of mind required to arrive at those "answers," making our thinking as scientists transparent. We need not show learners *what* to think, but rather *how* to think.

Modeling could include walking learners through a related but separate task, or talking them through today's activity highlighting key thinking points. In every instance, our purpose as a teacher when we model is to guide students through the thinking we want them to be able to do on their own. For example, say we are about to invite students to conduct their own experiments on the affect of cola on brine shrimp metabolic rates. Before we ask them to come up with hypotheses, we want learners to understand the nature of a quality hypothesis in general. We may start our conversation by inviting them to list the criteria for a good hypothesis, then suggest a related but different experiment—say, adding warmer water to a goldfish bowl. We can then model for students how we might develop our own hypothesis for the warm water-goldfish bowl experiment.

Peers are also powerful and important models. We may share student work from a previous year's class, or highlight the thinking of current students to support the class understanding of what is expected, and what they and their peers are capable of doing.

Rather than overwhelming the group with in-depth suggestions about the entire process of lab design at once, most effective modeling is specific and succinct. Building on students' background knowledge, an example should offer just one or two new ideas or thoughts. This modeling takes time, more time than simply saying to the kids, "Write a hypothesis," or "Design an experiment." But when we take the time, more learners are able to actually understand what writing a hypothesis or designing an experiment really means, and we empower them as scientists. In the long run, students benefit more when we progress slowly and build deep understanding each step of the way (for more on labs, see Chapter 6).

Thinking Aloud

A think-aloud is a specific way to model thinking. In a think-aloud, we essentially recite to learners our own mind's chatter as we walk through a thought process.

For example, thinking aloud to develop my hypothesis about the warm water-goldfish experiment, I might share as follows:

> The science question I am thinking about is, "What would happen to my goldfish if I added some warm water to her bowl?" Not too much, but just enough to make it feel tropical to her. I know that fish live all over the world in all different temperatures, but she is used to her room temperature water. I know I find taking a warm bath relaxing, so I wonder if my fish's metabolic rate will slow down if I warm up her water. My hypothesis is that if I increase the temperature in her bowl by five degrees Centigrade, she will decrease her activity level and heart rate.

I may go on to share my thinking about controls and variables, what data I plan to collect as evidence, as well as other aspects of experimental design, just talking aloud to the students in the same voice I use when mulling things over in my own mind. After this think-aloud, or modeling, I can review with the class the key points in my thinking process and make a checklist for learners as they work on hypotheses of their own (for more on thinking aloud, see Chapter 10).

During

While learners are busy working, it is tempting to turn to the array of unfinished tasks in every teacher's inbox: take attendance, check homework, organize supplies or copies for a later class, respond to emails from colleagues and parents, catch up on paperwork . . . the list goes on.

During students' work time, we need to be available and confer with them to promote thinking and learning. When we focus our attention on sitting and talking with individuals and small groups about science, rather than critiquing off-task behavior or poor work habits, we demonstrate that we care about and give attention to *learning*.

Confer

Precious work time when students are engaged in their own learning presents an ideal opportunity for us to connect with learners individually, assess their progress, and push their thinking. This can be done through conferring.

Conferring can take many forms; ideally, it entails short, individual conversation between teacher and student while the rest of the class continues their independent work. Conferring is *not* about giving answers. These conversations include three parts:

- information gathering,
- instruction, and
- planning the next steps.

For example, this conversation between a student and teacher about a physics experiment demonstrates these aspects of conferring.

> "How is it going?"
>
> "Fine."
>
> "What are you working on?"
>
> "Well, we think that a bigger ball will fall faster than a smaller, lighter ball, so we set up the timing gates on the staircase to test that. We dropped both balls from the second floor landing down the slot in the middle of the stairs."
>
> "And what did you find out."
>
> "Nothing, really."
>
> "What do you mean nothing?"
>
> "Well, a couple of times the tennis ball landed first, and a couple of times the Ping–Pong ball did."
>
> "Are you dropping them at the same time?"
>
> "No, one at a time, but based on their travel time, we don't have any conclusions."
>
> "What do you think a scientist would do in this situation?"
>
> "Try again."
>
> "What would that look like?"
>
> "We probably need to do a lot more trials and average the data."
>
> "Great plan. What do you need in order to get started?"
>
> "We need to set the gates back up."
>
> "Is there anything else you need?"
>
> "No."
>
> "You have twenty more minutes of work time; now is a great time to set those gates up and gather more data."

In this conversation, you see the teacher walking through those three steps. First, she assesses the team's progress and learns that they have a hypothesis and have tested it, but found their data to be inconclusive. Next, prodding with the question about how scientists handle such situations, she simply reminds them of the importance of repetition in the scientific process. This moment of instruction was created not by offering an answer but by asking a question. Lastly, she helps the learners to clarify their plan before moving on. In this way, within a short conversation, this teacher assisted a group in moving to the next level with their independent work.

We can record learners' thinking and progress in a variety of ways while conferring; some teachers I know use a small notebook with a page for each student or team, recording each conversation there. Other teachers will simply have the class list on a clipboard and use that as a place to keep notes. Whatever the structure, we need to have somewhere to keep track of students' progress over time to ensure that each opportunity to confer builds on the last. These notes also serve as useful assessment data (conferring is discussed further in Chapter 4).

After

After work time, students need to reflect on their learning, and to assess their progress toward the learning goals. This step, all-too-often skipped, ensures that students know where they themselves are in the learning process, and that teachers have sufficient information to be able to refine the next stage of instruction as needed.

Reflect

At the conclusion of any project, and at many junctures along the way, we need to pause and allow students opportunities for metacognition—that is, for learners to stop and think about their own thinking and learning: What do you understand? What questions do you have? How does this learning connect to your background knowledge, the big ideas? This important step, according to researcher Richard Stiggins (1997), ensures for all students greater possibilities of success. The questions need not be complex, but this is a source of valuable information to help guide future instruction.

Certainly the act of reflection is beneficial to the students themselves, yet reflections are a wonderful tool for teachers' assessment and planning, giving a window into learners' thinking at a given point in time, as shown in Figure 3.2. Some teachers have students record their reflections in science notebooks, while others use separate pieces of paper they call an "exit ticket" collected as students leave class.

Regardless of where learners reflect, this exercise produces its best results when teachers create time to read through—even skim—students' responses at frequent, regular intervals. Reading reflections helps teachers tailor their next class session to meet the needs of the group—which may mean slowing down, speeding up, or even taking a detour from the original unit plan to ensure all students meet the learning goals along the way.

> Overall, I think my weaknesses lie in recording my results. I often have trouble collecting all the quantitative data I need from my experiments, leaving holes in my data tables and graphs. I have been working on this, however, and my data-collecting skills have definitely improved. I think my strengths are mainly in taking observations and analyzing my results. I love to observe everything during an experiment, and it is fascinating to make conjectures about why things happened the way they did.

FIG. 3.2 *Student Reflection After a Lab Investigation*

These opportunities for metacognition and self-assessment are essential for science learners. In *How Students Learn Science in the Classroom* (Donovan and Bransford 2005), the authors share a case study on reflective assessment which demonstrated the efficacy of students answering targeted reflection questions after a learning experience. Compared to a control group asked to answer more general questions, the students invited to reflect on their understanding of the main ideas and of the inquiry process (as well as a variety of attributes of the task itself) exhibited greater gains in science learning (for more on reflection, see Chapters 4 and 5).

Some teachers like to end class with this final reflection on an "exit ticket," collected as students leave the class. Figure 3.3 suggests some potential reflection prompts, which can also serve as tools for assessment.

Assess

Formative assessment, including conferring, is the ongoing process of gathering data on student understanding. Some assessment is linked to grading, other assessment links to planning, and much links to both. Exit tickets, reflections, conferring notes, and class discussion participation can all serve as sources of formative assessment data, as can a teacher's own observations of students at work. This data is crucial fodder for thought for the reflective teacher ready to plan tomorrow's minilesson in response to today's learners' needs.

For example, one teacher I worked with created a geometry project to assist his students in understanding reflection and refraction. On the first day of independent work time, many students' work with protractors indicated that they were rusty on how to use one to measure or sketch angles. Vigilant to his students' needs and struggles, this savvy teacher adjusted his weekly plan to start the next day with a lesson on protractors, reminding the learners of the requisite skills for success in this task. In this way, ongoing assessment created an opportunity for responsive teaching that fostered student success.

Traditional tests and quizzes, products, presentations, models, performance tasks, and the like are all worthy demonstrations of student understanding. In Chapter 4 and

- Your biggest "aha" moment today
- A time when you were thinking like a scientist
- A question you have about what you learned today
- A connection between your learning today and a big idea of science
- The most important thing you want to remember
- Something you wish we had more time to investigate
- One thing you understand; one you are still confused about
- Assess your progress toward today's learning goal
- Feedback for the teacher about how today's class could have been even better
- What you say when your friends ask you, "What was science class about today?"
- If we were starting class with a pop quiz tomorrow, what would the questions be?
- What do you think we are going to do next?

FIG. 3.3 *Exit Ticket Ideas*

later chapters, we will look at various demonstrations of understanding and the role that rubrics can play as project maps guiding students to success.

For the purpose of workshop design, what is important to remember about assessment is that we need this data, this evidence. We need to get it from students during or after their work time. So, tempting as it may be to extend independent work right up to the looming bell, we must get into the habit of stopping earlier, giving students the gift of reflection before they move on to their next class.

Figure 3.4 offers an overview of all of these stages in the workshop model, and the suggested steps within each stage. The table indicates what both teachers and students should be doing each step of the way.

Planning deliberate workshop model science instruction does require an investment of time. Yet once you and your students hit the stride of this routine, it will flow easily before, during, and after each learning experience—and the benefits in terms of

	What does the teacher do?	**What do the students do?**
Before		
Purpose	Clearly explains the big idea and the learning goal of the work.	Understand what they are supposed to be learning, and how this topic relates to the broader field of science.
Engage	Piques student interest and investment in the topic.	Understand why the topic is meaningful to them; activate their own background knowledge.
Scaffold	Breaks task down into manageable steps, provides instruction around each step, and assesses students' progress before encouraging them to embark on the next segment of the project.	Understand the steps required to complete the project; recognize what the teacher expects at each stage before allowing students to move on.
Model	Demonstrates the thinking involved in completing the task at hand successfully.	Observe and hear how the teacher thought through a related task.
During		
Confer	Uses work time to connect instructionally with as many students as possible.	Work independently; enjoy opportunities to talk one-on-one or in small groups with teacher to share what they understand and receive assistance in areas of confusion.
After		
Reflect	Asks students to be metacognitive about the meaning of the work they are doing in class.	Have frequent opportunities to stop and think about their new learning, and to put it into the context of their background knowledge and lives.
Assess	Creates opportunities throughout as well as at the conclusion of the project for students to give and receive feedback.	Receive specific feedback from peers and teacher about their thinking and products.

FIG. 3.4 *Workshop Overview*

student engagement and student learning will prove your investment well worth the effort. Here are some planning questions to help you get started.

Designing Workshops: Teacher Planning Questions

Before

Purpose: What is the learning goal of this activity? How does this relate to a big idea?

Engage: What is the relevance of what we are studying?

Scaffold: How can I break the activity into small steps with checkpoints along the way?

Model: What will I need to model in order for students to be successful?

During

Confer: What questions will I ask students while they are working?

What will I be looking for to assess students' understanding?

After

Reflect: How can I invite reflection and sharing as we work on and conclude this task?

Assess: How will I know what students learned from this experience?

Dobetter Workshop

Ms. Dobetter had always used a water temperature exploration activity to introduce her thermal energy unit with her seventh-grade physical science class. In it, she asked students to follow directions on a worksheet, observe and record changes to the temperature of containers of hot and cold water over time, and to answer some questions about their explanations based on the evidence they gathered. In the past, she noticed that the activity did not really seem effective in introducing the unit, and that the students' completed worksheets did not reflect much thought. This year she considered searching out a new activity, but instead decided to stick with the old one yet implement the workshop model in an effort to bring it to life. Here is how she thought through the planning of her day's lesson using the workshop planning questions.

Before

Purpose: *What is the learning goal of this activity? How does this relate to a big idea?*

My goal is for students to understand how water temperatures can change over time based on environmental conditions.

Really the purpose of this activity—it is not really a lab, just an activity—is to get the students thinking about temperature and thermal energy, engage them in an experience that will hopefully help them to see where this next unit is heading, and motivate them to start thinking about the big idea: patterns of change.

Engage: *What is the relevance of what we are studying?*

We just always have done the thermal energy unit before the kinetic energy unit, but now that I think about it, thermal energy is really important to the students and their lives; cooking, for example, or running a car—these are times in our lives when we can benefit from an understanding of thermal energy. So I think it is highly relevant, but that the kids will not really see that unless I make a point of it. I am thinking I can tell some stories from my own kitchen to bring it to life for them: deciding how to defrost frozen stew on the stovetop—two small pots or one big one?

Model: *What will I need to model in order for students to be successful?*

Well, based on my past experiences with this activity, there are a few things the students don't always get that they should. Measuring with a graduated cylinder is a challenge for some, and if they don't do it correctly it can really throw off their results. I need to explain the meniscus. Also, reading thermometers is important to review. You would be surprised how many confuse Centigrade and Fahrenheit, and how unfamiliar they are with reading the mercury level. Those are the two skills that can really make or break this activity.

The one other thing I would like to convey is my expectations for quality in their written work. So often, these guys just turn in brief, shoddy things . . . a few words in answer to each question. I am looking for at least a sentence!

Scaffold: *How can I break the activity into small steps with checkpoints along the way?*

I am thinking that before they really get to do the activity they need to show me that they can read a meniscus and a thermometer. I think I will do a quick lab skills practical exam at each table before I hand over their materials. That would go a long way toward ensuring their success.

Also, I would like students to finish the whole task before they run ahead to the reflection questions; sometimes, they seem to think that those are all that really counts. So my new idea is to put the questions on a separate page, not on the back of that activity sheet, so that I can give questions out only after they are done collecting data.

During

Confer: *What questions will I ask students while they are working? What will I be looking for to assess students' understanding?*

I think I will ask them about their measurements, what they are finding, what they are thinking about how the change in temperature in the hot beaker compares to the change in temperature in the cold. Really, this will just give me a baseline on their thinking about thermal energy. I do not really know what they know yet since this is just the beginning of the unit, so conferring during this activity will be a great opportunity for me to preassess their understanding.

After

Reflect: *How can I invite reflection and sharing as we work on and conclude this task?*

I think I need to ask good, specific questions: What do you understand now about temperature? What patterns of change did you notice? How did this activity help you develop your understanding? What are you still wondering? I will give them each time to write, then ask students to pair and share their thinking.

Assess: *How will I know what students learned from this experience?*

In addition to assessing their lab skills and thinking about thermal energy during the activity, I will read all of their reflection answers and use those to make decisions about what to do next. If this task accomplishes our learning goal, we can move on. If students remain fuzzy, I will have to look for more ways to reinforce these key concepts before we take the next steps in our unit.

What Happens

Before

Ms. Dobetter's students file in, taking their seats with a modicum of enthusiasm. Rather than starting with the usual question of the day on the board, she elects to begin with a story about what happened at her house last night: her cousin was coming to dinner. Ms. Dobetter's cat had gotten sick and so she had rushed to the vet after school and, by the time she got home, she felt too tired to cook. She searched the freezer and found some delicious chickpea and artichoke heart stew she had made last summer and knew this was just the time to thaw and serve it. Here was the dilemma: she had two small Ziploc bags, both frozen solid. To defrost all of it, was she better off putting it together in one big pot or separating the stew into two small vessels on the stove?

She stops her tale there and invites the class to share their thoughts. Despite students' insistence, Ms. Dobetter does not tell them how she proceeded, but rather implores them to test their theories at home, then draw their own conclusions.

At this point, Ms. Dobetter introduces the purpose of today's work: "We are going to be looking at a pattern of change. Do you remember any examples of that big idea?" Students recall studying angiosperm life cycles and the cell theory last year as examples of this big idea. They review these topics for a few minutes, recalling the meaning of a "pattern of change."

"You can be thinking about how temperature changes relate to those concepts you studied in life science . . . my goal is that by the time the bell rings, you will understand how and why water temperatures change over time based on environmental conditions. If you can explain that in detail, we will each have done our job today."

The defrosting the stew story proves to be an engaging leaping off point for her brief explanation of thermal energy, its utility and import. Ms. Dobetter chooses not to belabor her point but instead leaps right into an introduction of the day's activity: on the overhead, she flashes a copy of the handout students are being given. She asks them to turn to their lab partners and read the activity sheet aloud to one another. When the classroom quiets, she points out a couple of things they will need to know in order to succeed at the task.

She had sketched a graduated cylinder on the board and invites a student up to explain what he remembers about the meniscus. Other students pipe up, and pretty soon the whole class seems to be recalling what they learned in elementary school about measuring fluid. She invites students to model the measurement strategies rather than doing so herself: she requests a volunteer to come up to the other sketch on the board and explain how thermometers are used; one girl, then another, comes forth to review the rudiments of measuring temperature using the mercury's meniscus. The class as a whole, Ms. Dobetter realizes, remembers a lot.

She explains that to ensure each person—not just the collective—is ready with these skills, she will go around quickly and quiz each pair aloud. While she visits with each team, she expects the remainder of the students to be getting out their homework from last night, and writing down the assignment for the next two days from the homework box on the board.

During

Once she checks their measuring skills, Ms. Dobetter invites each team to go to the back counter, pick up their materials, and get started. Students sit in pairs, watching the clock, reading thermometers, recording temperatures. Ms. Dobetter quickly makes her rounds and finds that she only has to reexplain these skills to two people in the room. She gathers all the homework on her way through the rows. Once work time commences, she is ready to confer with the teams at work.

"What are you finding?"

"The cold one is warming, and the hot one is cooling."

"Why do you think so?"

"Because it's too cold and too hot."

"What does that mean, *too* cold?"

"Well, it's colder than the room, so it is warming up from the room."

"Do you think so? How?"

"Well, everything likes to be room temperature. That is why the hot one is cooling off."

"Why? What is the pattern of change?"

By the time Ms. Dobetter has spoken with half of the groups, she starts noticing most teams are done gathering evidence, recording temperatures in their data tables, and have started to clean up their materials.

She calls the class's attention to the analysis questions designed to guide learners in developing their own explanations based on the evidence gathered from this activity. Ms. Dobetter spends another minute at the overheard modeling the kinds of thinking she is looking for in a quality analysis. She refers back to the conversation above where a student thought carefully about the cause of an observed temperature change, explaining that orally this girl demonstrated a great depth of understanding but what a darn shame it would be if all she wrote on the paper was, "Because." In this way, Ms. Dobetter conveys her expectations before again releasing the students to work.

After

With ten minutes left before the forty-five-minute bell, Ms. Dobetter asks students to break the studious silence, turn to a partner, choose any two analysis questions of the eight, and each share how they answered those. Ms. Dobetter encourages kids to change or add to their answers if the conversation changes their thinking or deepens their understanding in any way. The room is again abuzz with voices as students turn and talk.

Lastly, she asks students to flip their papers over and reflect on the day's work. On the overhead, she writes, "Assess your own progress toward today's learning goal. How did the task help you understand? What are you still wondering? Did you notice a pattern of change? How does this learning relate to what you already know about the big idea?"

As closure to the class, Ms. Dobetter grabs her can of Popsicle sticks and pulls out two. She calls on the students whose names are on those two to each share their "aha" for the day.

Evelyn says, "I had forgotten that whole thing about the meniscus, and so you reminded me of that. I guess that was the biggest thing."

Sabre explains, "I realized from collecting the data that everything tries to get back to the middle. Temperatures are temporary."

Ms. Dobetter acknowledges the class for their good work, stands at the door and collects their papers. As she glances down at the top of her pile, she is glad to see sentences rather than phrases and single words used to fill in the spaces after each analysis question. "Definitely better than last year," she thinks to herself.

So What?

In the example above, we see how Ms. Dobetter enlivened a mundane worksheet activity by utilizing the workshop model. Her class enjoyed an engaging opening discussion, was prepared for success during work time, and had an opportunity to reflect on their learning before the bell rang. Using the workshop model, she succeeded in getting the majority of her class thinking carefully about the content.

As you read each chapter in the "Variables" section, you will see a range of examples of how the workshop model could be employed—whether students are reading *On The Origin of the Species*, building egg-drop devices, or constructing rocket ships to the moon.

"Yah, but . . ."

- *My classes are only forty-two minutes long."*

We can think of the workshop model as contained in one class period, one day, one week, or one entire unit. While block scheduling offers ideal opportunities to implement all aspects of the workshop model on a daily basis, teachers with shorter classes can condense the "before, during, after" to fit into a daily lesson, or spread different parts of their workshops over several days, preserving just a couple of minutes to review yesterday and wrap up before tomorrow in each class period.

- *"When I sit down to confer, the rest of the class goes crazy."*

Independent work is a learned skill. When students have the purpose, modeling, and scaffolding they need in order to be successful, they are more likely to use the independent work time wisely. Still, you can start small with short chunks—just a few minutes—of conferring time. Remind students of your expectations and the value you place on conferring. Let them know that when they are doing the right thing, everyone benefits because their responsible participation means that you get to spend your time being a teacher, not a warden. Create a rubric for quality independent work time. Enlist students' understanding and support. Scaffold by practicing, giving feedback, and practicing again. Remind students of the real world value of working independently.

- *"How am I supposed to know what the students need before releasing them?"*

Past experience is often the best reference point to help a teacher understand how to head off student confusion. But we do not always have the benefit of repeating a lesson, and our best guess at finding the pitfalls can fail. In this case, we can stop and introduce a quick minilesson as the need arises. Some teachers call this the "catch and release" approach: catch students' confusion, clear it up, then release students to continue independent work. For more insight into how to make workshops work, I recommend Bennett (2008).

- *"I always run out of time for the debrief and reflection."*

There is always so much to do that it is tough to make yourself save those last five minutes of class for metacognition. Yet when we do ask students to reflect on what has gone on in class before their brains switch gears and run down the hall, we help them to synthesize and cement the day's learning experiences. Make those last five minutes sacred, and do not allow yourself to run into them with other work unless absolutely necessary. Saving time for reflection is a learned discipline.

Is these first three chapters, we looked closely at inquiry as an approach to promoting thinking, what we teach (important content linked to big ideas), and how we teach (through the workshop model instruction). In the next chapter, we will discuss assessment, how we know when students understand.

CHAPTER 4

Assessment

By clarifying conceptual understanding and skill competence goals before a learning experience, teachers can design effective formative, ongoing, and summative assessments and use data from these to maximize student learning.

Think Tank

- How do students know what I expect them to know?
- How do my students show what they know?
- How do I know what students know?

Tomorrow is Friday, and Mrs. Smith needs to prepare a test for her eighth-grade unit on energy transfer. She sits at her computer, a binder of lecture notes next to her, and flips through the pages selecting facts and vocabulary words to include in the final assessment. Most of the test is short answer ("Define convection") with a few multiple choice questions ("Which of the following is the best conductor: (a) wood, (b) metal, (c) glass, (d) water"), and one section where students are asked to draw and label a diagram ("Sketch and label a Thermos, and explain why it works"). She gets to her four-page limit and goes back to change the margins. The test ends up having thirty-eight questions, so she adds two more to make the percentage scores come out to even, round numbers.

The next day, Mrs. Smith sits at her desk and catches up on email while students silently sweat over the test, notebooks closed. As the period nears its end, Mrs. Smith reminds students to check over their work, and invites any who are done to submit their papers and begin to independently read the next chapter.

At the day's end, five piles of about thirty tests each wait on her desk. Over the years, she has developed a system to make the necessary evil of grading them a bit less painful: she checks everyone's first page first, writing the number of points earned in the bottom right-hand corner of the page, then checks over everyone's second page, records those points, and so on. Her final step is to flip through the four pages of each test and write a total score out of forty on the top. She lets students translate those points into percentages themselves.

Mrs. Smith looks at her regularly scheduled tests as a required classroom ritual, disconnected from her instruction. She feels like she ought to ask students to complete silent, closed-book, paper-and-pencil tasks at regular intervals before moving from one unit to the next. Many of her students endure routine failure on tests, knowing that by producing homework and participating in class, they can keep their grades up, even if they are unable to recall unit vocabulary reliably.

This week, when she finally gets to the step of adding up the points and entering them into her online grade book, she realizes that more than half of her students flunked the test. "Oh, well," she tells herself. "They will do better on the next unit."

Reflection

Why might these students have "failed" the test?

How did assessment drive instruction?

What does it mean to "fail"?

In the account above, Mrs. Smith and her students are flying blind; her students' test scores represent simply a scatter plot of memories from pages of lecture notes. Every week, Mrs. Smith and her students use precious learning time on assessments like this, and then she has to spend her limited planning time correcting papers.

A lot of teachers I know hate grading. It keeps them up late on weeknights and eats into their weekends. Counting up points and calculating grades can surely become tedious. For students, testing becomes a part of their school routine, but for many students test results are used only to calculate a grade, rather than diagnose holes in their understanding. How can we utilize assessment to expand science learning?

Assessment, data collection about what students know and can do, is integral to and integrated into quality teaching. Assessment *for* learning means using data to improve student outcomes. It is worth the time.

High Stakes

More than thirty states now administer standardized exams with science sections. For many schools and districts, this is the ultimate assessment of their performance. Teachers work hard all year to ensure that students will know what they need to do well on these tests. Standardized tests, often scoring students based on responses to multiple choice questions and limited constructed response opportunities, offer one snapshot of student achievement.

Denver Public Schools' recent switch to standards-based report cards in all middle schools shook up the points system in my city. All of a sudden, teachers had to find the time to shift gears and begin to assess for understanding. Conversations changed from,

"How many points is this project worth?" to "What do *we* really want students to *know*, and how will we know when they *get it*?"

Both of these—standardized tests and report cards—are endpoint assessments with serious implications for schools and students. In our classrooms, we have the opportunity to look at assessment incrementally, as something we do each day, week, unit, and semester to ensure that students are prepared to perform when the stakes are higher.

Assessment for Learning

I know from my own experience that teaching and learning do not always work in tandem. Early in my career, I taught one class of 32 eighth graders; 27 were boys who all seemed to love skateboards. I taught my heart out every day, but when test time came, they never showed much understanding of what I had been going on about at the overhead. I envied the teachers who could put their feet up and trust their students to meet the learning goals seemingly unaided.

Assessment *for* learning ensures that all of a teacher's good effort is not for naught. Assessment is an integral part of the learning process, as well as the planning process. As assessment expert Richard J. Stiggins (1997) explains, "Assessment and instruction can be one and the same if and when we want them to be" (18). To this end, we make the best use of our own and our students' time when we

- know and share with them our learning goals at each unit's outset;
- design opportunities for formative, ongoing, and summative assessment;
- communicate clearly with students about our expectations for quality work;
- provide descriptive teacher feedback at regular intervals throughout the learning; and
- include time for reflection—individual, collective, and one-on-one between each student and teacher—on the data gathered from these assessments.

This is like having Mapquest and a GPS for unit design: all along the way, students will know where they are, where they are going, and how far they need to travel to get there. In this way, a responsive teacher encompasses assessment as part of, not tangential to, the learning process.

Carefully planned science instruction and assessment work together to catalyze student learning. In order to promote this synergy, we must

- understand the distinction between conceptual understanding and skill competence;
- identify understanding goals connected to big ideas;
- identifying demonstrations of understanding and learning targets; and
- employ strategies for formative, ongoing, and summative assessment.

What Do We Assess?

Just as scientists do, we need to start with what we want to know—and then do the necessary fieldwork, experimentation, or research. We need to plan from the top down, starting with the benchmarks and understanding goals. In naming this process, Jay McTighe and Grant Wiggins (2005) coined the term "backwards planning" to describe beginning curriculum design "with the end in mind."

Based on our topic, we need to

1. clarify the connection to a big idea (as described in Chapter 2), then
2. specify our understanding and skill competence goals, and next
3. plan assessments, after which we can
4. break the unit down into learning targets, each addressed through one or more learning activities.

The big idea can remain a central driving force in planning both instruction and assessment. See Figure 4.1 for an overview of this process.

The goal of science learning is the understanding of science content linked to big ideas, and proficiency with science process skills necessary to engage in inquiry. These are what we need to assess.

Understanding

To support us in understanding what it means to understand, Wiggins and McTighe (2005) dissected the notion of understanding into six distinct facets: explanation, interpretation, application, perspective, empathy, and self-knowledge. These six, described further in Figure 4.2, present a menu of ways that we could expect students to "know" something.

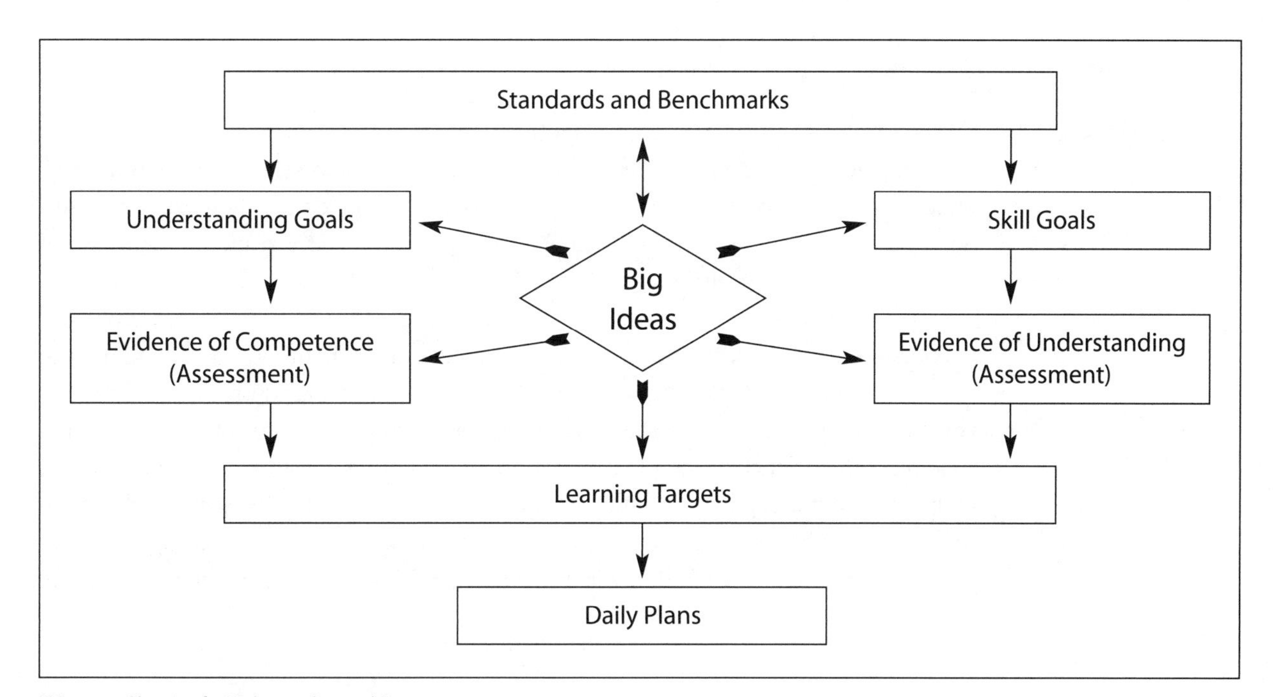

FIG. 4.1 *Planning for Understanding and Competence*

Facet	Definition
Explanation	Give detailed accounts and explanations
Interpretation	Make topic meaningful and accessible with images, models, or personal accounts
Application	Adapt and apply what is known to another context
Perspective	Consider the big picture and various points of view
Empathy	Explore a topic from the perspective of another
Self-Knowledge	Demonstrate awareness of what you do understand, as well as of impediments to full understanding

FIG. 4.2 *Six Facets of Understanding (adapted from McTighe and Wiggins 2005)*

Of these six facets, the first four seem most relevant to the work of scientists: we explain, interpret, apply, and consider the bigger perspective regularly in the course of a scientific inquiry. Empathy and self-knowledge, though, also have a place in our curriculum, as these invite us to consider our own and others' strengths and limitations. In addition to these types of understanding, there may be other ways of knowing that you, as a science teacher, value.

Skills

As well as understanding content, most science courses involve students learning the processes and skills of science. The specific nature of these skills may vary depending on the grade level or content, yet in order to work and think like scientists, students must develop competence in all of the following:

- experimental design
- observation
- measurement
- communication.

These skills are discussed in greater depth in Chapter 6.

Alongside assessing for understanding of concepts , we as science teachers are also often assessing for competence in process skills. For any given learning experience, we need a clear sense of our goals—both process and content—for student scientists, and a firm sense of what proficiency will look like.

If you think about it, assessment is a constant process in your classroom every day. Even as students walk in the door, you are assessing their mood, their readiness to learn, and whether they brought the appropriate materials. Based on this information, you may vary how you begin the class; some days diving right into content, other days sending students back to their lockers for books, still other days taking time to connect with kids about a pep rally or other schoolwide event. Nonetheless, you are already in the habit of gathering data from learners and adjusting your plans accordingly. Assessment for learning is no different; it just means tightening the focus on what data we are collecting.

Identifying Understanding Goals

Understanding goals are our opportunity to connect discrete content to the big ideas of science (see Chapter 2), as well as to hone in on what is essential about a topic. Understanding goals can be a bit more challenging to identify and assess than skill competence; it takes time to find out what a learner truly comprehends.

Standards, benchmarks, and other curriculum material are often generous in offering us course and unit goals, but can be less helpful when the ones provided are too broad to be useful or assessed. We need to be able to imagine what it looks like to us to demonstrate true understanding—not just memorization—of a content objective.

For example, the newly revised and updated Colorado Content Model Standards suggest among the benchmarks for Standard 3 (Life Science) that in grades 9–12 students should learn that, "(14.) Organisms are classified into a hierarchy of groups and subgroups based on similarities which reflect their evolutionary relationships" (Colorado Department of Education 2007). This is a very important idea. Students should indeed learn this concept, but what does it really mean? What would understanding look like, and how could it be demonstrated? These are the questions we need to ask ourselves in order to craft comprehensive understanding goals.

Identifying Demonstrations of Understanding

To meet the above-described benchmark I might decide that my evolution unit's understanding goals will include "Understand the structure of biology's system of taxonomy, as well as how biologists collect and use evidence to classify organisms." That still sounds like a pretty tall order, so now I need to ask myself, "What will that look like? If my students 'get it,' what will they be able to do?" That is the hardest question . . . so, hmmm, let me think aloud: I think that if they *really* understood Linnaean taxonomy, maybe they can do some classifying; or create their own system of classification; or sort out where a new, unknown specimen fitted into an existing system; or be able to tell the evolutionary story of a species based on its taxonomic relationship with others . . . I am thinking like this, brainstorming so many ideas of what the understanding could look like, how it could be represented.

After a few days of pondering, discussing with colleagues, and turning project ideas over in my head, I decide: Students will be able to look at a collection of beetles (a very few of the 350,000 known species), and—based on those animals' family, genus, and species—be able to create and explain a diagram showing their evolutionary history. If my students can satisfactorily complete the beetle task, will they have provided evidence that they can meet the previously quoted benchmark? I believe so!

So now that I know what the benchmark means for me and my students, it is my duty to communicate clearly, in students' language, the expected learning outcomes and culminating demonstration of understanding for the current unit. Then I need to consider the design of appropriate formative assessment to help us—my students and me—attain data about where they are at the outset of this learning process. Next, let me go and find some *Coleoptera* specimens!

It is not always easy to walk from a benchmark to an understanding goal to an assessment. But this is an essential skill that we must get better at; otherwise, the standards become a meaningless list.

Identifying Competence Goals

I am trying to teach my daughter to tie her shoes. That is a skill: she needs to know how to keep her tennies on all by herself without knotting her laces. It is a pretty easy goal to assess: either her shoes stay on, or they don't; either the laces can be easily untied, or they are tangled in knots that bring her crying to the kitchen.

While not always so simple, many science process skills are more straightforward to assess than content understanding: you can see the onion skin through the microscope, or you cannot. Still, for a given learning experience, it is important that we clarify the essential process skills we expect students to be able to use in order to succeed. Once those skills are identified, we must plan our instruction and assessment accordingly.

Selecting Learning Targets and Designing Learning Tasks

So first we identify the big idea, select understanding goals (based on standards and benchmarks), and choose appropriate skill competence goals for a unit. Next, we select appropriate formative, summative, and ongoing assessments. Now we are ready to break the units' broader goals into smaller building blocks: learning targets. These learning targets are stepping-stones toward those ultimate, broad goals.

Given manageable learning targets, we can design learning activities that will advance students' progress toward the stated goal. So rather than simply pulling my taxonomy unit binder off the shelf and photocopying some of last year's word searches and crossword puzzles, I am required to ask, "If I really want my students to know taxonomy and be able to sort beetles based on their lineage, what do they need to learn?"

In answer to this question, I need to start with formative assessment data: What do they already understand about evolution? What can they already do? Next I can consider what sorts of tasks will help us to bridge the space between what they know now and where we need to arrive together at the unit's end.

Selecting Learning Targets

How is a learning target different from an understanding or competence goal? Quite simply, a learning target is smaller, an incremental step toward the ultimate understanding. For example, in order that my students accomplish the beetle assessment described above, they will need to hone the skill of classification and understand the categories of the Linnaean system (kingdom, phylum, and so forth)—these need to be learning targets in and of themselves.

For learning targets to be helpful rather than headaches, they must be small, specific goals, which will build toward demonstrations of understanding the larger standards and benchmarks outlined by the curriculum, district, or state. While it may feel tedious to identify weekly or daily intentions, it does serve to streamline each task's work toward a specific purpose. Our planning, then, becomes about what students will *gain* from the lesson, rather than what they or the teacher will *do* to fill the class period.

Identifying incremental learning outcomes gives us a clear vision of what we want students to accomplish along the way. With these stepping-stones laid out, we can use frequent informal (or formal) assessments to gather evidence on students' progress. By gathering and using data along the way, we create multiple opportunities to intervene in the event that students do not understand the smaller learning targets. In this way, we ensure that we do not arrive at our destination, turn around, and find half the class back on square—or stepping-stone—number one. Stopping at each interval to confirm that all are, indeed, with us keeps the group on target to meet the benchmark together.

Big Idea: Evolution				
Standard and Benchmark	**Understanding Goal**	**Final Assessment**	**Learning Targets**	**Learning Activities**
• Standard 3: Life Science • Benchmark 14: "Organisms are classified into a hierarchy of groups and subgroups based on similarities which reflect their evolutionary relationships." (Colorado Department of Education 2007, 10)	• Understand the structure of biology's system of taxonomy, as well as how biologists collect and use evidence to classify organisms. • Skill Competence • Classification of organisms	• Students will be able to look at a collection of beetles (a very few of the 350,000 known species), and based on those animals' family, genus, and species be able to create and explain a diagram showing their evolutionary history.	• Understand the role of taxonomy in biology and other sciences. • Apply logical principles of classification. • Know the categories of the Linnaean system. • Understand the relationship between taxonomy and evolution. • Able to sort specimens based on recognizable traits.	• Compare and contrast three different classification systems, looking for strengths and weaknesses. • Slide show and song. • Read excerpt of *The Origin of the Species* and create concept maps. • Sort species cards and develop family trees.

FIG. 4.3 *Taxonomy Unit Overview*

Figure 4.3 presents a sample overview of this "backward planning" process, starting with the big idea, benchmarks and standards, and moving to goals, assessments, learning targets, and activities.

Thinking through a unit or project in this way invites us to design significant learning tasks or projects that can serve as true assessments of students' understanding and competence. When we take the time to know what we want students to understand and what we expect that understanding could and should look like, we are better teachers.

Now that we know where we are headed, the destination, and the stepping-stones, we can develop an assessment plan to monitor learners' progress along the way—gathering data at regular intervals before, during, and after learning activities, and using this data to refine instruction. This strategy of ongoing assessment for learning, advises Richard Stiggins (1997), will offer us maximal opportunity to close achievement gaps and support all students. Let us look at some helpful assessment strategies for monitoring each stage of the learning experience.

Preassessment

"Students come to the classroom with preconceptions about how the world works. If their initial understanding is not engaged, they may fail to grasp the new concepts and information that are taught, or they may learn them for purposes of a test but revert to their preconceptions outside the classroom," explains the National Research Council (2004, 14–15).

As described above, it is essential to begin each new study with an examination of students' background knowledge, whether correct or otherwise. The once-popular film *A Private Universe* (Harvard–Smithsonian Center for Astrophysics 1987) depicts the learning journey of one bright high school student who hung onto preconceptions about the phases of the moon even after her teacher explained the truth with words and models several times. In the film, we see that the learner needed to actually manipulate materials herself during individualized direct instruction in order to confront her own incorrect ideas.

As this example illustrates, if these preconceptions about science are not drawn to the forefront and confronted in a variety of ways, all well-intended instruction may be for naught. We must know what science learners know or *think* they know before we are ready to delve into, deconstruct, or build upon this background knowledge to create new understanding.

Formative assessments, or preassessments, are also an excellent opportunity to clearly communicate to students the understanding goals of the unit. Students who know what they are intended to learn from an experience, according to Marzano (2005), outperform those who do not. So for our teaching to be most effective and beneficial to our students, targeted preassessments are an essential step.

Some of us use written quizzes to preassess a unit or topic, but more often I observe teachers launching a study with popcorn-style oral sharing: "What do you guys already know about DNA?" In these casual class discussions, the few smarty pants who've heard about or read about or think they know about the topic at hand will chime in, a few others may voice questions or wisecracks, but the vast majority of students will sit silent—perhaps wondering if they should know something, have heard something, or are in the wrong class. Here are some alternate ways to introduce a unit with a preassessment.

K–W Charts

We can borrow the whole-class K-W-L charts embraced by our elementary school colleagues—which include columns for what students "Know" and "Want to Know" (completed before a learning experience) and a final column for what the student "Learned" to be filled in afterward. Alternately, we can create stand-alone preassessments that ask students individually to record "K: What I Know" and "W: What I Want to Know" about the upcoming unit of study. This is never a more interesting task than when introducing the topic of sex ed.

Give One–Get One

An improvement on brainstorming as a whole group, this structure gets everyone engaged in the conversation. Each student needs a piece of paper numbered one through ten. Ask them to draw a line under number four. Next, pose an open-ended question; for example, what are the sources of pollution in our town? Ask each student to record four answers of their own on each of the first four numbered lines of their paper.

Once they have had some quiet work time to do so, it is "give one–get one" time: Learners leave their seats, walk around the room, and exchange answers with their peers. Alberto shares one answer for Ben to record on his paper and vice versa before the pair splits to find new partners, share, and record again. Each student credits each idea he records by writing the name of the person he got it from. When they have each gathered ten ideas, students can signal this by returning to their seats.

As a way to share after everyone has collected ten or more ideas, invite learners to share with the class one idea *someone else* told them, and to credit that classmate by name for their idea. Then call on that named person to share an idea she or he got from a peer, and so on. In this way, everyone gets to celebrate the good thinking of others and no one is at a loss for words, since they have had many opportunities to gather ideas.

Labeled Drawing

Give students a blank piece of paper, and ask them to draw and label everything they know about something representative of what you are about to study: a molecule, a rift valley, or an ecosystem.

Concept Map

Concept mapping is a way for learners to gather and synthesize what they know about a given topic. It is all about understanding what a set of words and ideas have to do with one another. What I love about concept mapping is that you cannot look answers up in the glossary; in order to succeed at making the connection between what, say, inertia and gravity have to do with one another, a person needs to truly understand each. Concept mapping is appropriate before, during, and after a learning activity—as a preassessment or the review of a unit.

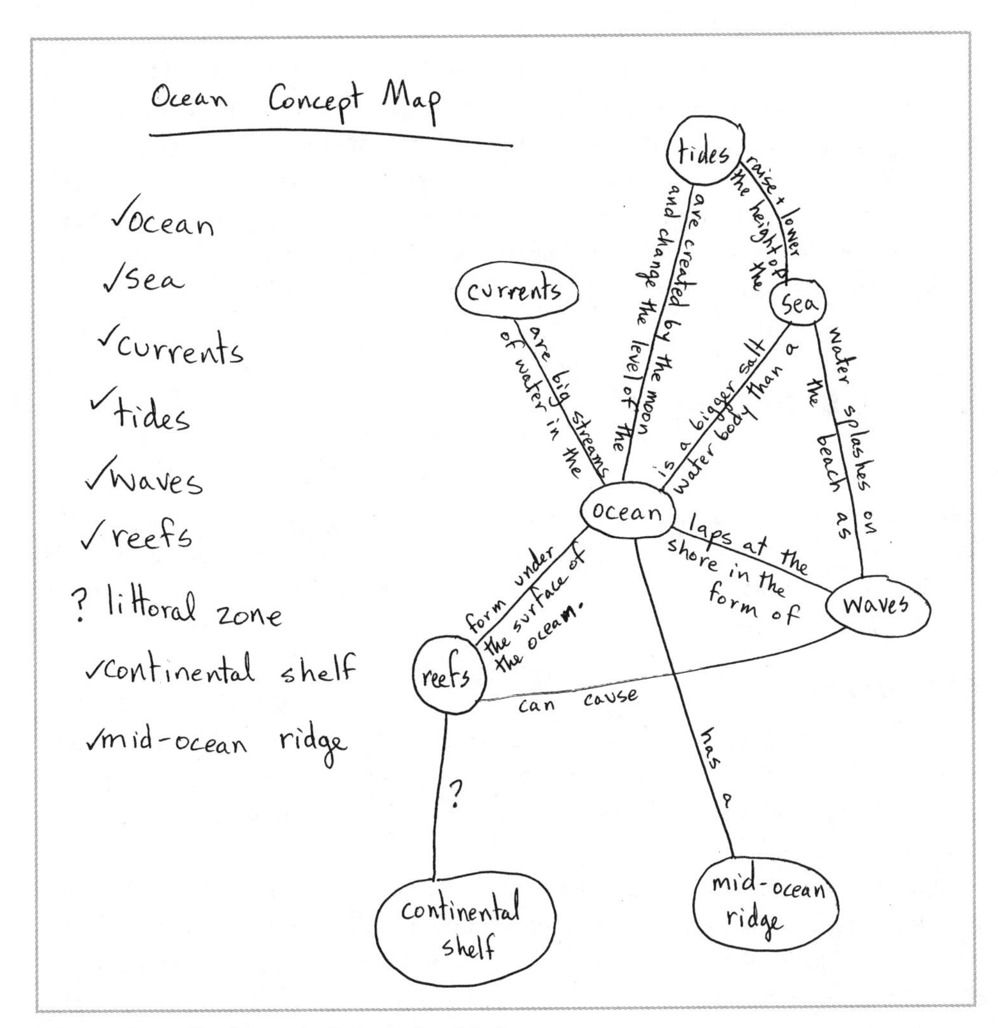

FIG. 4.4 *Concept Map Preassessing Understanding of the Ocean*

Before creating a concept map, teacher and students need to create a list of important words or ideas to be synthesized. For beginning concept mappers, it is easier to start with a large piece of paper and a small-tipped pen or pencil for optimal legibility of the final product. For example, if we were embarking on a study of oceanography, our preassessment concept map could include somewhat familiar terms: ocean, sea, currents, tides, waves, tides, reefs, littoral zone, continental shelf, and midocean ridge. How students are able to connect and explain these words is a window into their prior knowledge about the topic at hand. Figure 4.4 is a model of how these terms might be related using a concept map.

To create a concept map like this, each word or idea is placed in a circle and a line is drawn to connect it to related words or ideas. Along the line, the connection is explained in the students' own words. It works best to explain each connection before drawing the next line to avoid ending up with a wordless sketch of a spider. While creating the concept map, mappers need to explain each connection in as much detail as possible. One connection should be explained before others are added. Students can make a limitless number of connections. The map can be as complex as is appropriate. While mapping, learners may elect to add additional words or concepts in circles of their own to help make the connections stronger.

Teachers can score concept maps in a variety of ways, but attention should be paid to quality of connections over quantity; we want to discourage students from writing "ocean has current" in favor of their taking the time to really explain, "Ocean water moves around the globe in different streams, called currents." Sometimes, I read only a few connections on each concept map, so I encourage students to make each one as clear and specific as possible, in case it is the one I do examine.

K–W charts, give one–get one, labeled drawings, and concept maps are all examples of engaging, inclusive assessments that work well at the beginning of a unit of instruction, yet also could be integrated as ongoing assessments midstream. Below are additional ideas for assessment during a learning experience.

During Learning

Just as a professional scientist must keep an eye on the ultimate outcome of a study, learners must remain focused on the goals of our work together. Many of the strategies listed above as preassessments also can be used during a unit to assess learners' progress. Here are some other ideas to try during your unit.

Conferring

As introduced in Chapter 3, conferring is an excellent tool for instruction and assessment that can be employed throughout learning experiences. Conferring is an opportunity for us not only to coach students to independence, but also for us to learn about our students as thinkers.

My colleague Patrick Allen (2009) outlines the process of conferring with the acronym RIP: Research, Instruct, Plan. The following steps, adapted from a conferring format designed for reading instruction, can structure teachers' conversations with individuals or small groups during any learning activity.

Conferring: Research, Instruct, Plan (RIP)

1. **Research**
   - Recall what you already know about this student as a learner.
   - Observe the student. This may mean watching from afar, watching up close while the student works, looking at the notes she has made to hold her thinking, or listening in as he discusses a problem with a peer.
   - Interview the student to find out what she is thinking. Ask, "How's it going?" or "What are you thinking?"
2. **Instruct**
   - Start by noticing and supporting the learner's positive intentions and actions.
   - Teach the student one thing he can try that will raise his level of understanding.
   - Demonstrate how to use the strategy. Model the kind of thinking you want the student to stretch toward.
   - Have the student try the strategy while you are there to coach.
3. **Plan**
   - Ask the student to articulate what she will do or practice after you leave the conference.
   - Make a written record of the conference.

To get a better understanding of how the RIP structure for conferring looks and sounds, review the sample conferring conversation in Chapter 3.

As you confer, keep track of those conversations. This data is important documentation not only of individual students' progress but also of how the class as a whole is responding to the task.

Reflective Writing

Reflective writing is a wonderful and important tool for assessment and self-assessment, yet it can be overused. Learners, especially those less adept at narrative prose, appreciate when we intermingle this strategy with others. Written reflection prompts can vary, but here are some examples.

- Write a letter explaining how tornados are formed.
- Describe everything you understand about how weather fronts interact.
- Explain areas of confusion about cloud formation.
- What do you feel like you still need to know in order to understand how to accurately predict the weather?

Mind Map

Another form of reflection that could be used during or after a learning experience is the creation of a mind map. Mind mapping, similar to concept mapping, invites learners to cluster related ideas together—something like branches on a tree, sorting and categorizing processes or ideas. In this way, students can visually represent both what they understand about a topic and their journey to that understanding. The product can include illustrations, prose, or even digital photographs of students at work. Rather than an essay, this visual serves as an accessible way to invite students to depict their learning journey.

Using the data gathered from all of our selected assessments, we can adjust instruction at regular intervals, ensuring that all students are meeting learning targets and are well prepared to demonstrate proficiency of the understanding goal on our final unit assessment.

Final Assessment

In many schools and districts, the final assessment of students' science learning is a high stakes standardized test. In preparation for these exams, we do need to train our students in the skills of test taking and offer them experiences sharing what they know in test formats. In addition, we can use other forms of summative assessment for some units and learning experiences.

A final assessment should serve to present evidence of understanding of the unit's goals in direct proportion to their importance. Daily learning targets build toward the final understanding goals, demonstrated through quality work on a culminating product. In the forthcoming chapters of this book, you will consider a range of "product ideas," that can take you beyond the familiar tests and quizzes.

There are few things more unfortunate than standing by while a student reads verbatim from a PowerPoint presentation full of plagiarized text cut and pasted off the Internet and can answer no questions about the content. Sad, but this happens every day in American classrooms. I have watched. I have worried: what are we really teaching these students about what it means to "know" something?

To hop back on my soapbox, knowing must mean understanding. Let us look again at McTighe and Wiggins' (2005) Six Facets of Understanding and consider what sorts of products, aside from or in addition to exams, we might ask our students to complete. See Figure 4.5 for some possible learning and assessment tasks that incorporate skills and demonstrate understanding.

The final product of a learning experience must require individual skill and thinking—original thinking—about important content. The product must, by its very nature, be impossible to create *without* that essential thinking and understanding. Products of this description take some time to dream up, but you will feel wonderfully effective as a teacher when you develop a culminating activity truly poised to force original thought.

Facet	Sample Assessment Task
Explanation	Create a picture book designed to explain the process of a lunar eclipse to a third-grade audience
Interpretation	Develop and perform a skit representing how and why the seasons differ in the two hemispheres
Application	Make an "Earth Journal," documenting what you would see of the Earth each night if you were stationed on the moon for a month
Perspective	Write a letter to Cardinal Roberto Bellarmino making a case for Galileo's emancipation
Empathy	Taking on the role of Copernicus, gather evidence and prepare to debate Galileo
Self-Knowledge	Visually depict how your understanding of the structure of our solar system has grown and changed through the course of this unit

FIG. 4.5 *Sample Final Assessment Tasks Based on McTighe and Wiggins' Six Facets of Understanding (2005)*

Conveying Expectations

Once a final assessment task is defined, but before it is assigned, we need to take time to identify with our students how a quality product will look. We can do this with

- rubrics,
- scoring guides, and
- sample products.

When sharing a sample product with learners, you need not tell the class your own opinion of these pieces, but can invite students to assess the work based on specific criteria—yours or their own. This leads to valuable conversations about the expected outcome of the performance assessment.

Although more tedious to design than criteria lists and scoring guides, rubrics are a comprehensive and descriptive means to convey to our students expectations for excellence on a given task.

Rubrics

These days, many teachers turn to online rubric-makers that produce generic rubrics based on teacher input about the project type and categories to be assessed. While this approach may save time, it raises two concerns. First, making a rubric is a personal process where you as the teacher, knowing both your students and your content well, identify what you expect to see. Using an online source, or even another teacher's rubric, is skipping an essential step in clarifying your learning goals and product expectations for students. Second, most of the rubrics available online and through textbook companies take more of a checklist approach—that is, to get full credit a student would need to have five of these, four of those, and no more than two of the other. While this descriptive approach makes some sense, it reduces the task to a mere checklist. Other commercially produced rubrics look at student work from a deficit perspective, including language such as "includes few sources" or "many grammatical errors."

You need to make your own rubrics. This process helps you to clarify in your own mind the learning targets and what evidence of proficiency will look like. I used to start the school year by compiling my own rubrics, presenting them as drafts to students as we began a project. As I watched students work and think, I would often find ways to revise the rubrics to more accurately reflect expectations of quality. As the year went, I would invite students to participate in rubric making. Small groups would work together on each row of a rubric, identifying descriptors of quality for each aspect of the project. These groups' work, combined and revised by the class, would create a class-generated rubric, increasing student understanding of and investment in doing top-notch work on the project.

It took me a long time to learn to make rubrics that I liked. I went from generating two-pagers with so many categories that I confused myself grading every project, to brief overviews with pithy, nondescript qualifiers that confused my students as to how I possibly ever assigned their work to a given box in a page full of verbiage. These days, my rubrics fall somewhere in between—a few broad categories that I recycle, and plenty of room to wiggle.

Planning a Rubric

Flip through and take a look at all of the sample rubrics in this book. What do you notice?

These are all examples of additive rubrics. What I love about additive rubrics is that they outline specific expectations using positive language, crediting students for what they *do* do ("Label data table and graph with correct units") rather than offering them negative language such as "Does not state hypothesis in if-then-because form" or "Contains five or more spelling mistakes."

	1	3	5
		All of 1, plus . . .	*All of 3, plus . . .*
Understanding	• Represents time on another planet.	• Connects to Background Knowledge about Earth's calendar.	• Applies understanding of relationship between planetary and lunar motion, and increments of time.
Content	• Calendar is based on planet's rates of rotation and revolution.	• Basis of calendar (data) and source are included. • Relationship between planet's calendar and Earth's is clear.	• All increments of time are explained. • All calculations are included and explained.
Craftsmanship	• Represents data creatively. • Original, created by hand.	• Design accurately reflects data. • Free from mathematical or grammatical errors.	• Aesthetically impeccable and amazing.

FIG. 4.6 *Planet Calendar Project Rubric*

Before designing a rubric, start with a clear understanding of the task and the learning goals you wish to see met. Once you feel ready with a clear task description, you can break down the broad categories to be assessed.

Consider giving weight to product as well as process, to understanding as well as presentation. After you articulate each area of assessment, create an additive rubric by listing the most basic requirements in the first column, and adding in each subsequent column qualities that build on the prior with the language "All of 1, plus . . . ." Also, in my work with teachers, I have learned that it is helpful to skip numbers when assigning point values to each column: one, three, five. This way, we are allowed room to assign a score in between columns—a two or a four—without getting into fractions of points.

For example, Figure 4.6 is an example of a project rubric initially developed to assess students' work on the planet calendars project described in this book's introduction; in small groups, learners designed calendars for other planets in our solar system as a demonstration of their understanding of the increments of time. This rubric served as a tool for ongoing as well as summative assessment.

A quality rubric can serve not only as an assessment tool, but also as a project planning guide and a checkpoint for peer feedback. Long-term projects invite peer review at regular intervals, coupled with opportunities for revision before presenting the final product.

Keeping Track

Assessment requires the ongoing collection and analysis of data. There is a lot to keep track of. In addition to assigning scores to tasks and recording those in a grade book, here are some strategies for storing assessment information in useful formats.

- *Conferring Logs.* These can be kept on a class list or seating chart, or you can have a separate sheet of paper for each group or individual. One or more clipboards or spiral notebooks are terrific tools for keeping track of all this information. As a note taking format, you could use the RIP steps: research (describe the data gathered), instruct (note what you taught the group), and plan (jot what the group or individual intended to do after you left). In this way, you know exactly where to pick up with them next time you have the opportunity to talk.
- *Running Rubrics.* In advance of the project, you can label one blank rubric for each student or group; then, as students work, make note of their progress on their rubric. For example, there may be sections of your rubric related to understanding or process that are not as easy to assess based on a final product. By having these rubrics ready on hand as students work, you are able to note their proficiency in certain areas, then complete the rest of the rubric later.
- *Portfolios.* Portfolios are a fantastic assessment tool that deserve extensive discussion, but here I will only mention that they are a great system for gathering and presenting student work as evidence of understanding. For detailed suggestions on implementing portfolio assessment, I suggest Stiggins (1997, ch. 16).
- *Student Reflections.* Teachers can make copies and file significant reflections as evidence of students' progress.

Grades

Most teachers in most schools need to summarize a term, a semester, or a year of work with a single letter or numerical grade. Many teachers' grades are simply an average of the number of points scored on each learning activity. This system gives credit for consistent participation and effort but does not necessarily document understanding.

Standards-Based Grading

Consider using a standards-based grading system that credits learners based on their best recent demonstration of understanding of the units' learning goals.

This system is more parallel to real life. For example, a teen may have to take his driving test several times in order to pass. At each test, the examiner allows the student a clear slate, interested only that the teen is now, at present, capable of safely managing the vehicle. Imagine if drivers' tests were an average of all previous performances. This would mean a student would have to achieve numerous perfect scores on the driving exam in order to offset one unfortunate failure. What would be the point? All we need to know is, "Can he drive now?" Just as in our science classes, all we need to know is does he understand relativity *now*—regardless of what he understood in September.

A standards-based grading system gives credit to students when they are at their best, disregarding earlier trials. For some teachers, the transition to this system is alarming because it changes the nature of a grade from a collection of daily homework, participation, quiz, and activity points adding up to a cumulative total to a score based simply on one or more culminating demonstrations of understanding. In this new system, the role of grades in student motivation and classroom management shifts; consider the implications.

Let's Get to Work

To be a great assessor, you need to know where you are headed in terms of final assessment design, and to create checkpoints throughout students' learning experiences to confirm progress and address misunderstandings or confusion. To that end, here are some planning questions to help you reflect on your current and future practice in designing assessment *for* learning.

Assessment: Teacher Planning Questions

What do you want students to know and be able to do at the end of this unit?

How will students demonstrate understanding and competence through a culminating activity or final assessment?

What smaller learning targets are essential stepping-stones toward the unit goals and culminating project?

What preassessments will I use and why?

How will I know that everyone is with me as we go?

Dobetter Assessment

Ms. Dobetter is interested in how careful planning for understanding and skills goals, linked to preassessment and ongoing assessment, can maximize student learning. Let's watch how she revises her chemistry class' radiation unit so that she and her students are using assessment to support, as well as document, learning.

What do you want students to know and be able to do at the end of this unit?

I want them to understand that radiation is everywhere, a part of their lives. Radiation is an example of the big idea, energy, which is everywhere, ubiquitous. More concretely, learners need to know what types of radiation there are, and the benefits and risks of each. To understand this, they need to master some basic concepts, vocabulary, units of measure, and a bit of history. Our culture has a lot of fear of radiation, much of it unwarranted.

How will students demonstrate understanding and competence through a culminating activity or final assessment?

In the past, I have always ended the year unit with a test—sort of typical multiple choice, short answer—but now I am considering another kind of project or activity that will allow students to demonstrate more of their understanding . . . Perhaps they could write some sort of radiation guide for the general public. We could publish it online. It can include details on what kinds of radiation are good or useful, and those that are dangerous, and explain it all in layman's terms.

What smaller learning targets are essential stepping-stones toward the unit goals and culminating project?

They will need to understand what radiation is, energy, the terminology and units of measurement related to it, the sources and types of radiation, and the ways we use radiation in our everyday lives. Students need to see that radiation is useful and important in many fields—medicine, sustainable energy sources, carbon dating—as well as that radiation has its dangers (nuclear weapons, unsafe storage or power generation plant maintenance, and so forth).

What preassessments will I use and why?

I think I will by just asking them the K–W, what do you know? What do you want to know? Before that, maybe I will find out just what they think of radiation as a whole—is it dangerous, or beneficial? Most students are probably coming in with preconceptions about this.

How will I know that everyone is with me as we go?

One of the tough things with this unit is that it is so conceptual, not very visual, a lot of lecture is what I usually do for this unit. But I think I need to liven those up with more interaction, checkpoints, exit slips, and so forth. So many students have misunderstandings about radiation, I find, and if I don't get those out on the table and really confront them, we are wasting our time.

Assessing Radiation

In the past, Ms. Dobetter had always started this unit with some photographs of atomic bomb blasts. That slide show would get students' attention, but she realized that it also gave the wrong impression, put fear into students about radiation, and reinforced their bias that radiation is only dangerous. This year, she decided to start with a preassessment instead.

"Radiation," she wrote on the board. "This is our next unit, radiation," she explained. "My goal is that each of you understands what it is, where it comes from, how it can be useful or harmful. Let's get started by finding out what you already know about radiation. I am going to make some statements, and if you agree with one, I want you to stand up. Don't say anything; just stand up."

"Radiation is dangerous."

Almost the whole class stood up.

"Why?" she asked and called on a few students to share their thinking:

"A-bombs killed a lot of people in Hiroshima and Nagasaki."

"It causes birth defects, that's why they put the lead shield on you for an X-ray."

"I saw this movie about a nuclear power plant accident, and radiation can totally mess you up, make you puke and die."

"Radiation causes cancer."

"Yah, but doesn't it cure cancer?" one boy, himself standing, interrupted.

"Good question," Ms. Dobetter affirmed. "Let's try another one: Stand up if you think radiation is beneficial." A few students rose. "Why?" Ms. Dobetter prodded.

"Like Shaun said, it cures cancer."

"The sun produces radiation, and we benefit from that."

"But the sun is not radioactive!" interrupts a peer.

"Isn't it?" asks Ms. Dobetter, leaving another question lingering in the air. "There is a lot to learn here!" she exclaims. "I want you to document what you know now and what you are curious to learn about radiation. Take out a piece of paper, and make two columns." She models on the board as she explains. "On the left-hand side, list what you know. On the right-hand side, list questions that you have, what you want to know."

As students get down to work, Ms. Dobetter walks between the rows, glancing at their papers. She is astonished by how much students are writing in the left-hand column. At a closer glance, she is surprised by how much misinformation students have about radiation. One learner thinks bombs are radiation's only source. Another wrote that radiation from power lines causes brain tumors.

Ms. Dobetter gathers their papers, planning to read them through after school, then spends the remainder of the class building students' background knowledge. She draws out their thinking about the big idea, energy, then describes how radiation's diverse forms are examples of energy.

At the end of her lecture, and each day after that, Ms. Dobetter asks students to complete exit slips. Some days, her questions are about the content of her presentation; on other days, she asks students to write about their own understanding, what makes sense, what they need help to comprehend.

Each time she asks students to complete exit slips, she takes the time to read them before finalizing the plans for her next day's lesson. She begins each day by responding to the questions and comments from the previous day's exit tickets. As the week comes to a close, she decides to give students a good old-fashioned quiz. There are certain terms and content understandings they need to truly grasp in order to move on to the next task, working on the radiation guide.

Those students who scored well on the quiz are able to leap into the project the following week; those who did not demonstrate understanding need to visit with Ms. Dobetter for additional instruction and support so that they can pass the quiz independently. Soon enough, the whole class is on track, working in teams to author pages of their collective user-friendly online radiation information guide. Topics range from atomic bombs to nuclear power plant hazards, nuclear waste storage to X-ray safety. Ms. Dobetter gave each team a common format to follow in writing their research: explanation, opportunities, risks, and resolutions.

During a week of in-class and at-home work time, Ms. Dobetter supports students' work with minilessons on research, plagiarism, writing, and editing; she confers with teams during work time, assisting them with understanding their research and assembling original explanations of complex scientific information. After completing their first drafts on paper, students use a teacher-designed rubric to peer-critique one another's work, then revise theirs before submitting it to Ms. Dobetter. She assesses their work herself, and gives feedback to her students not only on their understanding and explanation of the science content, but also on their writing. After another round of revision, Ms. Dobetter's students assemble their work into a finished guide for all to read online.

So What?

The purpose of schooling is student learning. The purpose of assessment is sharing with students data describing their progress toward stated learning goals. When we are explicit with students about learning goals and include them in the process of self-assessment at regular intervals, time in class becomes focused on our shared pursuit of understanding. Learners remain in the driver's seat while teachers facilitate the process.

Effective assessment is assessment *for* learning. It is "for" learning because the assessment both evaluates what the student knows at a given time, and indicates to the teacher how to adjust instruction to ensure that learning is taking place continually. Assessment and learning are intimately linked to one another and to teacher planning.

In each of the "Variables" chapters in this book, I present examples of instructional strategies and appropriate assessments for each.

"Yah, but . . ."

- *"I am not supposed to write learning goals, just guiding questions."*

Many teachers use their understanding goals and big ideas to develop one or more guiding or essential questions: overarching or thematic queries that can be answered at different levels as learners build their knowledge about a topic. But you can use a guiding question to set the purpose for a unit, then for assessment at intervals throughout.

A good guiding question is one for which there is not a single right answer, and whose answer requires explanation and understanding beyond simple regurgitation of information, such as

- What is the relationship between evolution and taxonomy?
- What is the nature of time?

Guiding questions and learning goals are interrelated; we must take the time to identify both for a given unit.

- *"This all sounds fine for the average and low achieving students, but what about those high achievers who don't want to tiptoe from stepping stone to stepping stone?"*

While it is important to believe in and expect all students to achieve a certain level of competence and comprehension in science, the truth is that not all students are the same. Some need an extra challenge, while others need extra support. Differentiation is a critical approach for the skilled teacher striving to challenge all students appropriately. As Tomlinson and Allan (2000) explain, we can differentiate through three avenues: the content, the process, and the product. For more insight on differentiation, I recommend Wormeli (2006).

- *"Can't I just give quizzes? What is the big deal?"*

Sure you can give quizzes. Nothing wrong with a quiz. Still, it is your duty as the reflective teacher to review the students' work in order not simply to assign a grade but to identify areas of weakness that need to be revisited either by the class or individuals. Further, different kinds of learners need different kinds of assessments. Quizzes are great for some; why not mix it up, and see what happens?

- *"Who has time to implement all of this? Won't all of this assessment take away from time for student learning?"*

Assessment, when done well, is part of learning. When students are completing assessments, they and we are both learning what they know, and what they need to know. While we would not want to overassess at the expense of learning, assessment need not be perceived as separate from learning. The two tasks are interdependent.

Teacher Liza Eaton from The Odyssey School reports, "For me, naming the learning targets has reduced my assessment time because it forces me to narrow what I am looking for. Looking for one thing, even if it is more closely, takes less time, and I feel like I do it more effectively" (personal communication 2008).

So far in this "Constants" section, we have explored scientific inquiry by dissecting it into its essential features, delved into science's big ideas as a tool to tighten our focus on important content, discussed workshop model instruction designed to foster students' independence as scientists, and looked at how assessment can—and should—guide our instruction. In the next and final "Constants" chapter, Culture, I invite you to consider ways to enhance learners' sense of themselves as members of a community of capable scientists.

CHAPTER 5

Culture

Creating a classroom community of scientists engaged in a culture of inquiry increases students' science learning and prepares learners for success in all of their future endeavors.

> Think Tank
>
> - How do my students feel about themselves when they are in my classroom?
> - How are my beliefs and values reflected by what takes place in my classes?

"Smith, you're next."

"We're not ready."

"You're next. Get up here," a teacher barks as a pair of sulking teens drags their poster board to the front of the room.

By way of presenting their original research on the best paper towels, the eighth-grade boys read aloud (but not very loud) from the black trifold poster, their backs turned to the class. When they are done, they look up reluctantly. The teacher asks the student audience for comments.

A snappily dressed boy in the front row raises his hand. When called on, his loud question is simply, "Huh?" which seduces the class into a sea of laughter. The presenters attempt to return to their chairs, but the teacher is not done with them yet. As he makes notes on his clipboard, he surveys the failings of their project.

"Why weren't you ready? You knew the presentations were today." He leaves no time for a response and continues. "You did this research yourselves, so you should have been able to speak to us about it. You did not need to read right from your poster.

Where is the title? I can't even read it from here." The boys skulk back to the security of their chairs, grateful to stash their poster on the floor beneath their sneakers and put their heads down.

Reflection

How safe do you think the students feel in this science class?

What roles do peers play for one another in this class?

What kind of modeling does the teacher provide?

While you probably cannot imagine yourself enacting the caricature of humiliation narrated above, each of us still ought to stop and think about the subtext of how our classrooms operate. Amid the stress and frenzy of a school day, one can easily lose sight of students as individuals—their feelings, hopes, and fears. Yet when students feel criticized, teased, or demeaned in a classroom, they are unlikely to strive for excellence.

"One must understand that elements having nothing to do with curriculum often have the most profound effect on the lives of children," veteran teacher Ron Berger explains in his work *A Culture of Quality* (1996). Students thrive when they feel safe, supported, accepted, and encouraged; many can founder when these essential ingredients are missing from their school experiences. Creating a positive classroom culture does not mean refraining from offering critical feedback. A positive classroom culture is the product of believing in students' greatest potential and working hard every day to draw that forth from each individual.

Our students may go on to pursue careers in science—but statistically, it is more likely that they will not. Nonetheless, lessons from our classrooms can have a profound effect on their future endeavors. When we teach students to work and think and talk together respectfully, we not only create a productive science learning community this year, but also equip these same learners to succeed in their future roles as partners, parents, employees, voters, and leaders in all fields.

A Culture of Inquiry

A culture of science inquiry is a culture that respects and promotes scientific thinking. High levels of student engagement in a thinking culture are only possible when students feel safe and valued. Creating this environment in a school today can present a formidable—yet surmountable—challenge. Remember the popular story of teacher Erin Gruwell and the Freedom Writers, proof that all students can learn and care when taught with compassion.

For insight into what a culture of inquiry could look like, we can turn to the community of professional scientific research: science is a community endeavor moderated by a process of peer review; publicly funded researchers apply for grants, which are reviewed and funded based on their peers' input; study findings are presented in articles submitted to professional journals, which must first be reviewed by peers; at conferences, researchers deepen their own understanding by engaging in dialogue about what they are learning and would like to know. Professional science can be highly competitive, yet—in most settings—this competition retains a respectful, ethical tone. In this way, the science community serves as a resource and an accountability system, goading all of its members onward to greater discoveries.

The communities in our classrooms can reflect the norms of the professional community described above. First, though, our students must take science (and themselves as scientists) seriously. Here are some of the excuses I have heard from students and teachers who do not believe such a community of science learners is possible in their classroom setting.

Low self-esteem as learners. Students programmed by years of unfortunate schooling grow to think of themselves as unable to make positive contributions as learners.

Peer pressure to act dumb/not participate. Peer culture can powerfully sway students, convincing them that the goal of school is other than working hard to learn.

Cliques, "I can't work with/sit by her." Students permitted to practice unprofessional behavior in school settings expect to be permitted to remain in their social comfort zones.

Distaste for group work. Many students have not, in the past, had positive experiences with cooperative learning, and therefore shut down at the thought of another group project.

The visionary teacher can see the mind of a scientist within each child or teen. Understanding and insight are required to slice through years of habit patterns and ignite in all students a willingness to learn, a capacity to give, and a stance of compassionate critique toward peers' good effort. This is the most important gift we can give the learners who cross our classroom thresholds day after day.

If any of the above beliefs or challenges ring familiar to you, you are not alone. Creating positive classroom culture is a long journey and takes significant effort, but the learning rewards for students are great. In this chapter, I describe some ways to begin or progress along this worthy path.

- Believe in students' potential to collaborate and succeed.
- Ensure that your beliefs are reflected daily in your students' science learning experiences by establishing an intentional classroom culture through
  - classroom norms,
  - the physical learning environment,
  - the structure of learning activities, and
  - feedback systems.

Examining Our Own Beliefs and Teaching Behavior

Have you ever heard yourself sounding just like your own mother or father? I remember how shocked I was to hear myself one day tell my young child that his behavior was "not cute or funny." Those are the exact words my mother used to say to me when I was acting out! Somehow they had been stashed in my subconscious for decades and just leapt from my lips when my son pushed the right button.

This incident startled me into seeing just how quickly I can slip into autopilot with my words, behavior, and reactions to others. So many of us as teachers adopt the stance and structures we experienced as students, regardless of whether we believe in them or

If you believe . . .	Do you . . .
Each child is a capable scientific thinker.	Devote time to drawing out and celebrating each individual's thinking?
Students are responsible for their own learning.	Train students to develop their own standards, manage their time, and progress on their work?
Learning is a community endeavor.	Create opportunities for students to talk with one another about the content?
All students can meet the standards.	Expect high quality contributions from everyone?

FIG. 5.1 *Teacher Beliefs and Teacher Behavior*

not. I remember a high school math teacher of mine who spent most of each period at the board explaining equations. As I sat there in my chair day after day, I remember feeling less and less smart, less and less interested. Pretty soon, I dropped math altogether. Now my guess is that our teacher thought us all smart, but the way he set up the class made me feel like he was the expert, I was the innocent, and the safest strategy was to keep my mouth shut. The structure of the class did not communicate to us students that he believed us to be capable mathematicians.

Research suggests that our own teaching beliefs and values, unexamined, can undermine even our best efforts to reform our curriculum and instruction (Yero 2002). As you look over Figure 5.1, take the time to consider your teaching beliefs and how they are reflected each day in your classroom. What other beliefs do you hold about students, teaching, and learning? How does your teaching practice and the culture of your classroom reflect these beliefs?

Intentional culture requires time and effort to develop. Back to my math teacher—he probably was teaching us the way he himself had been taught, which is exactly what I found myself doing shortly after starting my teaching career. I had to work hard, and still do, to examine my beliefs and learn ways to integrate them into my work every day.

Intentional Culture

Culture and community are created. Through the learning environment, classroom expectations, the structure of learning experiences, and our processes for giving and receiving feedback we have multiple opportunities to convey our beliefs to students. Below are some culture-building approaches to consider.

Classroom Norms

As the community of professional scientists shares expectations and norms for participation, our classrooms must do the same. Some teachers enjoy using a group process to cocreate classroom rules—starting with students discussing times when they each felt safe and productive, extrapolating from there to develop a classroom code of conduct together. Depending on how much time and energy you want to invest in this process, this approach may or may not be appropriate.

One of my favorite sets of school rules was developed some years back by Director Rob Stein and the faculty of Denver's Rocky Mountain School of Expeditionary Learning:

1. You are responsible for your own learning and for supporting the learning of others.
2. Be where you are supposed to be.
3. Take care of our learning environment.

When you think about these carefully, you can see that they encompass a range of topics including classroom behavior, promptness, and equipment use. Whatever set of rules or expectations you choose to adopt, they must mirror your beliefs and values—your ideas about how you want your classroom to feel.

For a rule to be a rule, it must be supported with an appropriate consequence. These may differ depending on your setting and population, but it is worth taking the time to prepare consequences in advance of any infraction. My uncle, who taught middle and high school for decades in the Los Angeles Unified School District, advised me as I began my career that on the first day of school I should throw someone out of each class—the sooner the better. It would send a prompt, clear message, he told me, that I meant business. This worked pretty well as a way to communicate the unequivocal value I place on respect in my classroom. But this was not a long-term strategy for building community.

So in addition to throwing students out of class, we need to develop community-building consequences for an array of off-target student behaviors. These could include

- writing a letter of apology to an individual or group;
- repairing or replacing broken equipment;
- spending extra time caring for the learning environment (cleaning, organizing); and
- doing and sharing additional research to expand the class's knowledge.

Above are just a few examples of ways that we can make justice in our classrooms restorative rather than punitive (Cameron and Thorsborne 2001).

Naming Names

A secondary teacher today can teach more than two hundred students in a given week. These numbers make it difficult to develop relationships with each individual. Yet one important gesture we can make to support each individual student is simply to learn everyone's name as soon as possible. Use a seating chart, an old yearbook, memory tricks, visualization . . . whatever it takes, know everyone's name as soon as you can. This prevents the scourge of students becoming invisible.

Once you know those names, use them! Greet students by name as they enter the room. Call on students by name to share their thinking. Credit students by name when referring to previous comments, as in, "Just as Maggie was saying, the force of gravity is less on the moon than on Earth. . . ." Celebrate contributions by remembering who made them.

This simple gesture of knowing students' names (and pronouncing them correctly) conveys to all that they are noticed and appreciated.

The Learning Environment

Ms. Alexander's classroom walls are full of color, light, and thinking. Her displays include photos of students showing their recent projects, examples of high-quality student work, and a list a classroom norms agreed to by all of her students. Also, colorful charts and lists documenting student questions (and answers) about their current unit hang from the walls. Any learner entering her classroom will see a piece of himself on those walls.

Desks are arranged into tables of four, so all students have one shoulder to the front board while facing their peers. Materials are accessible on the back counter in neatly arranged bins. A few plants bring life to dark corners, and Ms. Alexander's desk is decorated with photos of her family and friends. Although the classroom is not pristine in its order, it conveys a warm welcome to all who enter. In fact, students often linger after class, enjoying the physical space.

How does the layout of your room reflect your beliefs about classroom community? While your science lab may have its tables anchored to the floor, you still have many opportunities to create a physical environment that demonstrates the high value you place on student thinking. Figure 5.2 presents some factors to consider in creating a student-centered classroom.

What other ideas do you have about using the physical space to support and celebrate thinking?

Supplies

Art teacher Anne Thulson helped me to understand the value of placing quality materials in students' hands. She explained that in doing so we convey to our students that

More Student-Centered	More Teacher-Centered
Walls full of high-quality student work.	Walls covered with commercially produced posters.
Student desks arranged in groups or a circular pattern.	Student desks arranged in rows facing front.
Front of classroom is on long side of rectangle, so no one is too far from it.	Front of classroom is on short end of rectangle, so there is definitely a "back" to the room.
Classroom is a warm, personalized space, with plants, photographs, and a personal touch.	Classroom is a cold, generic space.
Student supplies are plentiful and of high quality.	Student supplies are cheap and scarce.

FIG. 5.2 *Student-Centered Versus Teacher-Centered Classrooms*

we take them and their work seriously. In her art classes, students generate memorable creations.

When I began to follow her lead—and to the extent possible, offer my students real, quality science materials to work with—the results were clear. The quality of my students' work did improve; at the same time, a sense of calm and seriousness began to pervade our classroom.

It is hard to find the money to stock a science room with high quality, state-of-the-art supplies. Yet even in low-income communities, resources can be drawn into our classrooms in many ways.

- Recruit a parent volunteer, student teacher, or other interested person to coordinate acquisition of classroom materials.
- Create a wish list, and share it with students, parents, and community members. You never know who knows who or who has what.
- Make a standing request to local postsecondary institutions for donations of outmoded lab materials (not including secondhand chemicals, of course).
- Contact local businesses and community partners who may have an interest in science education, and request funding for particular projects.
- Apply for grants.

DonorsChoose.org

This is a fabulous website summarized by their slogan, "Teachers ask. You choose. Students learn." The founder of Craigslist created this site to invite interested donors to support specific, individual classroom projects. Teachers post their project idea online, then select required resources and materials from the online catalog. Through the Website, donors can select and contribute to projects that fit their interests. This is an amazing resource! Check it out at: www.donorschoose.org/about/history.html?zone=0

Gathering all the "stuff" we need in our classrooms can take a lot of time. As the years go by, you can assemble quite a quality collection of materials that reflect to students your belief in them as capable, competent, serious scientists. Just as we must model for students how to treat peers with respect, we also need to model for students how to manage the equipment with care. In many instances, I have seen students so honored to get to work with "real" science equipment that they treat it like pure gold.

Structure of the Learning Activities

In the "Variables" section of this book, I describe many learning structures designed to promote and honor student thinking. Most of these require collaboration, which (for some students) can be a stumbling block. Years ago, I remember reading of an employability study conducted by Canadian officials curious to know how well their school system was preparing graduates for employment. The study concluded that the number one reason young people were being fired from their jobs was *not* that they could not write, or complete math problems, or use their computers. The biggest shortcoming employers found with high school and college graduates was that they lacked the essential relational skills to get along with their peers and superiors.

Cooperation, communication, and conflict resolution are life skills that we can impart to our students through science (and any other class). As well as offering students essential experiences of collaboration, creating a community of learners in our classes results in a positive environment where people—adults and youth alike—feel happy to be and to learn.

Learning in Groups

Learning to learn in groups is one of the most difficult challenges we can offer our students. To support learners in being successful, we must be mindful of how the task design and group size complement one another. Fruitful group learning tasks require interdependence, not simply a sharing of equipment or supplies.

All students, regardless of their academic skills or English language knowledge, can be included in cooperative group learning. Think about the message we convey to our class when, rather than simply creating a separate, individual task for struggling learners, we invest our time in finding ways to keep everyone included in the group task. To this end, educator Mara Sapon-Shevin offers us the following simple steps:

1. think about the cooperative learning lesson
2. consider individual children, including those with IEP objectives
3. design modifications and adaptations that allow *all* to participate (Sapon-Shevin 1999)

Throughout the second half of this book, you will read about a variety of science learning activities that lend themselves to varying group sizes. Think about the learning you currently ask students to do in teams. Are your grouping strategies making best use of their time and minds? Consider Figure 5.3.

In addition to carefully calibrating the group size to the task, we need to explicitly teach students to be successful working in a group. After explaining expectations for full and equitable participation, we must teach and model those behaviors for our students, then offer them small opportunities to practice collaboration, as shown in Figure 5.4. These skills include

- sharing materials,
- discussing and deciding on action plans,
- being responsible to complete assigned tasks,
- offering one another constructive feedback, and
- remaining flexible, willing to adjust as needed for the groups' collective success.

While essential to successful collaborative science learning, these skills are also important throughout students' lives. How fortunate they are to learn these at a young age in our classes! Using the workshop model, offering ample modeling and feedback, we can scaffold learners' success with group work. These skills, though, must be taught explicitly.

Group Size	Types of Learning Activities	Examples
Solo	Use equipment designed for one	Use a microscope to observe amoeba and paramecium slides
	Read, write, graph	Record thinking while reading a text
Pair	• Discuss reading • Share thinking	Share an important conclusion you drew from a graph
	Conduct shorter labs with limited equipment	Conduct hands-on exploration of the differences between convex and concave lenses
Trio	Analysis tasks	Create a Venn diagram comparing tornados and hurricanes
	Extended investigations	Design and conduct a lab to explore how your eyes' pupils react to light
Quad	Creative thinking requiring multimodal output	Write and perform a skit to demonstrate DNA replication

FIG. 5.3 *Matching Group Size to the Task*

By the time they reach our classroom door, many of our students have already survived the gamut of cooperative learning experiences. Some of these may have left bad tastes in their mouths. To head resistance off at the pass, it can be helpful to lay all the cards on the table. One year in September, I asked my class to brainstorm all of the potential pitfalls of cooperative learning. We came up with about a dozen, including common problems such as partner expects me to do all the work, partner won't let me contribute, partner loses materials or resources, partner is absent . . . and so on. Next we split the list, and in small groups students discussed solutions to some of the problems presented. We developed a class strategy bank for making group work successful. This hung on our back wall and helped us all year long. When a student came to me complaining of a common problem, I could refer her to the list and encourage her to select from the solutions offered. Very liberating.

The most important way we can demonstrate our belief in the value of collaboration in our classrooms is not to give up. You might try a group project in October, be tempted to write it off as a flop, and never look back. Yet we can learn even from our failures. Edison did.

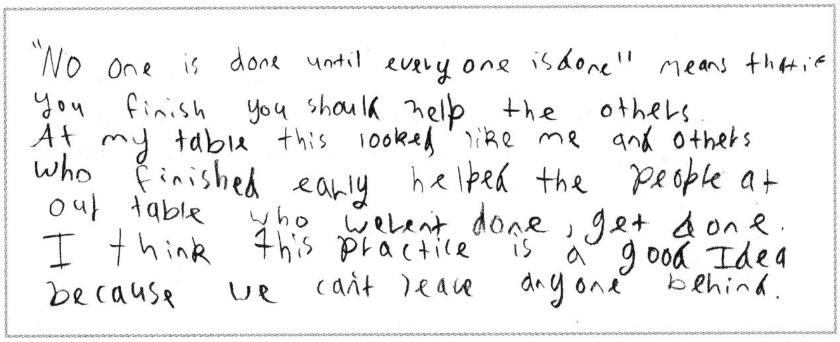

"No one is done until every one is done" means that if you finish you should help the others. At my table this looked like me and others who finished early helped the people at our table who werent done, get done. I think this practice is a good Idea because we can't leave anyone behind.

FIG. 5.4 *Student Reflection After a Group Project*

When things go bad, we need to stop and ask why, engage students in a sincere conversation, and then problem solve for next time. There is nothing wrong with permitting students to experience honest failure, as long as we take the time to find the learning from that experience, to teach the skills that were missing. When you have the nerve to try group work again, trust me, the students will do better. We all learn from our mistakes, and by allowing students another crack at it, we demonstrate that we do believe in their capacity to do good work together.

Tone

Liza Eaton's middle school science classroom at The Odyssey School is alive with positive feedback. Learners are constantly encouraged and complimented for their thinking: "Good idea . . . I like what you are saying about . . . Does everyone agree with . . . What are you thinking now?"

The words that come out of our mouths minute by minute reflect our beliefs. In order to cultivate students' confidence in themselves as scientists, we can begin by watching our own language. Here are some ways to say, "I see the Einstein in you."

- Greet students at the door by name when they enter the class.
- Call your students "scientists."
- Recognize publicly when they are thinking as scientists.
- Give specific, positive feedback.
- Compassionately give appropriate consequences when students fall short of their best.
- Refer to students' recent thinking during class discussions.
- Call on everyone, not only those reliable ones whose hands are constantly raised.

When applying this last suggestion, you will surely encounter the dear one who replies to your query with, "I don't know." Do you let him off the hook? If you do, you send him the message that you do not expect him to think or participate in the conversation. What if, instead, you drew him out? Offer him more time to think, invite him to get some ideas from people at his table, suggest that he share what he thinks the answer *might* be if he *did* know. Whatever he says, we need to celebrate his participation and effort until he grows in his confidence as a contributing member of our classroom's conversation. Demonstrate to him, to everyone, that we expect them to *know*.

Classroom conversations must reinforce to students that we take them, all of them, seriously as scientists. In Chapters 3, 4, and 9, I describe a number of structures for conversation that invite students to think and participate at a small group level, enhancing their confidence and ability to join in the whole class's conversation.

The tone we set with our own voice, language, and stance toward our students sends a strong message about our belief in them. When we see the best in them, when we find ways to encourage them, honor them, and celebrate them, students will come to see themselves through our eyes as capable scientists and contributing community members.

Feedback as Part of Learning

Hard as we work to set everyone up for success, we still need to monitor learners' process as they embark on the learning activities we design. Whatever the task, we support students when we create opportunities for ongoing conversation with us, and with peers, about their learning.

Teacher Feedback

In addition to conferring during work time (discussed in Chapters 3 and 4), we can give the entire group frequent feedback on their progress.

Renowned reading teacher Cris Tovani presents one easy structure for documenting learners' behavior and contributions during independent or group work time: she creates a three-column chart on an overhead transparency, similar to the one presented in Figure 5.5, and circulates around the room jotting notes to share when students come back together as a whole class.

With an empty chart set up like Figure 5.5 attached to a clipboard, you can circulate among working students and make notes on their participation. In the left-hand column, note down positive attributes; the middle column is a space to record direct quotes from students, examples of them thinking like scientists or demonstrating effective group behavior. In the third column, we can document any unfortunate behavior taking place—students off task, misusing materials, or disrespecting peers.

Toward the end of class, flip this transparency onto the overhead and share aloud with the students the data you gathered. Next time they see you circulating with a clipboard and an overhead pen, learners will likely try to let you catch them being smart scientists.

As we gather and then reflect this feedback to the group, we are modeling appropriate, honest information sharing about performance. Very few students have been taught how to give and receive feedback gracefully, especially from peers. Once we demonstrate our language and stance in giving feedback, we can create opportunities for learners to offer feedback to one another.

Peer Feedback

Giving and receiving peer feedback empowers students to take responsibility for their own learning. Sometimes I notice students are tougher on one another than a teacher may ever be. While as facilitators we must protect our students from unfair comments and set a tone of respect and kindness, this need not mean that we shield learners from

+	" "	–
• Adam agreed with Kira's hypothesis, then asked a clarifying question about the lab. • Martina let Lainie take charge of the materials, even though they both wanted to.	"Can you explain that again?" (Ben) "I think the data suggests that . . ." (Alonzo) "Why do you think so?" (Suzanne)	• Loitering at the sink • Putting down lab partner's thinking • Leaving paper towels all over lab station

FIG. 5.5 *Class Work Time Feedback Chart (adapted from Tovani 2004)*

the hard facts. It is a razor's edge to walk: if the presenter spelled "brain" incorrectly, peers would be fair to let him know, but it would be out of bounds to call that student scientist "dumb."

Here are a variety of structures for giving and receiving peer feedback about student work or student thinking. To ensure that all learners are engaged and thinking about a presentation, set an expectation that *every* student prepares feedback *every* time. You or student facilitators can elect to call on only those who volunteer, call on students randomly, or have everyone record their thinking on paper. As well as having students present, ask students to listen, watch, and learn from one another.

- *Praise.* Celebrate what you liked and learned from a piece.
- *Warm and cool feedback.* Share one thing you liked and one suggestion for improvement. You can't just say, "It was great." You must tell *what* was great about the work and *why* you think so. Cool feedback must also be constructive, not damning, offering specific ideas for changes or improvement.
- *Questions.* Create an evocative question to ask the presenter. The question should probe for understanding or expansion. Presenters do not need to know all the answers.
- *Sandwiches.* Tell one thing you liked, one question or area of confusion, followed by another thing you appreciate.

Self-Reflection

Even more important than hearing feedback from you or from one another, students need time to reflect on their own effort, participation, and learning.

At frequent intervals, we can stop and ask them to record how they see themselves as members of a learning group or the class as a whole, as well as what they are thinking, understanding, and wondering.

In Chapter 4, I suggest a variety of reflection questions designed to get students thinking about what they know and learned about science. Additionally, we ought to create opportunities for students to step out and look at their role in the learning process. Here are some possible reflection questions appropriate to a cooperative learning sequence.

- How would you describe your role in the group?
- How do you predict peers would describe your role?
- What benefits did you gain from being a part of this group?
- How did you contribute to the learning of others?
- What were your group's strengths?
- What could your group have done better?
- What is important for you to remember next time you work in a group?

With questions like these, we invite students to reflect honestly on their essential role as a learner and a teammate, and to share that thinking with peers. Through this process of analysis, students deepen their understanding of and capacity for collaboration.

Feedback to Teachers

In addition to creating time to give learners feedback, time for students to give feedback to one another, and to reflect on their own learning, we can allow chances for students to share their reflections on how we, as teachers, are doing. I like to do so at regular intervals, often before a holiday break. Some comments are predictable ("give less homework") but some are insightful and instructive. "Lay off the overhead," Loryn Isaacs told me. Only then did I realize how intensely I had begun to rely on that one piece of technology.

Our students spend more time with us than any staff developer or administrator ever could. When we invite their insight into our practice, we communicate to them that we, as they, are learners engaged in an ongoing process of improvement. We also, through this invitation, convey our respect for them and their thinking.

Far too few schools today are places where students want to be and learn. As teachers, we have a golden opportunity to create for learners a safe place where thinking is honored and encouraged. In doing this, we give to students the gift of faith, faith in them, which can grow into their own faith in themselves.

Every intentional community-building effort you make communicates loudly to students your vision of and for them as participants in a culture of inquiry. As exemplary teachers have demonstrated through the ages, great learning can take place when we believe in our students and their innate potential.

Whether you are prepared to start a new school year, or considering a midstream adjustment for your present classes, take time to consider your beliefs, your students', and how those are acted out in your classroom. Look for ways that you can

- adjust or reinforce norms,
- shift the learning environment,
- revise the structure of learning tasks, and
- modify feedback systems.

These together constitute the "hidden" curriculum of your class. Make sure that in every way possible you communicate to students a belief that they are capable, and that you expect from them the quality thinking and responsibility for learning befitting brilliant scientists. Here are some planning questions to help you hone your work around this important task.

Crafting Culture: Teacher Planning Questions

What do you believe about your students and their promise as scientists?

How would you like your students to feel about themselves as scientists?

In what ways do you think the following support or detract from students' experience in your classroom:

- norms
- learning environment
- structure of learning activities
- feedback systems

What changes do you feel inspired to make? How will you begin?

How do you or how could you help students take responsibility for building culture? What kinds of support will students need to be successful as community members?

Dobetter Culture

Halfway through the year, Ms. Dobetter realizes that her freshman biology class is not a place any student likes to be. The culture of the group is having a detrimental effect on students' participation and learning. It is time to make some changes, so she works with the planning questions to revise the culture of the class.

What do you believe about your students and their promise as scientists?

In my heart of hearts, I like to think there is an Einstein in every child, but I realize that sometimes their behavior gets me down, and I forget. I start to treat them like animals because that is how they behave, this class in particular. I don't like what I am doing or how I am thinking of them. I would like to get back to believing that they are all smart, but they have worn me out.

How would you like your students to feel about themselves as scientists?

I want them all to think that they can do this, be bright and capable. I think one of the problems is that this is considered a low-track class, not honors, so the students just act immature, disinterested, and negative. We have had a lot of issues with iPods and texting, so I just feel like they don't care.

In what ways do you think the following support or detract from students' experience in your classroom:

Norms?

I was pretty clear about setting up classroom expectations at the beginning of the year, but I guess I have watched those slide somewhat. The kids are not always very nice to each other, and I had to start picking my battles. I do think these are something I need to revisit with the class.

Learning Environment?

I went and sat in the last row the other day and realized that from back there it is pretty tough to see the board, and I think the kids sitting over there find it easy to disengage. I am considering moving the tables around, making the long side of my room the front, so they will have their backs to the windows. I would have to get someone to move my projector screen, but I think it would be worth it.

I also do not really have very many high-quality supplies. There is just no money. But I have been using that as an excuse. Maybe if I put some energy into it, I can drum up some materials that will help these kids feel like I take them seriously. I have a friend that works for the university. Maybe she can help me get some hand-me-downs.

Structure of Learning Activities?

Because these guys have been acting so goofy lately, I realized I have been trying to rein them in by grabbing more and more control of what goes on in class. And then it is a downward spiral because they rebel against that by acting out. I need to give them more responsibility, but they also need to handle it.

Feedback Systems?

Feedback is kind of a one-way street in my room. I give the kids a lot of feedback about how I think they are doing, and sometimes ask them to give comments to each other about their work, but I have not opened the door for them to give me any feedback. I guess I am a bit afraid of what they might say. But this would be a good starting point: I probably need to hear it.

What changes do you feel inspired to make? How will you begin?

Okay, there is a lot I can do, such as

- change my attitude about my students;
- revisit the classroom norms;
- switch my room around so the back is not so far back;
- talk with Pauline about getting some specimens, photographs, equipment, materials, or some other hand-me-downs from the university;
- find ways (that I can live with) to put students more in the driver's seat of their own learning; and
- probably the first thing I need to do is get their feedback, just level with them that this class is in rough shape and hear what they have to say about it.

That seems like a lot to do, but just making the list is sort of empowering. I have been feeling run down by the culture in that group, so I think I need to just go through this list one step at a time and see what we can do.

How do you or how could you help students take responsibility for building culture? What kinds of support will students need to be successful as community members?

I think that conversation is key, opening the door to their feedback, letting them talk about how they would like the class to be, then inviting their participation in making things better.

I think the most important thing I can do in terms of support is not to let go of those norms, not to let them off the hook. They are good kids; we have just gotten in a rut.

Shaking It Up

The next week when her students roll into Ms. Dobetter's room, no one is quite sure where to sit. The tables are all turned ninety degrees, and the back row is a lot closer to the board. When the teens finally settle in, instead of flicking on the overhead with her usual day-starter exercise, Ms. Dobetter perches on her stool at the front of the room and starts softly, "It is time for us to talk."

Surprised, students remain silent for a while, then realize she really does want to listen and begin to speak up:

"We never get to do any of the labs the honors biology class always talks about."

"You think we are dumb."

"This class is boring."

"Who cares about science, anyway?"

While these comments and the others that follow are hurtful, Ms. Dobetter jots them down, resisting the temptation to explain away the learners' concerns.

After she has the sense that students got to have their say, she begins to speak about her vision for the class—that they all be smart scientists together. Snickers. She apologizes for her own shortcomings as a teacher, and explains that this is not something she can change all by herself: she had stopped letting them do the labs because their behavior was so out of control. She wants to change that, she explains, but they will all need to work together. "So, we have a decision to make: do we want things to be better in here or not?"

Students signal that they do.

"Okay, then, what are we going to do?" Students brainstorm ideas, some feasible, some ridiculous. She writes them all on the board. After the list-making energy peters out of the group, she asks them to commit: "I want you to look at this list and choose the three things that you think would make the biggest difference in terms of our classroom culture, three things you can really commit to doing. I am going to read the list, and when I read the ones you think are important and are personally willing to do, I want you to stand up."

Students vote like this, on their feet, and Ms. Dobetter's risk in giving them voice proves worthwhile. As a group, they commit to respecting each other, doing their work, and leaving electronics out of sight during class. Simple measures, but these are some of the major battlegrounds that have consumed their teacher's energy all year.

In turn, Ms. Dobetter makes the group some promises herself: she will make positive presuppositions about students; she will work to create more engaging lessons where students will be in charge of their own learning; and she will try to get some more interesting materials for them.

The conversation ends with a calm tome of acceptance and optimism. Ms. Dobetter explains, "We are all in the same boat here; it is not fair to drill a hole under your seat, even if it is *your own* seat."

This conversation is not a quick fix, but it does catalyze new attitudes in the class. In the weeks and months to come, things slowly improve. There are setbacks, but Ms. Dobetter notices students more willing to be one another's keeper, reminding peers of their shared responsibility to make this class a positive learning environment. She works harder to plan interesting tasks for the group, but the students also work harder to learn with her. It is a win-win.

So What?

In this example, Ms. Dobetter demonstrated the courage to confront an unproductive classroom culture and takes steps to redefine it. Community is a work in progress. Processing thinking and discussing norms takes time, time that you may be reluctant to take away from important content goals. Yet when we strike the balance just right, community and content learning can mutually support one another. In the long view, the very long view, teaching students to think and learn together might just be more important than any other way we could possibly use their time.

"Yah, but . . ."

- *"My students hate school."*

How very sad that many students today do not appreciate the educational opportunities available to them, but also that some schools and teachers are not more effective in creating learning environments that truly address students' needs.

I remember that in the beginning of my first year as a teacher, I felt intensely hated by half of my homeroom class. I began to reach out to them one at a time, to talk with them, get to know them, ask questions, and find common ground. This took a long time, but eventually I won most of them over. Students began to care and learn only after we built this bridge. It is hard work.

- *"My students are not ready for group work. They do best working alone."*

Many of our students do, since often this is how they have grown accustomed to working. Yet to be prepared to participate in relationships, family, and workplaces as teens and adults, all of our students need to be prepared to collaborate, cooperate, and communicate, whether about science or what happened to the pizza ordered by table eleven. We do learners a great service when we create opportunities for them to practice the skills of community in our classrooms every day.

- *"How do I grade group work?"*

Teachers approach this issue in many different ways, all depending on their goals and values for the task.

  - Give everyone in the group the same grade; assess both product and process.
  - Create a combination grading system that takes into account a group grade on the final product and a process grade crediting each individual for his participation and contribution.
  - Grade individuals solely based on their work as part of the team.
  - Switch up the groups frequently and randomly.

- *"This is way too touchy-feely! I teach science."*

We all teach science, but more importantly, we teach students. These students will grow up to be thinkers of all sorts, not only scientists. By integrating into our curriculum and culture the values of respect, understanding, compassion, and excellence, we teach life skills which are transferable to all of their future endeavors.

Constants Checklist

Now that we have looked at each of these—inquiry, big ideas, workshop, assessment, and culture—under the microscope, let's lean back and consider the big picture:

It would be crazy to go through all of the planning questions from each chapter for each unit or lesson. That is too much to take on at once while you manage daily planning and instruction. Yet as chaos theorist Edward Lorenz describes, the beat of a butterfly's wing can eventually alter the path of a tornado. So any one of these "Constants" chapters you choose to focus on, to think about, will affect the entire learning system in your classroom. Start by working through one lens, and take your time.

To keep the constants in mind, review this Constants Checklist from time to time, a ready reference to prompt your big picture thinking.

Constants Checklist

1. Which feature of inquiry will I emphasize? How?
2. What is the big idea, and how will I bring it to life?
3. Which elements of the workshop model will I employ?
4. When and how will I assess students' content understanding and skill proficiency?
5. How will students build and experience community through this learning?

As you read through the chapters in the "Variables" section, each detailing a common instructional practice, you will see the Constants Checklist appear again and again, demonstrating how these constants can support all of the learning we hope for our students.

Variables

When we hold constant in our classrooms a stance of inquiry, an emphasis on the big ideas, a commitment to workshop model instruction, and use assessment *for* learning within a positive culture, we create fertile ground for science learning.

How we choose to pursue that learning with our students—whether through labs or lectures, demonstrations or discussions—can vary. This section describing common instructional strategies is, for that reason, entitled "Variables."

Whether visiting a fifth-grade class with a kit-based science program or talking with a ninth-grade teacher implementing an interactive physics curriculum, I have found that most science instructors select from a tried-and-true menu of learning activities each day:

- labs,
- demonstrations,
- lectures,
- discussion,
- reading,
- projects,
- activities, and
- fieldwork.

Each of these variables is featured in its own chapter in this section. Each chapter follows a similar format to those in the "Constants" section, and is designed to be a resource and tool for you as you develop or refine instructional plans.

All eight of these variables may already be a part of your class's experience; you may see your favorites and your instructional weakness in this list. While each of these chapters draws from the first five in the book, feel free to pick and choose from this section and read these chapters in the order that serves you best.

CHAPTER 6

Labs

Well-designed labs put students in charge of their own learning, support important content understanding linked to big ideas, emphasize the essential features of inquiry, and develop students' science process skills.

Think Tank

- What role do labs play in my instruction?
- How do I teach inquiry thinking?
- How do I teach science process skills?
- What ownership do my students have of their science investigations?

Students are deeply engaged, using droppers to transfer colored chemicals from one divot in their test plates to another. Slowly and carefully the seventh graders work. The room is calm and purposeful, and I am struck to find this impressively studious atmosphere in an otherwise chaotic urban middle school. I lean in to listen and watch one group, then another. After observing for a long time, I quietly ask one student, "What are you doing?"

"Moving this stuff," she explains in a hushed voice.

"Why?" I ask quietly.

"I don't know." She whispers and turns back to her work.

I probe a few other teams to get a sense of what they are thinking about this task and get similarly uncertain answers. As their teacher calls for cleanup, I go back to the girl I'd initially spoken with.

"What did you learn?" I inquire.

"I don't know."

The teacher overhears our conversation, and pipes up sternly, "Sit down, and I'll tell you what you learned!"

Reflection

How would you describe students' experience of inquiry in this class?

What are your hunches about why the girl in the story "did not know" why she was doing the task or what she was meant to be learning?

What suggestions would you offer to her instructor?

How frustrating for this teacher that he had gone to so much trouble to orchestrate an engaging hands-on lab experience, but that the students I spoke to did not understand what their work was about. All too often, hands-on labs offer students skill practice, yet fall short of supporting learners in understanding big ideas and related science concepts through an experience of inquiry.

In the introduction to *How Students Learn Science in the Classroom,* Donovan and Bransford (2005) describe a 1908 study on the value of learning with understanding:

> In one of the most famous early studies comparing the effects of "learning a procedure" with "learning with understanding," two groups of children practiced throwing darts at a target underwater. One group received an explanation of the refraction of light, which causes the apparent location of the target to be deceptive. The other group only practiced dart throwing, without explanation. Both groups did equally well on the practice task, which involved a target 12 inches under water. But the group that had been instructed about the abstract principle did much better when they had to transfer to a situation in which the target was only 4 inches under water. Because they understood what they were doing, the group that had received instruction about the refraction of light could adjust their behavior to the new task. (7)

This study demonstrates the importance of students understanding the big picture in order to transfer learning from one context to the next. For this reason, then, we must be transparent with students about the learning goals—both process and content—of lab tasks, and ensure that our investigations are designed to promote understanding of big ideas.

What Is a Lab?

Some teachers use the word "lab" to describe any occasion when students are doing something other than sitting and listening. To professional scientists, the word "lab" is short for "laboratory," the site of their scientific research. Research labs are filled with specific equipment designed for certain areas of investigation. As described by the traditional scientific method, a scientist investigates a question by

- developing a hypothesis,
- designing an experiment,

- conducting her research,
- gathering data, and
- synthesizing this information to further clarify the hypothesis.

Competence with this investigation process requires proficiency with the five essential features of inquiry described in Chapter 1, as well as mastery of certain process skills.

Setting up and conducting high quality labs takes a lot of planning and instructional time. As astute science teachers, we must sort through our lab choices and devote time only to those that both

- illuminate important science content linked to big ideas and
- engage students in the thinking skills of inquiry.

In order for learners to be able to do those two things independently and well, we need to teach them science process skills.

Labs should maximize content learning in the context of big ideas. Unfortunately, there are textbooks and kits containing "labs" that are little less than activities related to the topic at hand. A high-quality lab needs to emphasize important concepts from our current studies, not just involve related vocabulary or equipment. Be sure that the labs you choose will help you drive home understandings about science, rather than simply entertain your students.

For example, my students have achieved wonderful learning outcomes about evolution and speciation through the Beak Lab, an experience where they use different tools—tweezers, spoons, popsicle sticks banded together like tongs—to attempt to pick up a variety of "foods" (beans, seeds, leaves). Though students' hands are busy manipulating materials, and their science notebooks get filled with data tables, the main emphasis of this lab as I design and conduct it is on *explaining* the data, understanding what this experience has to teach us about how birds and other animals find their niche—all of which helps us to access the big idea, evolution.

Thinking and Understanding During a Lab

During a lab, then, our students ought to conduct scientific research of their own: pose questions, gather and analyze data, and so forth—experiencing each of the features of inquiry. While we may not be prepared to invite our young scientists to design and conduct entirely original investigations for every unit, we can ensure that all lab tasks include some occasions for scientific questioning and the experience of discovery. Through these sorts of labs, students come to understand the nature of science, and science as a way of knowing in and of itself.

Through labs, we can also teach the process skills of science. Some science teachers feel obliged to set weeks aside each year to teach measurement, microscopes, and the like in the absence of science content. Asking students to memorize steps of the scientific method, names of lab materials, and features of a quality lab report out of the context of a real investigation is, in my experience, something like trying to teach math without using numbers. Science process skills can be learned within the context of inquiry-based labs addressing science content standards.

Inquiry-Based Labs

Each year when I teach my class on science methods for preservice teachers, I bring in the film *Apollo 13*. We watch the segment about the carbon dioxide filter problem, the part where the NASA engineers have to figure out how to fit a square peg into a round hole to ensure that the astronauts aboard Apollo 13 have enough oxygen to make it back to Earth safely. In the film, after the engineers on Earth have assembled a system to solve the problem, they document its construction and then dictate the step-by-step procedures for the astronauts aboard the spacecraft to replicate.

After watching this film clip together, I ask my students who was behaving like a scientist in the movie. They usually all say that the NASA engineers were being scientists because they were figuring something out. Then I ask about the astronauts; some students think the astronauts were, while others say they were not. We talk together about how being a scientist can include

- creative problem solving,
- following a series of scripted steps, and
- analyzing the outcome of your work.

In the instance depicted in the film, the engineers were the problem-solvers, while the astronauts were investigating whether they themselves would live or die if the procedures were followed. Although the astronauts' role was simply to follow directions, the *outcome* was not a foregone conclusion.

Labs and Inquiry

Labs are an ideal and very practical opportunity for us to promote scientific thinking among our students. In each lab, we can ensure that students experience one or more of the essential features of inquiry:

- engaging in scientifically oriented questions;
- giving priority to evidence in responding to questions;
- formulating explanations;
- connecting explanations to scientific knowledge; and
- communicating and justifying explanations. (National Research Council 2000)

These features need to be modeled, practiced, and discussed within the context of a lab. In this way, students can learn the science content as they come to understand science as a way of knowing.

If a "lab" task does not ask students to engage in at least one of these features, it is time to revise.

The problem we encounter with some commercially produced science "labs" is that they do not ask students to think like the NASA engineers *or* like astronauts. The difference between what happened aboard Apollo 13 and what students are asked to do in "cookbook" labs is that the results on Apollo 13 were unknown and uncertain; conversely, students are often asked to follow scripted steps in lab sheets which then tell them the outcome of the experiment. These cookbook investigations leave little room for student thinking as described in the essential features of inquiry detailed in Chapter 1.

Process Skills

A science student needs to know certain process skills in order to succeed in conducting labs independently. It is important to note that these skills—some demonstrated in Figures 6.1 and 6.2—should be practiced in support of content learning and inquiry thinking, not as an end unto themselves.

The process skills, mentioned in Chapter 4, include

- experimental design,
- observation,
- measurement, and
- communication.

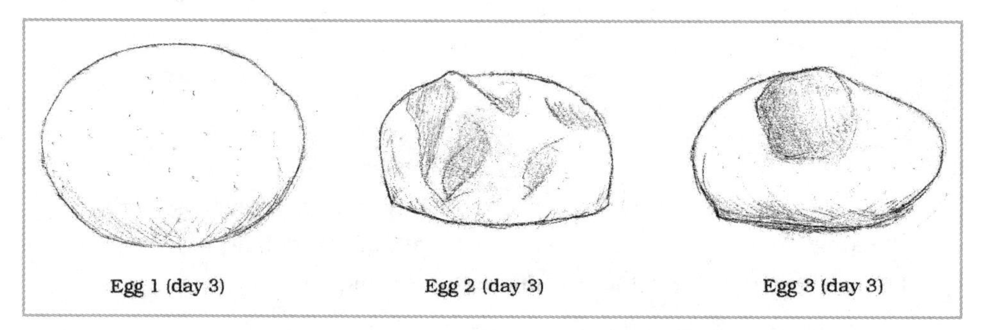

FIG. 6.1 *Data Gathered by a Student Scientist as She Soaked One Egg in Each of the Following: (1) sugar water, (2) corn syrup, and (3) both sugar water and corn syrup*

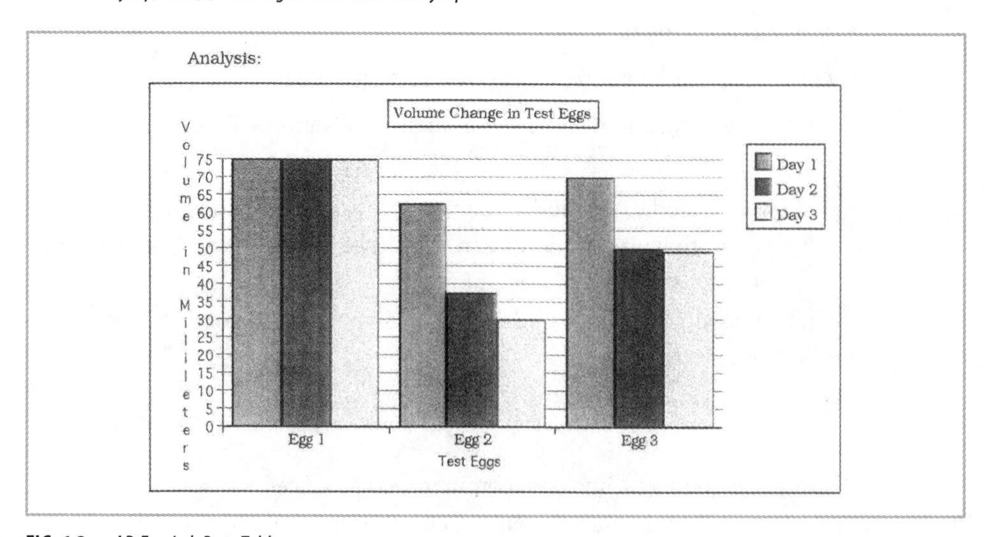

FIG. 6.2 *AD Egg Lab Data Table*

	What should students know and be able to do?	How would a student demonstrate proficiency with this process skill in the context of a tropism experiment?
Experimental Design	Write a specific, testable hypothesis as an "If-then-because" statement	"If I take a young plant and lay its pot on its side, then the stem will start growing upward, away from the Earth, because plants have geotropisms."
	Use controls and variables to test a hypothesis	"To test my hypothesis, I will use four runner bean plants, give them each the same soil, water, and sunlight. These are my controls. I will place two upright and two on their sides; this is the variable."
	Design replicable experimental conditions	"I will keep track of seed type, the room temperature, pot size, volume of water, watering schedule, and soil type so that my experiment could be repeated precisely."
Observation (Qualitative Data Collection)	Use and care for the tools of observation	"I will also document the plants' growth with photography. I know how to use, care for, and store the camera."
	Remain objective while gathering data	"In addition to documenting measurements, I will collect the following qualitative data: leaf texture, color, and strength. For each quality, I will establish a scale of reference. I will avoid writing that the plants 'look tired' or other interpretive comments."
	Record observations in a variety of formats—narrative notes, data tables, sketches, life drawing—as appropriate to the task	"I will keep narrative notes of qualitative data, and print out the photos for use in my lab report."
Measurement (Quantitative Data Collection)	Work with the metric system of measurement	"All measurements will be recorded in millimeters."
	Use and care for the tools of measurement	"I will use a ruler and a protractor to measure my plants and the angles of their stems. I will store these in the classroom so that I can use them each day."
	Understand and use correct units	"I know that there are 10 millimeters in a centimeter, and that since my plants are growing slowly, millimeters will be the best units of measurement for this data collection task."
	Use mathematics to calculate measurements as needed	"I will convert between centimeters and millimeters as needed."
Communication	Write clear, detailed procedures	"1. Gather materials. 2. Fill pots with soil to 2 cm below rim. 3. Place one seed 6 cm below the surface of the soil in each pot . . ."
	Create organized data tables	"I will have one data table for each plant. Each data table will have space to record the plant stem's length (from soil to tip), the angle (if any) in the stem, and the height of the stem after the angle. I will have space to record this data every day for two weeks."
	Construct accurate graphs	"I will plot three graphs based on my data over time: stem length, stem angle, and height after angle."

FIG. 6.3 *Science Process Skills and Examples*

In Figure 6.3, I describe these skills in greater detail. Each of these skills can be taught in the context of a laboratory investigation.

If we stop after teaching these process skills, we are training students to work only as lab techs—not as research scientists. We must build from a foundation of skills, then devote our energy to promoting *thinking* based on these skills. This means learners spend at least as much of their time making meaning of their results, analyzing, and explaining data as they do making observations or taking measurements.

Comparing Sample Labs

To bring these ideas to life, let us look at three sample lab tasks in Figures 6.4, 6.5, and 6.6. All are designed for seventh-grade life science classes beginning their study of the circulatory system, yet they differ in their structure. As you read each lab, consider these questions.

- What important science content will students learn through this task?
- Which of the essential features of inquiry will students experience through this task? For each feature, where would you place the task on the continuum from teacher-directed to student-directed (see Figure 1.6)?
- What science process skills will students practice during this lab?

There is a time in the school year and a place along the continuum of inquiry for each of these labs. Yet you can see the progressively increasing opportunities for student thinking and independence with process skills as you move from Lab A to B to C. Figure 6.7 summarizes the differences between the three labs based on the essential features of inquiry.

In Lab A, students are spoon-fed background information and then told exactly the steps they should follow to complete the lab. The data table is already created for them, and essentially all they are being asked to do is follow directions and write down some numbers. The first two conclusion questions invite elementary reporting of data, while the third question—referring to the crux of the lab—is actually answerable from simply reading the text at the top of the page. A student in this class will experience little more than reading and following directions. Perhaps she or he will come to understand the relationship between exercise and pulse rate, but that understanding is not integral to her completion of this task. Ultimately, what this task says to a student is "Don't worry about thinking like a scientist. Just follow directions."

Lab B is a reinvented or "hybridized" version of Lab A, designed to invite students to think about and design their own investigations along prescribed lines. A teacher created this lab by crossing the traditional "cookbook" lab (Lab A) with the open-ended Lab C. This new lab, Lab B, opens the door to student thinking and creativity without losing sight of the learning goals of the task. Success with Lab B requires the support of workshop model instruction (described in Chapter 3) and represents a stepping-stone for students ready to move from Lab A to Lab C.

Lab C, requiring a high level of self-direction, keen understanding of inquiry, and competence with process skills, mirrors the work of independent scientists. Some of our secondary students are prepared for this level of autonomy without scaffolding, while others may founder if presented with the assignment tomorrow.

Name ______________________ Date ____________ Assignment # ____________

Pulse Lab A

Background Information

Your heart is the most important organ in the circulatory system. It pumps blood throughout the body, delivering oxygen and nutrients to each cell, then carrying away carbon dioxide and waste products. When you exercise, your heart beats faster to deliver nutrients and oxygen throughout the body more quickly to meet the increased demand. In this experiment, you will find out how much faster your heart beats when you exercise.

The average adult's heart pumps between sixty and one hundred beats per minute. You can find your own pulse most easily in the arteries of your upper arm, upper thigh, or neck. Most medical personnel like to check the pulse in the wrist because this is less invasive. When measuring a pulse, feel for it with your fingers, not your thumb, because the thumb has a pulse of its own, which can be confusing. To calculate your pulse, you will need to count how many times your heart beats in ten seconds, then multiply that number by six to find the number of beats per minute.

Procedure

Step 1: Find your pulse.

Step 2: While seated and relaxed, take your pulse. This is called your resting pulse. Remember to count your heartbeats for ten seconds, then multiply that number by six. Record your data in the table below.

Step 3: Do jumping jacks for one full minute.

Step 4: Take your pulse again. Record your data in the table below.

Step 5: Do jumping jacks for one full minute.

Step 6: Take your pulse again. Record your data in the table below.

Observations

Resting Pulse	Pulse after one min. of exercise	Pulse after two mins. of exercise
Beats/Minute	Beats/Minute	Beats/Minute

Conclusion

1. How much faster was your pulse after one minute of exercise than your resting pulse?
2. How much faster was your pulse after two minutes of exercise than your resting pulse?
3. Why does exercise make your pulse go faster?

FIG. 6.4 *Pulse Lab A*

Getting from A to C

Many teachers I meet find themselves doing Lab A with their students yet feel like they ought to be doing Lab C. This is a frustrating predicament because it is not an easy leap from A to C! How do we take mundane "cookbook" labs like this and transform them into challenging thinking exercises for young scientists like Labs B or C? How can we fold essential process skills into inquiry experiences? Here are some suggestions to guide your planning.

Name ______________________ Date ______________ Assignment # ______________

Pulse Lab B

Big Idea: Stability

Question: How does exercise affect your pulse?

Planning Questions

1. What is a pulse rate?
2. How can you measure your pulse?
3. What is your hypothesis about how your pulse changes when you exercise?
4. Design a short (ten minutes or less) experiment to test how exercise affects your pulse. Write step-by-step procedures describing how to conduct the experiment. Before gathering data, create an empty data table to record the observations.

CHECKPOINT:
Show your teacher your experimental design and data table before conducting the experiment.

Conclusion

1. What was your hypothesis about how your pulse would change when you exercised?
2. Was your hypothesis correct? Use your data to explain.
3. Compare your data to your classmates' findings.
4. How do these findings relate to the big idea of stability?
5. What questions do you now have about the relationship between pulse and exercise?

FIG. 6.5 *Pulse Lab B*

Name ______________________ Date ______________ Assignment # ______________

Pulse Lab C

Design and conduct an experiment about how exercise affects your pulse.

Your investigation must include the following:

- Question
- Hypothesis
- Experimental Design
- Procedures
- Data Table
- Data Analysis
- Conclusion

FIG. 6.6 *Pulse Lab C*

Features	Lab A	Lab B	Lab C
Learner engages in scientifically oriented questions.	No question is posed, only implied.	A "how" question is set out for the students.	Learner is responsible for formulating question.
Learner gives priority to evidence in responding to questions.	Learner collects, but analyzes it only superficially.	Conclusion questions ask learners to reflect on hypothesis in light of data.	Learner is responsible for gathering evidence.
Learner formulates explanations from evidence.	Text does the explaining in the "Background Knowledge" section.	Conclusion questions foster formulation of explanation based on evidence.	Learner is responsible for formulating explanations.
Learner connects explanations to scientific questions.	Learner is not asked to make connections.	Conclusion questions refer learner to the main question of the lab.	Learner is responsible for making connections.
Learner communicates and justifies explanations.	Conclusion questions ask learner to communicate.	Conclusion questions ask learner to communicate and justify.	Learner is responsible for explaining and communicating.

FIG. 6.7 *Comparing Labs A, B, and C Based on the Five Essential Features of Inquiry*

Keep the Focus on the Science Content

All labs should feed important understanding goals and connect content with big ideas. Be sure to state the purpose for students up front and to draw out students' background knowledge about the topic. Invite learners to connect their thinking and learning back to the big idea on a regular basis through conversations, reflection writing, and other quick reminders. Ensure that the science content does not get lost in the "wow" of using equipment or the minutia of recording data.

Instruct for Inquiry

While all of the five essential features of inquiry are integral to labs, the following two lend themselves most easily to direct instruction within a lab experience.

Engaging in Scientifically Oriented Questions

Within the context of lab design, discuss with students what a scientifically oriented question is, and practice question writing with them. Teach them the skill of asking good questions. Discuss how narrow a question must be in order to be answered sufficiently through a lab investigation as well as what makes a question "testable" (pursuing these questions is inquiry itself). Rather than giving students a question and a hypothesis, ask learners to develop their own.

Formulating Explanations Based on Evidence

Rather than telling kids what they learned (or were supposed to learn), ask them to explain, to justify, and to demonstrate their understanding. To the extent possible, keep investigations open-ended. After students have gathered their data, work together to make meaning both of their individual data sets and all the information gathered by the class. Look for anomalies. Brainstorm, discuss, and critique explanations. Support students in developing their logic as scientific thinkers. Resist the temptation to explain away their confusion or curiosity.

Practice Process Skills

Rather than writing detailed lab instructions, let students write original ones. In order to engage in scientifically oriented questions, students must understand experimental design, observation, measurement, and communication as described in Figure 6.3. Consider teaching one or more specific process skills within each investigation, slowly building students' proficiency with the full range.

Handing Over Lab Design, One Step at a Time

Some science teachers I have met approach lab design as an all-or-nothing affair. Perhaps once each spring they turn students loose to design investigations for the science fair, but for the remainder of the year take responsibility for assigning professionally scripted lab tasks. Instead, I suggest a gradual release of responsibility—carefully training students over the course of the entire year and during each unit of content study, to take charge of their own lab designs. This transition is supported through workshop model instruction, detailed in Chapter 3.

Within each lab, we can instruct our students in one inquiry feature or process skill through targeted teaching and modeling. These minilessons, followed by practice and reflection, can be folded into the overall science content learning experience.

For example, you may start the year with your "Mixtures and Solutions" unit, and take time throughout to train your students on the skills of objective observation and all aspects of writing a quality conclusion, including explanations based on evidence. During the next unit, you may shift your inquiry focus to connecting explanations to scientific knowledge, still expecting students to take responsibility for conclusion writing, and so on. In this way, students will increasingly own the process of lab design (as shown in Figure 6.8) until—from hypothesis to conclusion—they are practiced experts prepared to design their own labs from start to finish.

Of course, for some investigations—chemistry, in particular—it would be quite hazardous to offer students the materials and invite them to design their own lab. Yet in many other instances, even given specific learning goals and clear safety guidelines, students are quite capable of designing significant aspects of their investigations given appropriate guidance and support.

	Fall	**Winter**	**Spring**
Inquiry Skills	Developing explanations based on evidence	Connecting explanations to scientific knowledge	Developing scientific questions and designing means to answer them
Process Skills	Observation	Measurement	Communication

FIG. 6.8 *Sample Timeline for Teaching Inquiry and Process Skills in the Context of Labs*

Planning Labs So Students Direct Their Own Learning

In addition to planning what students will do and understand, and how scientific inquiry and process skills will be folded into their learning, it is important to consider students' needs over the flow of time. Initially students may need to know who is going to select their lab partners, while later they begin to wonder how their work will be graded. Management issues always come up: is it okay to text message with the Bunsen burner on? If you anticipate and plan for these issues, you will be delighted to watch your students succeed. To this end, supports and accountability are an integral part of any activity design.

Labs and Workshop Model Instruction

The workshop model offers us an ideal framework for supporting student scientists in designing and conducting labs. Consider these opportunities to promote thinking before, during, and after a lab.

Before

Most lab activities require some background knowledge in order to be meaningful. Rather than just explaining that information to our students, we can draw out their prior knowledge and construct understanding with them. In small groups students can discuss their questions and hypotheses, then share their thinking as a class to ensure that everyone has a basis of understanding before embarking on investigation design. In this way, students are asked to engage—to think—from the get-go about the content of the task.

With this groundwork laid, student scientists are ready to design their own lab in response to a specific question, theirs or yours. Learners can discuss and design their own experiments, considering controls and variables, measurement techniques, and data collection systems. Before being released to conduct investigations, students can engage in a process of peer review and teacher conferencing to ensure that their design will provide results relevant to their hypothesis.

During

While students conduct their investigations, the teacher's role is to be on hand conferring, promoting thinking each step of the way. Teacher Hector Ibarra offers us some useful lines of questioning to guide learners as they design and conduct investigations.

- Clarifying: Can you be more specific?
- Focusing: Can you give me an example?
- Probing: What do you think will happen?
- Prompting: What can you do . . . ? (Ibarra 2006, 76)

By encouraging students along these lines, rather than solving their dilemmas or answering their questions, we empower them as scientists to deepen their thinking and improve their work.

After

After gathering data, students can reflect individually on what they learned about the content, as well as the process, of science. Learners can share their findings and thinking in small groups, then report out to the whole class to explore difference, and arrive at a class consensus about the meaning of our data, its relevance to the topic of our unit, and its power to illuminate our big idea.

With the support of workshop model instruction surrounding a lab experience, students are invited into the thinking process from the outset. Rather than being left to their own devices, their work is structured and supported in small steps to ensure that they develop an understanding of what it means to think as scientists engaged in investigations.

Supports

Each group of students is diverse. Some come to us with the confidence to replicate the work of Benjamin Bannecker while others are hesitant to lift their voices. Naturally, when you invite students to take charge of their own lab work, you will meet with a range of responses and needs. Be prepared with some systems to support learners who need more assistance getting started and keeping rolling.

- Use the workshop model (see Chapter 3) as you introduce and conclude each lab.
- Provide targeted minilessons to support students mastering the essential thinking and process skills required to succeed.
- Build checkpoints into the lab planning so that you can keep track of each group and help them to stay on course.
- Create opportunities for students to share and compare their results, and reflect on their learning experiences.

Checkpoints

Most teachers are accustomed to circulating and visiting with teams as they work. But a checkpoint gives you a formal system to ensure that you see what each team is doing before they go from, say, step three to step four. Usually I do this type of check before anyone gets their hands on lab materials.

A checkpoint offers you a chance to screen for safety concerns, probe for understanding, and familiarize yourself with individuals' thinking. I like to use a rubber stamp to give our brief conversation a sense of officialness, letting students know that once they have that stamp they are free to move on.

To Support English Language Learners

While all of us are actually constantly learning English, an increasing proportion of the student population in the United States comes from homes where they speak a language other than English. To ensure these students maximum access to science content during a lab, you can take a few approaches.

- Offer nonlinguistic reminders on your lab design form to prompt students' memories of vocabulary words such as "hypothesis." Clip art of a mind thinking might signal that a prediction belongs here; a numbered list could indicate the space for procedure writing.
- Invite linguistically diverse students to write procedures and record data in their first language. They can translate this text into English later, but language need not interfere with thinking.

To Support Learners Who Struggle with Independence

In every class I have ever taught, there are the chargers ready to run with a project from the moment I mention it, the stragglers ready to distract themselves with any possible alternative, and students everywhere in between. To ensure that all have equal opportunities to learn, try these strategies.

- While the whole class is working to plan the student-directed portions of their lab, pull together a small group of students who may need more assistance planning theirs.
- Do *not* rescue struggling lab designers by offering them a cookbook lab. This communicates to them, "Never mind. I don't expect *you* to figure it out." Expect them and support them to do the thinking.

Accountability

Independent scientific research requires great responsibility. In addition to offering students the necessary support to learn the habits of success, we also need to develop appropriate assessments of their learning and consequences for any unfortunate behavior.

Labs and Preassessment

An original hypothesis is a wonderful preassessment not only of a student's content knowledge but also of her reasoning skills. For example, when preparing to conduct a lab testing conservation of matter and energy, what could you tell about a student's understanding based on each of these hypotheses?

- Jane: If we freeze 25ml of water and then melt it again, then there will be less water because freezing takes energy.
- Tomas: If I take 25ml of water, freeze it and then melt it, there will be more water afterward because water expands when it freezes.
- Vincent: If we freeze 25ml of water, then let it melt again, there will still be 25ml of water because matter cannot be created or destroyed.

How could you ensure that students' incorrect background knowledge is dispelled through the lab experience?

Assessment

As with any learning experience, science learning through labs is enhanced when we take time for preassessment, create opportunities for ongoing assessment during work time, and gather summative assessment data, as outlined in Chapter 4.

A rubric is a useful tool not only for assessing student work on labs but also in designing instruction around inquiry and process skills. Below is a rubric I developed over my years of teaching. I shifted from creating separate and distinct rubrics for each individual lab to reusing a generic one. My students appreciated this consistency; labs were a known genre in my classroom, and though the content changed, the expectations remained the same from unit to unit.

I designed the rubric in Figure 6.9 to assess a student's final product as well as to document the quality of his work over the course of the lab investigation. (See Chapter 4 for more on rubric design.)

Consequences

Invariably, some students want to test the limits, especially when they are being offered more self-direction than they may be accustomed to. Be prepared with appropriate consequences to help everyone stay on track. In addition to the usual repertoire of behavior management skills, I have seen teachers use several consequences for off-task behavior during labs.

- *Loss of access to equipment.* This may mean a student can only watch and listen while others conduct the lab, or it may mean the student needs to come in and conduct the lab alone, later, with close supervision.
- *Alternate task.* Rather than reaching the stated learning goals through work on a lab, the student is given an alternate, less glamorous, task such as reading or research—but is still expected to attain the same understanding.
- *Lab equipment apprentices.* One of the most challenging things about conducting labs is the amount of equipment and setup they require. Students who make poor choices during a task may "volunteer" to assist with cleaning up, organizing, and caring for this equipment.

Labs are a wonderfully integrated science-learning experience: through well-designed labs, our students can learn science content alongside science process and scientific thinking. When we utilize the workshop model to provide direct instruction, then allow opportunities for independent practice (followed by sharing and reflection), students grow in their capacity to work alone as scientists. Here are some planning questions designed to get you started designing or revising your labs.

	1	3	5
		All of 1, plus . . .	*All of 3, plus . . .*
Inquiry			
Experimental Design	• Conducts experiment • Collects data	• Hypothesis is testable • Uses scientific method • Data collected provides evidence useful for evaluating hypothesis	• Demonstrates a thorough understanding of inquiry • Completes lab with precision and care • All data recorded accurately and completely
Use of Time	• Works on lab during class • Attends class discussions	• Completes experiment in the time provided • Focuses during class, small group, and paired conversations	• Makes excellent use of all independent work time • Participates thoughtfully in all class discussions and peer critiques
Science Content Understanding	• Aware of the topic of study	• Understands the main science idea addressed through this activity • Understands relevance of this experiment to his or her own life	• Deeply understands stated science learning goals • Contextualizes learning from this investigation within the field of science
Product/Presentation			
Communication	• Serves as evidence of work on investigation	• Documents hypothesis, procedures, data, analysis, and conclusion accurately and in some detail • Completed on time	• Provides audience with a clear, complete, and comprehensive understanding of all student's related work
Craftsmanship	• Created by the student	• Demonstrates effort and care	• Professional quality

FIG. 6.9 *Generic Lab Rubric*

Dobetter Lab

As she embarked on her sixth-grade friction unit, Ms. Dobetter had a time-tested lab poised ready in her file cabinet. The original task asked students to test blocks with different surfaces (glossy, smooth, rough) on a plastic ramp at different angles of inclination. The handout included step-by-step instructions for setting up the ramp and conducting the experiment—including a data table ready with empty boxes, and some questions asking students to explain results.

Ms. Dobetter decided to revise the task to allow more opportunities for student thinking. Here Ms. Dobetter shares her thoughts as she plans her revised friction lab.

Designing Inquiry Labs: Teacher Planning Questions

Task Design

What do I want students to experience as scientists?

What important ideas do I want students to understand?

Instructional Planning

What background knowledge will students need in order to succeed in this task?

How knowledgeable and comfortable are my students with the inquiry thinking and science process skills (developing hypotheses, writing procedures, designing data tables, collecting data, analyzing data, formulating conclusions, and so forth)?

What can they do independently?

Which skills shall I teach them through this activity?

Management

What supports and accountability can I design to ensure that all learners succeed?

What do I want students to experience as scientists?

I want them to mess about with ramps and blocks until they understand how friction and gravity work in opposition to one another. They will design their own investigations, working with variables and constants, to explain and defend their results to our community of learners.

What important ideas do I want students to understand?

Students should understand how friction and gravity work in opposition to one another, and that the coefficient of friction changes depending on the surface material of two faces. Since we will be heading into our simple machines unit, I want learners to understand friction as an example of the big idea of "systems and interactions."

What background knowledge will students need in order to succeed in this task?

Students will need to think about their own experiences with friction—sledding, skateboarding, and so on—and use their common sense. They will also need to remember what they know about the scientific method.

How knowledgeable and comfortable are my students with the inquiry thinking and science process skills?

- *What can they do independently?*

By this point in the year, most of my students are good at developing explanations based on evidence, and are able to write high quality conclusions.

- *Which skills shall I teach them through this activity?*

I plan to focus on the idea of controls and variables as the process teaching point for this investigation. I will tell them the acne story, and take it from there.

What supports and accountability can I build into this activity to ensure that all students get on the right track and stay there?

I will check everyone's hypothesis before they move on, then check their procedure, and then everyone's data table before they get to work. We will use peer critiques and whole-class sharing as a way to ensure that each student gets some feedback each step of the way.

I will facilitate frequent whole-group conversations at each critical point to give everyone a chance to share and hear others' thinking. This always brings learners along. While students are working, I will confer with as many teams as possible.

Usually, a warning is all that my students need to get back on track. But there is a chapter introducing friction in our text that I was going to skip since we are doing this lab. I think I will have any student who cannot engage with the lab read that chapter and answer the questions in it instead.

Ms. Dobetter's Constants Checklist

1. *Which feature of inquiry will I emphasize? How?*
In this lab, students are recording data, evidence, and then using their evidence to develop explanations. I will emphasize and model this explanation in my minilessons each day.

2. *What is the big idea, and how will I bring it to life?*
"Systems and interactions" is the big idea. After students are done gathering data and analyzing it, I will introduce this big idea and ask learners to connect their experiences to it.

3. *Which elements of the workshop model will I employ?*
I will use the workshop model in its entirety, both surrounding the investigation as well as daily—by starting each day with some brief, whole-class instruction, and ending each day with a few minutes for reflection.

4. *When and how will I assess students' content understanding and skill proficiency?*
In addition to the final assessment, I will confer during work time and check in with each group as they plan their investigations.

5. *How will students build and experience community through this learning?*
Students will work in pairs, participate in peer critiques of their lab designs, and share and analyze their collective findings after their investigations are complete.

Setting the Stage

In looking closely at the old version of the lab, Ms. Dobetter decides she is happy with the activity and feels confident that it will lead students to understand the concept of friction. She also realizes this will be a great opportunity to introduce the notion of variables and constants in the context of the investigation.

Instead of handing out the many-times mimeographed original form of the lab, Ms. Dobetter decides to start by engaging her students in a thought experiment. "We are each scientists every day, investigating what will happen if we wear this, eat that, or apply a particular cream to our face." She shares a story about herself as a teen trying to manage acne. "As a tenth grader, my explanations for why I had pimples included genetically bad skin, eating too much chocolate, not getting enough sun, and stress.

"As a high schooler, I decided to address my acne by changing my behavior. I quit eating chocolate, started eating lunch outside every sunny day, and borrowed my mom's relaxation tapes, which I listened to almost every night before going to sleep. I also bought Oxy 5 at Walgreen's and started using it religiously.

"Sure enough, in a week's time my face was significantly smoother. I looked so stunning that Alvin Alvarez invited me to the prom. My friends bought me a huge chocolate cake to celebrate, but I did not know whether I was safe to enjoy it.

"Where had I gone wrong?"

The class discusses the problem that young Ms. Dobetter had created for herself by changing too many things at one time. Together, they work to design a better experiment to assess the cause of her zits. Linking this personal example to their upcoming physics study, Ms. Dobetter illustrates the necessity of controls and variables in an experiment.

Getting to Work

The next day, Ms. Dobetter brings out the blocks and ramps and gives students an overview of the investigation. She writes a broad question on the board: "How does the force of friction interact with the force of gravity?" Next she asks students to work in teams using the materials at hand to design experiments investigating this question. Her goal for the day is to have each group design a viable experiment, complete with a testable hypothesis, appropriately planned controls and variables, and an empty data table.

During work time, Ms. Dobetter circulates among the students to ensure that groups are on task and making progress. As they plan, each student records her thinking. Toward the end of work time, Ms. Dobetter asks teams to pair up and give each other feedback on their experimental designs. The peer critiques are to double-check that their classmates' experiment addresses the question and uses controls and variables in a way that will yield useful results.

The next day, Ms. Dobetter starts class by asking each group to share their data table with a peer. Finally she permits learners to test their hypotheses by conducting the experiments they planned. While the groups work, Ms. Dobetter circulates and asks individuals about their thinking based on their findings so far.

She asks questions like, "How does that compare to your other data?" "Are those the sort of results you expected?" "Why or why not?" and "What are you thinking now?"

Most groups stay focused on the task, but a couple of students receive warnings for their behavior and then make wise choices to get back to work, rather than head across the hall to do a tedious alternative assignment.

Sharing Learning

The final day, students share their groups' findings, compare results, and develop a unified theory of friction based on their collective data. Ms. Dobetter starts the class with the question, "So what do we know now about friction?" Students write independently, then share aloud, while Ms. Dobetter records their conclusions on chart paper.

"Gravity pulls against friction."

"Heavier things need more friction to stand still."

"A steeper ramp has less friction than a shallow one."

She next leads a discussion of the points raised, asking the class to verify whether they agreed with each. By the end of class, students support several concepts unanimously. Other concepts require additional research.

Throughout the investigation, Ms. Dobetter's students are engaged, excited by their ownership of the inquiry process. They handle materials with care, document each trial, and think critically about the evidence they are gathering. As an exit ticket after their last day of work, Ms. Dobetter draws in the big idea, "How is your experiment an example of the big idea of systems and interactions?"

As a final assessment of their learning, she creates a real-life friction problem for her students to analyze and solve individually: The city's parks department is designing a new water slide and wants to ensure that it is safe for youngsters as well as fun for teens. Write a letter to the parks department recommending a process for designing, testing, and regulating the safe use of the new attraction. Through this assessment, students are able to demonstrate not only their understanding of the forces of friction but also their prowess with scientific problem solving.

In contrast to the friction lab activity Ms. Dobetter had offered students in the past, the task she designed this year required more student thinking. They are invested in understanding the inquiry process, designing their own investigations, gathering original data, and reporting their findings to the class to contribute to the group's unified understanding of friction. Also, the audience for their learning is a real live committee making a decision about the future of their own city's park. Based on her assessments, Ms. Dobetter finds students capable of explaining friction and the inquiry process in thorough detail.

So What?

Ms. Dobetter was able to take a task she and her colleagues had repeated successfully for years and tweak it to invite more student thinking in her class. She carefully selected one teaching point about the scientific method—variables and constants—which dovetailed naturally with students' study of friction. In this way, she can continue to weave content learning with process learning all year long, developing increasing occasions for student investment and engagement in investigations.

Look over the labs you currently use to find opportunities for improvement. There is no wrong way to go about this shift from teacher-centered to student-centered lab investigations; if students are thinking more, you are doing it right.

"Yah, but . . ."

- *"My team has all the labs planned out; we rotate equipment, and I cannot change what my class is doing."*

Most teachers work within some system of school, district, or state-mandated learning goals. While your students may be obliged to do the same learning as your colleagues' students, you probably have more freedom than you think about *how* to achieve those learning goals. As in the above example of Pulse Labs A and B, it would be easy to take some of the common labs your team conducts and revise them within the constraints of equipment, time, and learning goals. In fact, once you demonstrate how to enhance a familiar lab with deeper thinking opportunities, your teammates may be keen to borrow your work.

- *"What about science notebooks?"*

Science notebooks are a useful structure for documenting students' thinking. Many teachers have students use a composition book divided into specific sections—notes, labs, vocabulary, and so forth—as a tool for keeping track of what goes on in science class. With it all recorded in one place, it is easy for learners to refer to prior work and make connections.

If you use notebooks already, you can ask students to record their inquiry work on labs in those notebooks. If you are not using notebooks and would like to start, there are many websites, articles, and books available to give you some structural ideas. If notebooks don't appeal to you, paper will be just fine. The main thing is that students are constantly documenting their good thinking.

- *"These students cannot behave during lab work time."*

As we hand over increasing amounts of responsibility to our students, the workshop model becomes a crucial tool. We must set students up for success. While they work to design their investigations, we have opportunities to confer with teams about their plans, and to engage the whole class in conversations about quality work. Yet freedom also has its risks, and management becomes increasingly important.

One wonderful thing about being a science teacher is that you have a lot of cool equipment most of the students are interested in using, or at least more interested in using than they are interested in seat work. You are like the PE teacher who can stop the game by taking away the ball. So after you clarify your behavioral expectations at the outset, you can point out that you have some very boring task prepared for which you are looking for five volunteers. In this way, you let the students know the consequences for not using their time wisely.

Ultimately, though, if behavior problems persist, each of us is obliged to look at his own curriculum and ask how it could be made more accessible and engaging to students.

- *"Inquiry labs take too much time."*

It is true. Inquiry takes more time than following directions. Thinking takes time. *Teaching* thinking takes even longer. But what better use of our time in science classes than to train young scientists to think and think and think? Even if we are not able to cover every bulleted standard of the content listed for our grade level, if through our labs we teach students to think like scientists, our time has been well spent.

CHAPTER 7

Demonstrations

Teachers can design demonstrations as model inquiry experiences with rich opportunities for students to think as scientists and document that thinking in a variety of ways.

Think Tank

- What role do demonstrations play in my class?
- What kinds of thinking do I ask students to do before, during, and after demonstrations?

All eyes are on Mr. Johnson, who stands on his desk at the front of the room—a book in one hand and a sheet of paper in the other. "So if I drop these two at the same time, let's see what will happen." He drops both. The class stares. The book hits the linoleum with a smack as the paper gently drifts to the floor. Students scratch notes. Mr. Johnson hops down and retrieves his equipment. "Then, when I put the paper on the book and drop them. . . ." He demonstrates the result: the book zooms to the ground, the paper along with it as though glued to the book's cover.

"What is happening here?" Mr. Johnson asks.

"Air resistance?" propose a few brave students.

"Correct!" barks Mr. Johnson, pleased with his students' ability to guess it right. He leaps down from the desk, jumps to the whiteboard and begins sketching labeled diagrams of the two demonstrations he just performed. He launches into a lecture on air resistance. Students sit silently, taking notes, while he talks for the remaining forty minutes of class.

Reflection

Who was thinking like a scientist during the class described above?

How were students' minds engaged before, during, and after the demonstration?

What might Mr. Johnson have done differently?

"Watch what I am going to do, and listen to me tell you what it means." That is how most of us probably were taught physics, as well as a great many other things in school. I remember taking physics in tenth-grade: every day we would come in and our teacher would be doing something cool, like touching a van de Graaf generator—you remember, the one that makes your hair stand on end. Sometimes we would get turns to try the stuff out. It was a pretty engaging way to start the period, but then I remember spending much of the rest of the time tucked in behind a desk taking notes. He didn't ask us to explain the phenomena we witnessed. But I wonder what we might have said and thought and believed about ourselves had we been asked to try.

"Experience in itself is not sufficient. Experience and understanding must go together," states the National Research Council (2000, 14). To this end, we can turn exciting demonstrations of scientific phenomena into true learning experiences for the young scientists in our classrooms by ensuring opportunities for students to think as scientists about the science content.

Demonstrations are a wonderful way to illustrate important content or create a discrepant event to jar students' preconceptions. Demos also can be excellent opportunities for students to practice thinking like scientists. Well-designed demonstration-based lessons can engage students in all five facets of inquiry described in Chapter 1.

Best Uses of Demonstrations

Demonstrations are a worthy and important strategy in the science teacher's repertoire. While not all scientific phenomena can be illustrated by a real-time demonstration that fits inside a classroom, a great many can. If used wisely, demonstrations can create key opportunities to engage students and promote their scientific thinking. Yet we need to choose wisely when and how to present a demo.

Yesterday, my two-year-old went exploring in the garage and came out carrying a putty knife. He was calling it a "shovel" and promptly put it to work trying to dig up the backyard. Now he was managing to fling a bit of dirt into the air with the thing, but if he or any of the rest of us had serious digging to do, a putty knife was clearly not the tool for the job. Similarly, with demonstrations or any other instructional staple, we must choose wisely the best tool for the job. Demonstrations serve a purpose, but they are not a panacea.

Well-planned demonstrations do create opportunities for students to experience the essential features of inquiry:

- engaging in scientifically oriented questions,
- giving priority to evidence in responding to questions,
- formulating explanations,
- connecting explanations to scientific knowledge, and
- communicating and justifying explanations.

Yet demonstrations also have drawbacks: some teachers I have observed start the class with a demo virtually every day. While this routine may be comfortable, it occasionally forces a mediocre demo just to fill space, or can create student apathy since learners are used to starting class by watching the teacher perform a "show." Furthermore, if demos are always used in the place of labs, students miss the opportunity to play the role of "scientist" themselves, which indirectly sends the message that they are mere observers of the process of science.

Labs Versus Demos

Neither teacher habit nor a need to maintain control are good reasons to stick with a demo. When, then, ought we best use a demo rather than a lab? Here are some good criteria for deciding when a demo may be the best educational choice.

- *Safety concerns.* Demonstrating the electrolysis of water with a lantern battery and a fish tank full of water is an ideal adult task.
- *Nature of the topic.* Some topics just makes sense to demo either because they are very important, highly complicated, require intimate attention to detail, address a lot of student misconceptions, or require super-high levels of care.
- *Time constraints.* If the setup of an egg osmometer by each student would take an entire period, but you really just want learners to observe the results, a demonstration allows you to complete the setup once and invite students to learn from the fruits of your labor.
- *Equipment shortage.* If a hood is necessary to conduct a chemical reaction safely, and your classroom or building only has only one, it makes sense that you would demonstrate the procedure while students watch.
- *Special equipment.* If a very delicate bell jar or other breakable is involved, it may work best for you to be the one whose hands are on the work.
- *Equipment costs.* Given your budget, it may not be reasonable to supply every team in the class with the appropriate tools to conduct this particular investigation themselves.
- *Equipment calibration.* It takes a lot of time to set up some types of very sensitive equipment—such as Geiger counters, certain scales, electronic timers—and you may not be able to provide a working set for each student team.
- *Efficiency.* If a new and time-consuming procedure is involved in the task, it may be easier simply to model that during the demonstration, knowing that students can be held responsible next time for doing it themselves.

These types of considerations, not ease or convenience, ought to be at the forefront of your mind when deciding whether a topic is best taught through a lab or demonstration. When practical, labs are a preferable choice, yet demos run a close second in their effectiveness at communicating important science content visually and memorably.

Making Demos About Thinking

Demos can be just as inquiry-based as labs, offering students numerous opportunities to practice the features of inquiry described in Chapter 1. In order to make them so, we need to dedicate some planning time to organize what the students will be thinking about before, during, and after the observable event. Many structures can engage students as scientists observing the demo by recording the process in the form of

- noticing and wondering,
- listing claims and evidence,
- picture(s) with caption(s),
- the scientific method, and
- POA (predict-observe-analyze).

Each of these structures provides a documentation format that requires students to think with you as scientists while they watch.

Demonstrations as Workshops

The workshop model is a wonderful structure to wrap around a demonstration—think of the demo itself as the "during" portion of the learning activity. So then before the demo, you want to set a clear purpose, engage students, and model the types of thinking they will be doing while they observe. And after the demonstration there should always be time for in-depth reflection and assessment. Remember, the demo is not the thing—the *thinking* is the thing.

Noticing and Wondering

Noticing and wondering involves two thinking skills—gathering data and questioning. *Noticings* are any observations students make about the setup, process, or results of a demonstration. *Wonderings* are questions that arise before, during, and after a demo. Some of these may be answered through the demo, some may serve as launchpads for future studies, and some may continue to linger when the unit is done. Noticing and wondering are types of thinking we do every day; in a demo situation, we are applying those to the context of science.

These noticings are a simple opportunity for data collection, a chance to review the senses and their roles, and the differences between quantitative and qualitative observations. Wonderings are simply questions—in this case scientifically oriented ones, as described by the first essential feature of inquiry.

Claims and Evidence

This format—claims and evidence—popular in many elementary level science programs streamlines student thinking in two other arenas: "what do you think?" (claim) and "why?" (evidence). This can serve as shorthand structure for promoting scientific thinking while watching a demo. Students can be invited to make claims—develop explanations, draw conclusions—based on what they see, then to provide evidence in the form of data to support those claims. For example, if I demonstrated to my class that a Geiger counter clicked more rapidly closer to the smoke detector in my classroom, they could make claims about why, based on evidence from my instrument.

In making claims based on evidence, learners are asked to work through the third essential feature of inquiry: formulating explanations based on evidence.

Picture(s) with Caption(s)

Like a *Far Side* cartoon, a picture and caption is worth far more than a thousand words. When observing a demo, students can create one or more frames sketching what they see, as well as describing their observations and thinking in a narrative caption. You can prescribe the number of frames, or not. This strategy works best when students have ample time to draw and to reflect on how to best explain their representations. Figure 7.1 is an example of a student's observations and thinking presented as a picture and caption.

Scientific Method

During their years in school, many students memorize the "scientific method" several times over. Here is an opportunity for them to put it to use as a format to record what they see happening in a demonstration. In its simplest form—problem, procedure, observation, and conclusion—the scientific method invites thinking about why a demonstration is being conducted (problem), how the demonstration is being conducted (procedure), what the demonstration shows (observation), and what students learned from the experience (conclusion). These four prompts—when answered independently by individuals, discussed in pairs or small groups, and synthesized as a class—have the power to engage students' minds as they watch a scientist at work.

While the verbiage of the scientific method may differ in different contexts, it remains a reliable structure to document a procedure and promote students formulating explanations based on evidence, the third essential feature of inquiry.

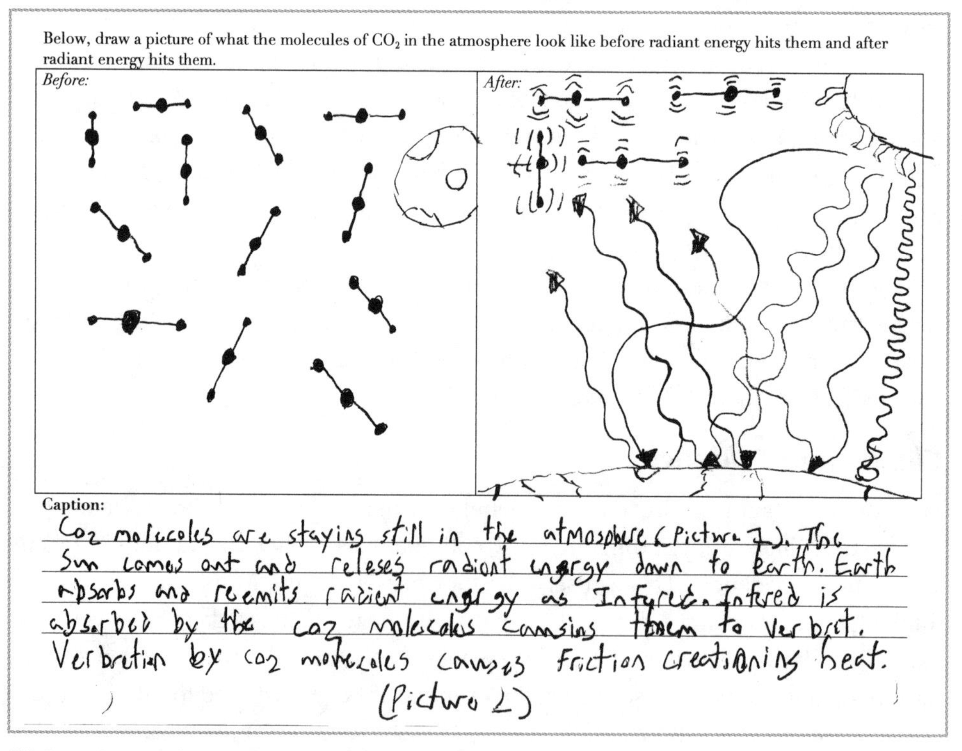

FIG. 7.1 *Picture and Caption: Radiant Energy to Thermal Energy*

POA: Predict, Observe, Analyze

Not unlike the scientific method, POA is a simple formula for thinking and recording the process of a demonstration. I use this a lot with my middle school students, inviting them to think, talk, and write before (predict), during (observe), and after (analyze) a given experience.

Predict. Before asking students to predict, I explain the setup of what they are about to observe. For example, we are going to be putting some pennies into vinegar and leaving them there overnight. Once my students know what they are about to witness, I can ask them to forecast the outcome.

This thinking task invites students to "engage in scientifically oriented questions," the first essential feature of inquiry. Although in the instance of a teacher-planned demo students are not asking the question, they are invited to consider an original prediction in answer. Predictions are answers to "What if . . ." questions that describe the setup of the activity.

Observe. Before beginning an experiment or demonstration, I discuss with students the sorts of observational data we might plan to collect as we watch. Here is an opportunity to talk about quantitative and qualitative data and offer students structured formats, such as sketching or data tables to record what they witness. Once a format for documentation is in place, students are ready to observe and record what happens. In the experiment described above, the pennies turned green!

Observing, students gather evidence in order to check their predictions. In this way, students are prepared to experience the second essential feature of inquiry: "Learner gives priority to evidence in responding to questions." The observational data gathered serves as evidence that can be used to answer or ask further questions.

Analyze. Once students have gathered data, they can compare their findings to their predictions and develop their own explanations for these events. Why did those pennies turn green instead of get shinier, as one may have hypothesized? In developing their analysis of how the data gathered compares with their prediction, students are experiencing the third essential feature of inquiry: "Learners formulate explanations from evidence."

Analysis is also an ideal time to invite students to link their observations to a big idea and connect what they are learning now to their scientific background knowledge.

With any of the structures described above, students experience some facets of inquiry without engaging in a full-scale lab. You can model the thinking behind any set of steps using the workshop model (see Chapter 3).

Further, learners can talk through the demonstration in pairs, small groups, or as a whole class, and consider ideas for further study along these lines. It is important that each student takes responsibility to record her thinking in some form of independent writing.

Over the course of the year, through demonstrations and other activities, students learn and practice the scientific habits of mind of making predictions, gathering and recording quality data, formulating explanations based on evidence, and linking learning to big ideas and the broader field of science.

Who Explains?

Once all of the data is in from a demonstration, it is time to make meaning of it. This explanation, or meaning making, is the most important step in the thinking process. Yet it is one we teachers, anxious to explain and move on, too often zoom through on fast-forward.

I know I slipped many times in my own classroom into the easy habit of doing all of the explaining. It is so tempting! After all, I went to grad school and know so very much! I could catch myself believing, "I was hired to be the teacher; surely I must be the one to tell everyone everything." But wait! If I explain everything, then what thinking do the students get to do? It took me a long while to learn to let the students do the work, the work of thinking and explaining and debating and justifying and learning in my class. But that was a very important lesson for me, one that benefited all of the learners I met. Telling the answers is a hard habit to break, but here are a number of strategies to help you develop new habits:

- *Talk less, listen more.* Create wait-time between speakers in your class—time for all to think. Specifically, count to ten in your head to allow silence after asking a question or hearing a student comment. Smile while you wait.
- *Ask open-ended questions.* "Why do you think so?" "Does everyone agree with Mavis?" "Did anyone have a different idea?"
- *Turn students' questions back to them.* "What do you think?" "How might you figure that out?"
- *Allow time.* If, at the end of the period, the group still has not landed on a full, correct explanation, extend the discussion into the next day, rather than short-circuiting it by telling the class the answer.
- *Resist the temptation to rescue.* When you hear students stumbling down the wrong road in their thinking, bring them back with probing questions rather than instructional answers.

Yes, it takes time to construct meaning like this with students, and learners may initially be annoyed with our reluctance to just tell them the answers and get on with it, but, in the long run, what would we really be teaching them if we did that?

Whether conducting labs, demos, or engaging in other learning activities, the thinking—student thinking—is the most important step.

Documenting Thinking

All of the wonderful questioning, data, and analysis of a demo is lost if not recorded. Just as professional scientists are responsible for documenting and sharing their findings, we can train our students to systematically record what they are thinking and learning through demonstrations and other learning activities. This recorded thinking can serve as a resource to individual students as they continue in their studies in this unit and others, as artifacts for teachers striving to understand what an individual knows, and as resources for peers who may benefit from another telling, another example, or simply sharing notes. Thinking and learning during demos or labs alike could be documented in a number of ways.

- *Note-taking sheets. Not* worksheets (which have a distinct closed-ended identity) *note-taking* sheets are just that, a structure for students to take notes. These can be particularly helpful when introducing a new system for thinking through a demo: for noticing and wondering, you may provide a two-column chart; for claims and evidence, you may provide a graphic organizer representing the claim in one large circle with the evidence in small circles touching and surrounding it; for a picture and a caption, you can go ahead and offer students the frame and lines for writing. When using the other structures suggested, it may simply make sense to list the prompts (problem, procedure, observation, conclusion; predict, observe, analyze) leaving space for writing about each. Symbols representing the sort of thinking each prompt invites can be helpful supports to assist students for whom these words are unfamiliar vocabulary. Be creative and develop a note-taking structure or graphic organizer that best serves the needs of the demo and the thinking involved.
- *Science notebooks.* These individual record books are a great spot to document a demo in any of the formats described earlier or in one that you develop yourself. In some cases, it makes sense to allow students to draw as well as write in narrative form. Like cartoonists, learners can sketch the setup of a science task and then describe their pictures.
- *Collective records.* We can document the finds of a whole class either on chart paper or electronically. Large poster paper hung in the classroom is a great place to gather and store student thinking. They pile up fast, and you may find yourself flipping through the stack of posters generated collectively by your different classes—yet these can be wonderful records of students' thinking and learning. Alternately many teachers use computers and projectors or smart boards to electronically store and share each class's thinking. Predictions, for example, can hang in the room on a chart or wait on a hard drive until all of the data is in, and then be revisited in light of outcomes.

Making Demos Inclusive

In addition to offering an opportunity to teach the thinking skills of inquiry, demos also create chances for us to teach the process skills of science discussed in Chapter 6—how to handle equipment, take accurate measurements, or make detailed observations. The instructor need not have exclusive presentation rights when it comes to demonstrations. While in some instances it makes sense for the teacher to remain the sage on the stage, we can also invite students to assist in presenting demonstrations in a number of ways.

- Teacher conducts demo with the assistance of a student. For example, the teacher may light the candle, but allow a student to toss a pinch of flour into the flame.

- Teacher sets up the demo, yet invites an untrained student to conduct it. For example, a teacher might hand a pair of students a candle, a matchbox, and a cup of flour and talk them through the demonstration with the class looking on.
- Teacher trains students to present demo. Outside of class time, students can learn and practice the demo before presenting it to the class. During lunch, for example, a team of rotating volunteers may come in and learn how to set up and talk through the demonstration. This structure creates an opportunity for students at all levels of achievement to take turns being the "expert."
- Teacher gives learning target, then students design demo. For example, the teacher may ask a team or teams of students to develop a demonstration illustrating how surface area affects flammability of certain substances. They could work on these during or outside of class time, then present them to the group.

All of these levels of student involvement in staging a demonstration not only hook the audience by mixing up the format, they also remind students of our belief in all of them as scientists, and as members of the community of learners in our classrooms (see Chapter 5 for more on culture).

When learners get to do the work of thinking before, during, and after a demonstration—or get invited to play a role in creating a demonstration—these learning experiences become rich opportunities for students to think as scientists.

Assessing Thinking About Demonstrations

You really have two ways to know what students are thinking—what they write and what they say. Learners may be thinking great thoughts, but if not shared in either of these formats, you are at a loss to understand the depth of an individual's understanding. Let your students know this regularly.

It is a lot easier to keep track of written evidence for assessment purposes, although conversational data collection is important in reflective teaching. If you settle on one or more formats for students to use while thinking about demos, you might create a generic rubric to which students can refer each time they are invited to, for example, develop claims and evidence. In this way, students become adept at these thinking skills, and your expectations for quality can be reinforced regularly. Figure 7.2 presents a sample rubric I developed for the predict, observe, and analyze format of documenting thinking.

This rubric details one of many ways you could engage your students in thinking and documentation when you choose to demonstrate important science concepts in class.

When deciding to demonstrate, choose wisely. Include students in presenting and thinking about demos at every possible juncture. During demos, require all learners to document their thinking in specific formats that can be assessed. Here are some planning questions to help you get ready.

	1	3	5
		All of 1, plus . . .	*All of 3, plus . . .*
Prediction	Hypothesis based on experimental design	Prediction is justified	Scientific background knowledge and logic are used to support prediction
Observations	Documents events	Important qualitative and quantitative details are recorded with words, pictures, and numbers	Description is so vivid that readers who did not witness the actual event can picture exactly what took place
Analysis	Reflects on connections between prediction and observation	Explains similarities and differences between prediction and observation	Justifies outcomes with accurate logic and knowledge

FIG. 7.2 *Sample Rubric for POA*

Designing Demonstrations: Teacher Planning Questions

What is the learning goal?

Why does this learning goal lend itself best to a demonstration?

How will I invite student thinking before, during, and after the demonstration?

How will I make the demonstration inclusive?

How will I assess learners' understanding?

Dobetter Demos

Ms. Dobetter is ready to put these new ideas to work revising her class demo on eclipses for her ninth graders. In the past she has had students read about the topic, then carried out a quick demonstration of the content herself. Student learning outcomes were mixed, and she is ready to make a change. Let's see how she illuminates the topic.

What is the learning goal?

We will study the solar system through the lens of stability, a big idea. I usually do a demo about eclipses. Last year, the day after my demo, a student wrote on her quiz that a solar eclipse happens when the sun goes between the Earth and the moon! When I read that, I knew that I had to do a better job helping students understand. So the learning goal is for kids to understand that a solar eclipse takes place when the Earth enters our moon's shadow.

Why does this learning goal lend itself best to a demonstration?

Well, I just thought that showing the kids rather than telling them, or having them read it in a book, would make a lot more sense since we are talking about the movement of tactile objects here. Last year, when I showed the students, I used the light from the overhead projector to represent the sun. I think that worked well, and since there is only one projector I guess I will keep using it like that. I could, I suppose, turn the lights off and give every team a flashlight and some balls to mess about with, but students have so many misconceptions that I feel it is better to present this topic in a more controlled way.

How will I invite student thinking before, during, and after the demonstration?

I will adopt something like the POA format, but with sketches, not just narrative: I think I will ask the kids to draw and write, along the lines of the picture and caption idea. I will give them each a piece of paper with three rectangles, one box for each of the three steps. In the first box, I will ask them to sketch what they believe is the arrangement of the sun, Earth, and moon that creates a solar eclipse. Next, while they are watching us represent the movement of the Earth and moon (each represented by small balls) relative to the sun (overhead projector), I will invite them to record in the second box what they see in terms of the arrangement and the lights and shadows. In the last frame students will write, comparing what they drew in their first two boxes. I will need to do some modeling for students to encourage them to sketch and label drawings carefully.

How will I make the demonstration inclusive?

Well, I really like the idea of letting the kids do the demos, so I have started inviting a team from each class to come in over lunch the day before a demo to figure it out, and to practice how to present the concept to the class.

The day of the demo, I will lead the whole class through the three thinking steps, then invite the team of presenters to simply show their classmates how the eclipse works, using the light from the projector and two small balls to show how the Earth orbits the sun, and the moon orbits the Earth—and when things are lined up just so, we get an eclipse.

As a whole class, we will discuss what we predicted, observed, and how it all makes sense. I will do my best to let the kids do all of the talking by using questions to draw them out.

How will I assess learners' understanding?

I think the written work students do individually will be great evidence of their thinking about the demonstration. I think I will use the same quiz as I did last year, asking the students, the day after the demo, to sketch and explain the eclipse. I will be hoping to see answers that indicate that students understand the paths of the Earth and moon relative to one another and the sun, and that they can show how these bodies align to create an eclipse.

Ms. Dobetter's Constants Checklist

1. *Which feature of inquiry will I emphasize? How?*

This demo is about answering a scientific question, "What causes an eclipse?" Presenters will be sharing what they learn and know about eclipses, and students will all be expected to answer that question.

2. *What is the big idea, and how will I bring it to life?*

For our solar system unit, the big idea is stability. This demo is tied to this idea in that the orbits of all celestial bodies are stable and predictable. I need to encourage my demonstrators to point this out.

3. *Which elements of the workshop model will I employ?*

There will be a "before, during, and after" for both the presenters and the audience. Presenters will practice and prepare with me, then share what they know, answer questions, and respond to feedback. Students in the "audience" will experience a preassessment, observe the demo, then reflect on what they learned.

4. *When and how will I assess students' content understanding and skill proficiency?*

The whole class will record how they understand eclipses before the demo and then again after. This will be the primary assessment of their understanding. The skill they will be practicing is accurate communication through writing and drawing.

5. *How will students build and experience community through this learning?*

The structure of this demo, being done by students for students, illustrates the interdependence of our science learning community.

Eclipse Demo

This year, Ms. Dobetter decided to honor students by their birthdays (or half-birthdays for those born in the summer) as demonstrators for the month. So in January, all the children born in that month or in July become her team, and she asks small groups of them—two or three at a time from each class—to come in about once a week at lunch to learn the demos she wants help with.

This week is all about eclipses, and when they meet together at lunch, she realizes this small group has a lot of confusion about what an eclipse really is. With an apple, a tangerine, and her overhead projector, she explains the celestial bodies' relative sizes, reviews the periods of their orbits, and illustrates the Earth's path around the sun (and the moon's similar path around the Earth) to clear up their confusion before talking about how they will present to their classes.

After about half an hour of small-group, hands-on instruction, each student is competent at representing how the moon (tangerine) moves relative to the Earth (green apple), and how the Earth moves relative to the sun. Next, each gains an understanding of how, from the perspective of Earthlings, the sun or moon appears to temporarily vanish. And they can show these things with the fruit and light provided.

And what do eclipses have to do with the unit's big idea, stability? Ms. Dobetter works with her team of demonstrators to ensure that all understand that the stability of our solar system allows for the predictability of eclipses. Great!

In preparing for the next day, Ms. Dobetter creates the three-box graphic organizer described in her plans and is ready with a copy for each student.

"Did anyone see the solar eclipse last fall?" she asks the group. A few hands go up. "What is a solar eclipse?" she asks as she writes the term on the board. Learners volunteer to share what they know about the sun getting blacked out for a few minutes. "How does that happen?" she asks as she passes out her note-taking sheet.

A few hands go up, but she does not call on anyone. Instead, she directs them to their paper. "Draw," she instructs, "in the first box, a sketch of what you think takes place to cause a solar eclipse. Your drawing should include the sun, Earth, moon, and any other important objects. Please label each."

Some students are quick to lean forward over their desks. Others make a show of rustling for pencils, wasting time. Ms. Dobetter circulates to check up on their progress. Once she calls time with her chime, she observes, "Some of you have a lot of background knowledge about eclipses, while others of you have not yet shown me that you understand how they work. We have some colleagues today who are going to walk us through the special circumstances required for a solar eclipse."

The student demonstrators head to the front, picking fruit up off their teacher's desk on their way to the overhead. "In a few minutes, I am going to give you time to revise the drawing you just sketched, but for now, just listen," she directs the class to the demonstrators and slips to the side of the room.

"Let's say this is the Earth," Jerrell begins, holding up the apple, "and this is the moon, okay?" holding up the tangerine.

"And here is the sun," Nicole clicks on the overhead projector. "The Earth goes around the sun." Jerrell takes a walk around the overhead cart. "That is a year, right?" he says when he gets back to where he started.

"And the moon goes around the Earth." Jerrell holds the apple still and circles it with the tangerine. "So we know these things happen over and over. Our solar system is stable, right? That's the big idea."

"So, usually," Nicole explains, "we don't really notice the moon during daytime, maybe just at sunset when it might be bright. But the moon is going around the Earth kind of slowly. Sometimes it ends up to be right between the Sun and where we are on Earth, so it can block out some of the sun, like, make a shadow." Jerrell adjusts the fruits in his hands to show that the light from the projector is being partially blocked from hitting the apple by the tangerine.

"The Earth is bigger than the moon, so not everyplace in the world will see a solar eclipse at the same time, but a lot of places can see a partial solar eclipse on the same day."

"You guys got it?" Jerrell asks.

"I can't see" comes a complaint from the back.

"Come on up here. Come up if you can't see," Jerrell invites with a glance at Ms. Dobetter who nods consent. About half the class moves forward, and Jerrell moves the fruits again to show how the moon blocks light from hitting the Earth.

"Questions?" Nicole invites.

"So why doesn't that happen every month?" one student asks. Jerrell and Nicole look at one another and shrug. They turn to their teacher.

"What a super question!" she affirms. "I am going to record it right here, and we'll see if we can't learn more about that during this unit."

"Other questions?" Jerrell asks.

"What's a lunar eclipse?"

"Oh, well, we're not really supposed to talk about that yet," Jerrell glances at his teacher. She wags her head, as if to say, "Go on."

"That is when the Earth blocks the sun's light from hitting the moon," Jerrell explains. "You can have a full moon like this," he sets up his fruit for a full moon, "but then, when the Earth gets in the way, there is no light for the moon to reflect, so we can't see it."

"Lunar eclipse is when you can't see the moon. Solar eclipse is when you can't see the sun," Nicole clarifies.

"Okay, can you guys show us the solar eclipse one more time?" Ms. Dobetter asks.

"Sure." Jerrell takes charge and talks his classmates through it once again.

"Let's give these presenters a hand and take our seats!" Ms. Dobetter calls, and the class claps and heads back to their chairs.

She pats both presenters on the back, bites into the apple, and turns to the group. "Now, back to your notes, in the second box, I would like you to draw a new, labeled picture representing a solar eclipse." Students work in silence.

After a few minutes, Ms. Dobetter asks learners to look at their two pictures. "How many of you drew the exact same picture twice?" Two hands go up. "How many of you drew different pictures?" Most hands go up. "In the last box on your page, take a few minutes to explain why your new picture is different from your first. What is it that you understand now that you did not before? What new ideas do you have about eclipses? If you drew the same picture twice, use this time to record any new learning you gained from Jerrell and Nicole's demonstration."

Ms. Dobetter circulates and sees widely divergent drawings on students' desks, yet most depict clearly the correct alignment of the sun, Earth, and moon to result in an eclipse. From reading students' notes in their third box, she knows that many have gained new understandings about the conditions that create this astronomical phenomenon. She feels pleased. Again, she thanks her demonstrators for the quality explanation they provided and notes to herself how relaxing it is to let the students do more of the work.

So What?

In this example, Ms. Dobetter illustrates a few simple changes that made her demonstration more engaging and evocative: by supplying students a structure for thinking and note-taking before, during, and after the demonstration, and by inviting students to present and explain to their peers, she maximized the learning opportunity and ensured that students understand how and why a solar eclipse is produced.

"Yah, but . . ."

- *"I use demos as quick intros. Who has time for all of this thinking?"*

I have never met a teacher who complained of having too much time and not enough content to cover! We all suffer from this sense of pressure, yet if we are going to take the time to present a demo, I think it is only fair to factor in the necessary time before, during, and after to ensure that students are extracting meaning from what they see. Once students learn these systems of thinking—whether noticing and wondering, or any other you present—they become adept at slipping into that mode with little set-up or modeling required.

- *"Students will only pay attention to a demo if I am the one who conducts it."*

This is a bad habit many students learn of disrespecting their peers. And this habit must be broken through persistent high expectations, explanations, and consequences. See Chapter 5 for more ideas on community and culture building. Having said that, I know that we teachers sometimes feel we must have the final word, the last turn to emphasize what is really going on here and why it is important. If you feel passionate to do so, follow your conscience, but work hard to do it in a way that honors, rather than brushes aside, student presenters and student ideas about the demonstration.

- *"Slowing down to do all of this writing and thinking will ruin the magical 'ooh!' moment of my demos."*

We do *not* want to take away the magic, only to learn from it! How can we do both? I think there is a time and place for thinking and writing—but then, if it suits you, you can create a pencils-down, lights-off, hold-your-breath atmosphere for the actual moment when you unveil the celery stick that spent the night in red food dye. Of course, after the "wow!" you are duty-bound to get your students back to talking about "how?"

CHAPTER 8

Lectures

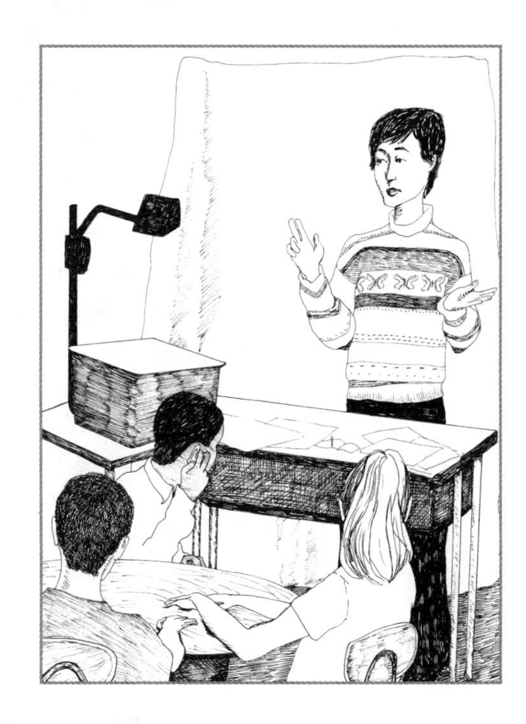

By setting a clear purpose, creating ways for students to document their learning while listening, and offering frequent opportunities for learners to stop, think, and share, teachers can ensure that lectures are engaging experiences for all students.

Think Tank

- When and why do you choose to use direct instruction?
- What are your students doing while you are talking?
- How do you know what they understand from your lecture?

As Mrs. Olson turns to the page containing her osmosis notes, one of the holes in the binder paper tears. She skims the paper as she props the old notebook up against her computer to read while writing on the board. Even though she has used this lecture for the past several years in her freshman biology class, sometimes she skips over a point or two, so she is in the habit of keeping her notes handy as a reference.

Students file in, and she begins her delivery: "Yesterday, we talked about membranes, different types of membranes, and today we are going to take a closer look at osmosis." On the board, she writes the word *Osmosis* as she speaks. Of the students who have their notebooks open and are making some effort to take notes, all record the word *Osmosis*, but after that their notes diverge. Mrs. Olson goes on to describe what she means by the definition; students look down, some able to copy her words verbatim, others paraphrasing, and still others just catching and writing a few words now and again. A handful of students let the word *Osmosis* stand alone on the page of their notes. Two boys at a back table spin their pens without paper in sight.

Mrs. Olson sketches the cell membrane and gives several examples of conditions where osmosis would occur. She makes big gestures with her hands, and raises her voice for emphasis, "Like *diffusion, osmosis* is the movement of *water* from an area of *higher* concentration to an area of *lower* concentration. Concentration of *what*? Not *water*! Sugars, salts, carbohydrates, macromolecules! Water wants to even the score . . ."

The next day, she decides to toss out a pop quiz, just to make sure the kids were awake. Less than half the class passes. Mrs. Olson feels frustrated; these kids just don't listen, she tells herself.

Reflection

What were the students doing while Mrs. Olson was talking?

How would you explain the students' quiz scores?

What suggestions for improvement would you offer Mrs. Olson?

Many veteran teachers acknowledge that traditional lectures, the style of teaching and learning which were staples for generations, are no longer effective for many of our students.

Our students are changing. The impact of electronic media—television, music players, the Internet, and cell phones—have changed the way their minds work, according to Jane M. Healy, author of *Endangered Minds.* Additionally, consumption of toxic or unhealthy foods and living a sedentary lifestyle are hazards to the brain's ability to focus, listen, and learn (Healy 1990).

Meanwhile, the population of linguistically diverse students enrolling in American schools is skyrocketing; between 1992 and 2002, the number of English language learners enrolled in grades 7–12 has grown by 70 percent, and 10.5 percent of all students enrolled in American schools today are speaking English as a second or third language (Hoffman and Sable 2006). These students, working hard to make meaning of challenging science content without the familiar cadence of their native tongues, need additional supports—realia, schema, images, and examples to support their comprehension.

It is time to reevaluate when and how we lecture to our classes and to find ways we can maximize the benefit of those presentations for all learners. While we as teachers cannot control our students' language proficiency, the amount of television they watch, or how many Spicy Hot Cheetos they eat, we can meet and engage their minds—especially while using a direct instruction format. In addition to creating a classroom culture of rigor and participation, we can present material in ways that invite students to connect and understand.

Deciding to Lecture

Each teacher must find for himself the equilibrium among teaching modalities that work best for learners at his level and in his content area. While many instructors have moved away from an emphasis on lecture-style learning toward more hands-on activities, there is still a time and a place for stand-and-deliver teaching.

Lectures can be a valuable format for conveying important information. You may decide to lecture in order to

- build learners' background knowledge,
- clarify how a topic demonstrates a big idea,
- explain important content vocabulary,

- contextualize a current event,
- relate current studies to the broader field of science, or
- summarize a learning sequence.

Students must be engaged with their ears and minds open during the lecture in order for any of these goals to be accomplished.

Some students have difficulty synthesizing information while sitting and listening. This need not mean that we abandon the lecture format, but rather that we improve our lectures to make them more understandable by

- starting with a preassessment and a hook,
- delivering a multimodal presentation,
- interspersing the presentation with opportunities for students to think, talk, and write,
- closing with a reflective task.

When lectures are focused in this way, they become an effective tool in any teacher's instructional tool belt.

Designing Direct Instruction

You can think of direct instruction as having three parts, based on the workshop model—a distinct before, during, and after.

- *Before* presenting the lesson's content, we must engage learners' minds and preassess students' understanding of the topic. This hook needs to provide a link between science content and the students' life experience or interests. The preassessment provides essential information to support the teacher in tailoring her presentation to address students' background knowledge or preconceptions.
- *During* the presentation, we set our purpose and present material using a variety of visual, auditory, and kinesthetic strategies addressing the learning styles of all students. Amid these varied presentations, we must pause to invite students to synthesize new information by thinking, speaking, or writing at frequent intervals.
- *After* the presentation, we need to ask students to document and reflect on what they learned and retained through their participation.

With these three essential components—before, during, and after the presentation—we can hone our lectures to promote thinking and understanding.

Starting with a Preassessment

The "opener," "question of the day," "day starter," or "dispatch" is a common routine in many classrooms—students come in, the question is on the board and they take out their notebooks or question logs and write silently for a few minutes until the teacher starts talking.

Often the question asks a review from the previous day's work, sounding something like: "What are the three types of rock?" "Define covalent bonds," or "Describe the difference between a virus and a bacteriophage."

While each of these questions does solicit students' background knowledge or misconceptions, none of these questions connect the learners' lives to the classroom. In order to truly hook students' minds with a question, strive to author one that relates science to them personally, or vice versa.

- What types of rocks have you used today?
- How is your life affected by covalent bonding?
- If you are ill, how will you know whether antibiotics will help you?

By asking questions about students' relationship with the content, we invite learners to share their background knowledge and preconceptions with us, as well as challenge student scientists to think about how the topic at hand actually does relate to their lives.

As an alternative to the day-starter question, some teachers use comics, photographs, slide shows, or drawing prompts to get students thinking and sharing. Any of these can kick off the class, as long as we take the time to link the learning goals to our learners' lives, rather than let the content dangle alone in the middle of the room.

As we know from *How Students Learn Science in the Classroom,* all students arrive in our classes with their own notions about many science topics (National Research Council 2005). Often students *do* have accurate background knowledge about a subject, while at other times they have picked up odds and ends of information and assembled them in a manner that only hazily represents reality. The student who believes all earthquakes are as fatal as Sichuan province's 2008 catastrophe, the learner who swears that combining Pop Rocks and Coke involves a nuclear reaction, the teen with faith that you can't get pregnant the first time—all of these students have some background knowledge to bring to the table, as well as some inaccurate information that must be addressed and dispelled (see Chapter 4 for more on preconceptions).

In addition to giving teachers valuable information about where students are starting from in their thinking, preassessments can invite students to engage with the topic—to share personal connections, memories, or experiences. In this way, students are getting their minds on the work before anyone starts explaining anything.

If you do take the time to ask students to write about a topic or question in the form of a "day starter," also take the time to find out what they wrote, either by reading over their shoulders, inviting sharing aloud, or structuring another kind of reporting. Too often, teachers ask students to sit and write, but then learners close their binders and move on to the next task without a conversation. This format reduces the day starter to a time-filling routine rather than any sort of preassessment.

Why Should I Care?

In the first few minutes of any science class, especially when we plan to use direct instruction, we need to hook students' genuine interest. Just like giving a speech at the Toastmasters' meeting, we need to start with a joke, a story, a familiar current event, a novel idea—a reason for our audience to keep listening.

Many young people have grown accustomed to passively observing the television while it entertains them. I have visited classes where students seemed to behave as though the teacher were a television program. Their instructor carries on presenting material while learners sit in their chairs, eyes at half-mast, daydreaming, sneaking snacks from their backpacks, or sending text messages from concealed cell phones.

School is not television. Learning is not a passive activity. How can we awaken students' minds to science?

Some perky learners sit up and listen regardless of how dry or abstract the topic may be. Most learners, though, need a reason to care about the content, especially if it is being presented in a way that does not invite their active engagement. So we need to think this question through as a teacher: Why *should* they care? What is it about this subject that relates to learners' lives? How can I make it *meaningful* for them?

For a smattering of possible content connections to students' experience and interest, see Figure 8.1. While the connections proposed may not be the focus of your unit, each could serve as a possible entry point, connecting students' background knowledge and curiosity to the area of study, increasing their engagement from the get-go. The third column of the table is left open for you to brainstorm your own ideas on linking this content to the learners you know.

The better you know your students, the easier it will be to find ways to make your topics meaningful to them. The ideas in Figure 8.1 are just a start.

"Clickers"

In addition to calling on students to share thinking the old-fashioned way, many teachers now enjoy using personal response systems, often referred to as "clickers," to gather students' thinking at regular intervals. These clickers, one small device per student, report answers into a central computer that tabulates the students' responses and can generate data reports numerically or graphically in a matter of seconds.

Clicker questions can be used to assess knowledge (Komodo dragons are a) lizards, b) reptiles, or c) mammals). Or they can be used to gather opinions about content (Endangered species should be a) protected, b) left to compete for survival). And clickers can be used to gather feedback on student interest (Rate today's topic: 1 (low) to 10 (high)). This data, quickly gathered and efficiently shared, can provide a wonderful preassessment or closing assessment—or a checkpoint in between. If you have access to clickers in your classroom, consider their uses at regular intervals during a lecture presentation.

The first phase, then, of direct instruction is not exactly about instruction just yet: we must win students' interest and assess their prior knowledge before moving forward to teach.

Presentation

Preassessment data points to the starting point of our presentations. We need to start from where students are. Learners' background knowledge, their life experience, their interests, and their misconceptions—all of these are important to integrate in the earliest minutes of our presentation in order to make that essential connection.

For example, if I were ready to begin lecturing about eagles and DDT, I may begin by listening to students share their understanding of pesticides (background knowl-

Science Topic	Possible Connections	Other Ideas
Anatomy	cardiovascular health, reproduction	
Botany	food production, seed germination	
Chemistry	pollution, medication, ozone depletion, global warming, clean water	
Ecology	trash and recycling, conservation at home	
Electricity and Magnetism	how cell phones, CD players, and other electronics work	
Genetics	inherited traits, genetic disorders	
Geology	precious metals and precious stones, natural disasters, erosion	
Meteorology	memorable storms, climate change, winter sports	
Newton's Laws	vehicles, sports, rocketry	
Oceanography	whales and migrations, coral reefs, depletion of fish stocks	
Zoology	pets, rainforests, food production	

FIG. 8.1 *Making Connections*

edge), their experience with thick or thin eggshells (life experience), or their inaccurate preconception that eagles are already extinct. Any of these entry points would welcome students into a connected conversation.

In moving from the engagement and preassessment stage, our presentation needs to:

- provide a focus or goal for learning;
- present information in multimodal formats; and
- invite students to stop, think, and document their learning at frequent intervals in structured ways.

Focus

I remember being a middle schooler. One of our favorite sports was getting teachers off the subject, asking leading questions drawing our able instructors away from the lesson plans they had prepared. Students today enjoy similar games, yet it is our duty in the classroom to present with purpose, to set the focus of learning at the beginning of class, to communicate that intention clearly to students, and to ensure that all of the day's experiences relate to that purpose. Knowing and sharing our learning goals with students, as assessment expert Richard Stiggins (1997) implores, helps students to engage in the learning process and make the most of their time with us. For this reason, we must set and adhere to a focus for each presentation.

Multimodal

Here is where the fun begins. Multimodal presentations might include

- photographic slides,
- graphic representations,
- models,
- real objects,
- songs,
- skits, and
- kinesthetic activities.

Multimodal presentations serve all of our students, but especially linguistically diverse students who benefit from nonlinguistic representations (Hill and Flynn 2006). We need not punctuate our class with burlesque every five minutes, but important content deserves convincing representation, so we need to develop lively means to tell the important stories of science to our classes.

While speaking, we convey meaning through body language, facial expressions, and gestures that assist English language learners in understanding our presentations. Above all, enthusiasm is infectious: if discussing the topic invigorates us, chances are that students will catch the curiosity train too.

Holding Thinking

As we are speaking, we must give students a real job to do. Graphic organizers facilitate note taking by structuring students' documentation of their learning. While our year-end goal may be to free students of reliance on such a tool, many students do come to us needing support in note taking. For this reason, we may begin the year by providing structured formats, then gradually release to our students the responsibility for documenting lectures in their own ways. For linguistically diverse students, graphic organizers with pictographs and other nonlinguistic prompts can be a source of connection and support.

Holding thinking is different from taking notes. Taking notes is a process of simply noting down what is said. Holding *thinking* means taking the next step, considering what the new information means to you, how it relates to your background knowledge, and why it is important. Students could do this on paper at their desks in a variety of formats.

- *Two-column notes.* Use the left side for new information, right side for my thoughts and questions about that information.
- *Three-column notes.* Use the left side for new ideas, middle column for pictorial representations, and right column for connections to my life.
- *Diagrams.* Relating concepts to one another visually.
- *Reflective note taking.* Space for recording information, space for restating or explaining in my own words.

Stop and Think

Every seven to ten minutes, we need to create opportunities for students to stop and think for themselves about what we are saying, what it means to them, and what they understand. This keeps students' minds on the subject, as well as allows them to self-assess at regular intervals—lest they waste precious time in a fog of confusion because we had been unclear about the real difference between tRNA and mRNA. We can ask students to stop and think on paper, with a partner, or out loud as a whole group. Prompts could include:

- What do you understand *now* about . . . ?
- What questions do you have?
- What is confusing?
- How would you explain this to your family over dinner?

Give students the gift of time to think, synthesize, and make meaning—then check their understanding before moving on.

During these interludes, revisit students' preconceptions. Give learners a chance to rethink what they said earlier, and invite them to integrate new information in a way that makes sense. Check in with individuals to ensure that their preconceptions are being addressed and confronted by the content of the lecture.

"What Questions Do You Have?"

When addressing the whole group to check for understanding, try this experiment: Ask one class, "*Any questions?*" My guess is that often not a soul will speak up. But, when posed, "*What questions* do you have?" students will often drum up something to ask. This second prompt, you see, assumes questions, assumes that students are sitting there thinking and wondering, and encourages them by its very syntax to voice curiosity. Try it out.

Ongoing, Inescapable Assessment

In asking students to stop and think at regular intervals, we can also use these opportunities to check for attention and understanding. It is easy to fall into the trap of calling on the same brave volunteers who raise their hands over and over again in our classes. While it is important to encourage the enthusiastic learners, it is also necessary to send a message to the class that all voices need to be heard.

Now this may be a controversial thought, but I believe it is fair—and important—to call on any student in your class at any time once each has had an opportunity to gather her thoughts. After students have paired and shared, after they have done a quick write, after they have filled in their graphic organizer, after any opportunity they receive to pull their thoughts together, I think we must randomly call on them (a few of them) to share their thinking. Why?

First of all, this is an opportunity for us, as teachers, to find out whether what we are talking about is making sense. Secondly, many students benefit from hearing content explained in new ways, and often peers are able to rephrase explanations more accessibly than we are. Yet perhaps more importantly, calling on all students indicates to every learner in the room that we expect each person to be ready to share her thinking at any time. This is a very important message: I expect you to be paying attention, to be using your conversation, writing, and reflection time well, to gather your thoughts and be ready to share them. Some teachers may balk at the idea of putting students on the spot, but this is not exactly that; we are giving them an opportunity to prepare, and we are expecting them to do just that. Whether lecturing or teaching in any other mode—call on your students randomly and frequently, I say; invite them all, each, often to speak.

In order to do so, I suggest creating a system for calling on students arbitrarily. You might use names on index cards, or popsicle sticks randomly drawn from a box or a hat, or seat numbers selected by a roll of the dice—whatever the method, random calling on students prevents any individual feeling "picked on" by you personally. It could happen to anyone, attentive or not, outgoing or not. The message is loud and clear: be ready! Also, once students have been called on, don't take their name out of the hat—this suggests that they only need to pay attention until that fateful day their name is called, and then they can coast. Wrong! You want them participating and prepared every day, right? Keep everyone's name in the hat.

Now what about Billy, who will always say, "I don't know"?

Well, if you say "Okay" and call on the next person, what are you telling Billy? That he does not need to know. If, on the other hand, you give him some time, invite him to share what he does know, allow him to call on a friend to help him, encourage him to refer to his text or notes, you are letting Billy know—and the rest of the group as well—that you do indeed expect them to know at least something. Do not let Billy off the hook. Once you do, you will never get him—or half of the class—back on.

This strategy of ongoing, on the spot assessment, when explained clearly and used fairly, is a wonderful tool to let students know you expect them to be with you all the way. In addition to intermittent assessments interspersed within a lecture, we need to save time for a closing assessment and reflection.

Closing Assessment and Reflection

After all of our hard work is done, we have hooked student interest, addressed their preconceptions, and presented in a multimodal format with frequent checks for understanding, we need to have a few minutes left over to answer two important questions.

- Assessment: What (did you learn)?
- Reflection: So what (does it mean, have to do with anything)?

These can be asked in a variety of formats—on paper, aloud, alone, in small groups—but please save those few minutes at the end of class for some sort of summative assessment and metacognition. Before walking out your door, learners need to remind themselves of what they did in class, what it means, and why it is important. For ideas on exit tickets, look at Chapter 3.

So, in order to plan effective lectures, we need to

- start with a purpose, a preassessment, and a hook;
- develop a multimodal presentation;
- offer students ways to hold thinking, integrate new information, and reconsider their preconceptions during the lecture;
- assess and invite students to reflect on what they learned.

To help you start planning with these ideas in mind, here is another set of planning questions.

Direct Instruction: Teacher Planning Questions

What is the learning goal? What is the big idea?

Why is this learning material best suited to a teacher presentation?

How does this content relate to my students' lives?

How will I draw out students' background knowledge and preconceived ideas?

How will I communicate the focus, stop to invite students to think, and make the presentation multimodal?

What sorts of graphic organizers will I offer students?

How will I know what they learn?

Dobetter Lectures

Ms. Dobetter is using her learning from this chapter to revise a dry photosynthesis lecture. In the past, she has watched her sixth-grade students' eyes glaze over as she lectured on the chemistry of combustion, respiration, and photosynthesis—and their relationship to the greenhouse effect. This year, she is hoping her presentation will wake them up! Let's see how it goes.

What is the learning goal? What is the big idea?

The focus is photosynthesis—what it is, how it works, why it is important. This is a foundational concept in biology, and supports students' understanding the big idea of systems and interactions.

Why is this learning material best suited to a teacher presentation?

Well, I have read about "experience before explanation," you know, when people say kids should do something before you go and explain to them about it. Sometimes I think that works, but I don't really want to put a bunch of plants in the closet and let them die. Photosynthesis is something that happens (first of all) slowly and (second of all) on a molecular scale, so I don't really think this content lends itself well to labs and demonstrations right off the bat. I just want to give them a clear explanation, and then we can take it from there.

How does this content relate to my students' lives?

Photosynthesis is the basis of the food chain, the basis of life as we know it. No photosynthesis, no us. It's that important.

How will I draw out students' background knowledge and preconceived ideas?

Well, I think I will go ahead and use an old-fashioned day-starter question, but I will make it about them. Something like, "What did you eat for lunch? How do plants get their lunch?" I know my students are all interested in food, and the part about how plants eat will draw out any prior knowledge, or lack thereof, about photosynthesis.

How will I communicate the focus, stop to invite students to think, and make the presentation multimodal?

After we discuss the starter question, which is usually when I set the purpose, or focus, for the day. So I will do that. And stopping to let them think, I am not very good at that because I usually feel like I have so much to cover, but I will work on that, let them do some writing and talking to each other at intervals during the lecture.

I have been thinking of a lot of ideas for making it multimodal. I was thinking to show them models of the molecules, how they break apart and recombine—also I am trying to make up a good song. Remember "School House Rock"? I can still recite the Preamble to the Constitution because of those jingles, so I am wondering if I can make up a jingle about photosynthesis that will be a great memory tool for them. Also, I might do some kind of skit, let the kids act the parts of the water, plant, and sun. They always like seeing classmates up front involved in the presentation, even though it can lead to some amount of pandemonium. It gets their attention.

What sorts of graphic organizers will I offer students?

I can make a note-taking handout, but I think I will keep it simple, just some space for definitions and equations. I will make a copy for myself on a transparency and use that to write the notes. That way, they will know what is the least amount of information to write down. "Your paper should look like my paper," I always used to say, but then I need to leave some space for their own interpretations and reflections on there as well. I want them thinking, not just copying.

How will I know what they learn?

Before the students leave, I will ask them a very important question: what would the world be like without photosynthesis? If they can answer and explain their answer to that, they will have understood the main idea—life as we know it relies on photosynthesis.

Ms. Dobetter's Constants Checklist

1. *Which feature of inquiry will I emphasize? How?*

During this lecture, my focus is on the fourth feature, helping students to connect with and understand what scientists already know about photosynthesis and its importance in the food web. This will build their background knowledge and help them with their explanations throughout the unit.

2. *What is the big idea, and how will I bring it to life?*

Systems and interactions. That is all photosynthesis is, but I think I need to highlight that term and refer to it during my presentation to bring it to life.

3. *Which elements of the workshop model will I employ?*

Before my lecture, I plan to set a purpose and engage everyone. There won't really be much conferring, but I can listen in when they pair and share. There will be some whole group conversation and interaction during the presentation. Afterward I am planning time for reflection and assessment.

4. *When and how will I assess students' content understanding and skill proficiency?*

Students' written work before and after the lecture will serve as my preassessments and postassessments.

5. *How will students build and experience community through this learning?*

Though I am really the star of the show today, I plan to get students turning and talking to peers frequently, and some students will help to present the small skit, so hopefully we can together, as a community, enjoy learning. That is really it.

Teaching Photosynthesis for Understanding

Students roll into the room as the lunch period ends. On the board are two questions.

"Why do humans eat lunch?"

"Where do plants get their lunch?"

Students know well enough that their job is to take their seats, open their notebooks, and get started thinking and writing about these two prompts. Ms. Dobetter mills between the tables as students write, peeking over their shoulders, affirming aloud examples of good thinking. After a few minutes of independent work time, she calls for the group's attention and invites everyone to pair and share. Next she asks students to share with the whole group any thoughtful ideas they heard from a peer. She records these ideas on the board.

Reasons Humans Eat Lunch

- we're hungry
- we need energy from food
- it tastes good

- our body needs nutrients to grow
- if we don't, we'll get sick.

She moves on to the second question, again recording ideas as students share their peers' thinking.

Where Do Plants Get Their Lunch?

- from dirt
- from water, from their roots
- they don't need lunch
- from the sun
- from nutrients that come from the soil.

Ms. Dobetter goes back to that fourth answer, "from the sun."

"So how does that work," she asks, "that they get food from the sun?" No one is quite sure. She writes a word on the board.

PHOTOSYNTHESIS

"Heard of it?" she asks. A few hands tentatively wag in the air, but there is not a student ready to explain the concept. She turns to the board and rewrites the word as two.

PHOTO SYNTHESIS

"*Photo*. What does that remind you of?" Students share connections to the prefix: color, camera, photography, photon, light. She moves on to *synthesis*, and students come up with more related terms: synthesizer, synthetic. "You see?" she points out, "You already know Greek! *Photo*, you are right, is about light; and *synthesis* is about combining things, mixing things, like music on a synthesizer, or in this case, chemicals, to make something new. So 'photosynthesis' means 'making something out of light.' What are these plants making? Lunch! Sugar for lunch? Wouldn't you love to eat sugar every meal of the day?"

The class giggles a "yes."

"So how does this work? That is our purpose today: to understand what photosynthesis is, how it works, and why we need it. You should be able to explain at least that before you leave here. To get us started, I need some volunteers." She calls on a girl in a green top to come up and be the chloroplast, a boy with a water bottle to bring that to the front with him, a known chatterbox to serve as carbon dioxide, and a boy in orange to play the sun in a quick skit at the side of the room. She takes a minute to huddle with them before their very rough performance:

> "Green . . . green, green, green," cautiously sings the green-shirted girl chloroplast (to the tune of "Dream"). The boy with the water bottle holds it up high, pretends to pour it on the chloroplast's head and makes the sound of raindrops with his mouth. Chatterbox shows up and blows what he calls hot air onto the scene. Then the three—chloroplast, water, and carbon dioxide—accompanied by their teacher, sing to the sun, "Oh, Mr. Sun, Sun. Mr. Golden Sun, please shine down on me." Mean-

> while, the sun, standing on a chair, waves his arms exuberantly over them all, and a gleeful shout of "Sugar! Sugar! Sugar!" springs from their mouths. It is corny; the class is laughing, but you couldn't be in the room and misunderstand what was taking place: some materials were getting together with sunlight to make sugar.

Ms. Dobetter thanks the actors profusely before inviting them to return to their seats. "It is an interaction! It is a system! Are you seeing that?" Ms. Dobetter then asks each student to turn to a neighbor. "In your own words," she instructs, "tell your partner the story of what you just saw. What was going on in this skit? What was the interaction? Where is the system?" She ambles around among them as students share their thinking, affirming their comments and ideas as she can, clarifying when necessary, celebrating always.

In drawing the group back together, Ms. Dobetter calls on one astute but slightly shy student to tell the class what he just told his partner. "I can call on anyone I like now," she explains, "because I just gave you time to rehearse in your seats." He stands and shares, and the class listens attentively.

By way of transition, Ms. Dobetter pulls down from the chalkboard a huge piece of craft paper to reveal a collection of colorful cut-paper shapes. "To understand photosynthesis," she begins again, "we really must go down to the atomic level. What is an atom?" She picks up a piece of paper and begins to tear it, first in half, then in half again, and so forth, dramatically, as she explains. "In ancient Greece, scientists began to wonder what would happen if you took something and kept breaking it into smaller and smaller parts. They used the word *atomos,* meaning *indivisible,* for the smallest piece of a material that could no longer be broken down further." She holds up a shred of paper from the sheet she started with and proves that even with her nails, she is unable to tear it again. "Atomos." She holds it up.

"Today, we have the word *atom,* meaning the smallest particle of an element, indivisible by chemical means. Two atoms of oxygen, for example, or carbon, or uranium, have the same properties as a balloonfull, or a pile of the same." She refers students to their graphic organizers. "Atom." She restates her definition and encourages students to write it in their own words.

After a moment, Ms. Dobetter writes her definition on the overhead transparency as well, to support those students who had yet to synthesize their own. Then she turns to the colored, lettered paper squares and points out that each represents an atom—carbon (red paper reading "C"), hydrogen (green, "H"), or oxygen (yellow, "O"). "Molecules," Ms. Dobetter goes on to explain, "are two or more atoms chemically combined." She gives the familiar example of water and points out where water molecules are represented by the clusters of paper squares behind her. "It takes energy to hold a molecule together!" She explains, calling a volunteer from the front row up to help with a quick demonstration. She links arms with her student. "It takes energy to hold on. That is where the energy is stored, in the chemical bonds between atoms that make molecules." She thanks the student, then asks students to define "molecule" on their own paper, again waiting a few moments before sharing her own definition on the overhead.

"The last term that we need to be clear about before we can understand photosynthesis is 'chemical equation.' A chemical equation is the story of how atoms and molecules combine or break apart. There are simple chemical equations and very complicated ones." She tells the story of water by way of example, then invites students to record their own definitions for "chemical equation." She adds hers again to the overhead and turns back to the paper squares representing the equation for photosynthesis.

"The equation for photosynthesis is much more complex than what happens in the formation of water, but the idea is the same. Some atoms get together to make a new compound. Here's the story." Pointing to the representations of carbon dioxide and water on the board, she talks about where plants get those materials, then describes how sunlight and water play into the equation, and asks for the class's patience while she reconfigures the paper squares on the board into photosynthesis' products: $C_6H_{12}O_6 + 6\ O_2$. Then, once she has rearranged the molecules, she invites a student to help clarify, "So what just happened?" A few volunteers are called on to tell the story in their own words, then Ms. Dobetter writes out the equation as scientists would:

$$6\ CO_2 + 6\ H_2O \xrightarrow[\text{chlorophyll}]{\text{sunlight}} C_6H_{12}O_6 + 6\ O_2$$

Next she asks the class to look to their own paper (Figure 8.2) and record the equation, as well as present it in pictures and their own words.

Ms. Dobetter circles the room while students write, complimenting their explanations and encouraging clearer thinking as needed. In calling the group back together, she invites one person from each table to share his or her description of the process of photosynthesis and marvels at the diverse but accurate explanations she hears. She highlights links students are making to the big idea of systems and interactions.

Confident that everyone is clear on the story, Ms. Dobetter reveals that they are in for a special treat. "I made up a song for you. And I am not a very good singer, but I think it is worth a try. Songs can really help us remember things." She whips the transparency with the typed words onto the overhead, explains where the tune came from, closes her eyes and begins (to the tune of "Candy Girl"),

> Hungry? *Photosynthesis time!*
> Gotta make some sugar! *Photosynthesis time!*
> Look to my chloroplasts,
> That's where it's happening!
>
> Start with water—*photosynthesis time!*
> Add carbon dioxide. *Photosynthesis time!*
> Hit it with the bright sunlight,
> And I've got my sugar!

The class listens in silence, shocked that she is serenading them about science. Once Ms. Dobetter opens her eyes to signal the song's end, they crack up. "Now, let's sing it together!" Some join the chorus, some just listen, but the tune is catchy and can be heard echoing in the halls for weeks to come.

So What?

With careful planning, Ms. Dobetter transformed a typical lecture into a memorable, thought-provoking, connected event in her students' lives. She started with an engag-

Name ______________________ Date ______________

Photosynthesis Notes

Atom—

Molecule—

Chemical Equation—

Photosynthesis in Pictures

Chemical Equation for Photosynthesis

Photosynthesis in My Own Words

FIG. 8.2 *Note-Taking Sheet*

ing hook, linking their learning to the source of students' own lunch, wove in a brief vocabulary lesson, and went on to explain photosynthesis verbally, graphically, and kinesthetically. While she may have gone overboard in creating many multimodal avenues to explain the content, she demonstrates in this lesson the many opportunities and strategies that can be employed to bring learning to life.

Far more engaging and accessible than a traditional lecture, this presentation offered students multiple points of access and a variety of assessment checkpoints. Their teacher did work hard to assemble this unique learning opportunity, but she can continue to refine and present this favorite lecture for years to come.

"Yah, but . . ."

- *"This is crazy. Why can't I just explain without all the bells and whistles?"*

You can. But before you explain, stop to find out what students understand. As you explain, think about modeling the content in a few different ways—visually, kinesthetically, and so on. And stop to make sure students are making sense of what you are talking about. That is all. The point is not bells and whistles—the point is understanding.

- *"When my class gets too lively, my students get out of control."*

Unfortunately, students unaccustomed to an interactive, multimodal presentation format may not know exactly what to do when presented with the liveliness modeled by Ms. Dobetter—yet as with all things, we need not use their inexperience as an excuse; we can train them, lay out our expectations for their behavior, be prepared with consequences, and take things one step at a time. In my experience, students love when the usual routine is mixed up, and a simple explanation that you can only keep the class lively if their behavior can endure often suffices to quell their overexuberance.

- *"What about vocabulary?"*

What *about* vocabulary? We must teach vocabulary, and there are a variety of means to this end. One is direct instruction, as described above. Notice Ms. Dobetter took the time to teach the students the root words that comprised *photosynthesis*. Science is riddled with long words derived from Greek and Latin roots, so we develop in our students the skills of lifelong decoders of scientific text when we arm them with a lexicon of prefixes and suffixes and the capacity to decipher compound terms (see Chapter 12).

Some teachers create "word walls," or bulletin boards covered with just such word parts and refer to them throughout the year as students build their confidence and competence as readers of science words.

- *"I am not that creative. Where am I supposed to get ideas?"*

It is not necessary to include a skit, song, model, demonstration, slide show, and interpretive dance every day of direct instruction. Choose just one or two new modes to add to the lecture. Come up with the best idea you can, and try it out first period. If it falls short of your hopes, you have time to revise. Experience is the best teacher of teachers.

You can also get students' input, and add their creative ideas to the recipe. They come up with wonderfully memorable demonstrations and explanations.

- *"College will not look like this at all. Why should I put on a dog and pony show now?"*

Students choose to go to college. Once in college, they choose their courses. Middle and high school students, except juniors and seniors, are a captive audience, and so can need a bit more outreach to get engaged. They are younger, less mature than college students and may not have their own sense of purpose for attending your class. Give them a reason to feel excited and motivated to be there and to participate!

CHAPTER 9

Discussion

Discussion is a life skill that can be explicitly taught. Teachers can structure and facilitate discussions in small or large groups to promote students' thinking and reasoning about science content.

Think Tank

- When is it appropriate to invite students to discuss information?
- How do I structure discussions to promote thinking?
- What is the role of the teacher during a discussion?

"Take out your homework, and discuss your answers to numbers six through ten with the people at your table." Students seated in clusters of four dig in their binders and backpacks to extract a worksheet about chemical equilibrium. Some tables get started more quickly than others.

"What do you have for number six, 'Designate the Brønsted-Lowry acid for NH_3'?"

"I totally did not get that one."

"Me neither. What's a Brønsted-Lowry acid?"

"NH_4^{+1}."

"Okay, cool."

"How about number eight? What's a Lewis acid?"

One student leans in and tells his tablemates the answers to the questions they skipped. His neighbors copy gladly.

In another group, students disagree about how to calculate the pH of an aqueous solution of 0.0150 M NH_3. "That's not what I got."

"Me neither."

"Okay, gimme yours. Lemme copy."

"Buy me a pop."

He hands over the paper.

"What are you doing this weekend?"

"Tonight, Darla and I are going to a movie, and tomorrow I have a game."

"Cool. What time?"

"I think it's at three."

"Do you want to do something after?"

Their teacher spends these ten minutes at the back sink rinsing glassware from the previous class. When he is done, he calls time; a few voices protest—"Not done yet!" (copying, that is) while most students shuffle to face the front of the room.

Reflection

What science did these students learn through their conversations?

How would you describe the quality of these discussions?

What suggestions do you have for their teacher?

While the teacher in this vignette offered his students an opportunity to discuss their work and their understanding of chemical equilibrium, students in the classroom described above spent their time comparing and copying without necessarily checking their understandings of the content. Often small group discussions can devolve into empty air time for students to shoot the breeze. Without buy-in, norms for participation, and a clear system of accountability, students quickly run to topics of greater interest. These are lost opportunities.

Discussion is an essential skill, not only for scientists, but for participants in any relationship, organization, or democracy.

Students need to learn how to use discussion time to share and refine thinking in order to advance their understanding. Teachers can support quality discussions by explicitly teaching conversational skills, monitoring student engagement, and assessing learners' understanding after discussion opportunities.

Discussion Gone Awry

I have witnessed many a small and large group discussion run amuck. Most memorably, my own students': one year early in my career, I inherited a class of spunky seventh graders who had enjoyed memorable class discussions the previous year. They began to ask, then pester me, to let them have a "debate" in our class about our current topic of study, genetics. Specifically, we decided, our discussion (as I called it) should focus on cloning. One day, I bravely asked for their help in pushing the tables to the back of the room so that we could circle our chairs for this "discussion" (I insisted; "debate," they asserted). I put the topic on the table—"Should we clone humans?"—and away they went.

What took place next was astonishing to me—a handful of students spoke up expressing strong opinions on one or another sides of the issue, then two students locked heads and bantered back and forth for a full fifteen minutes. No one interrupted. No one moved. We all just listened to these two argue loudly, something along these lines:

"Why would anyone want to clone *you*?"

"Well, *I* would. What if something *happened* to me, I got a disease, had an accident. I could use my clone as an organ donor."

"That's horrible! You would kill it to take its organ? How would that person feel to know they are really just a backup for you in case you get hurt?"

"Well, we wouldn't have to *tell* him."

"Yah, right, what are you going to do, just strap him to a hospital bed one day, and say, 'it's been nice knowing you,' cut him open and take out his heart? I don't think that's *legal*. Besides, he's a *person*!"

The two made some good points, and presented some garbled logic. After letting it run twice as long as I probably should have, I interrupted the students' argument and asked them to give the other students opportunities to talk. Reluctantly, they fell silent. No one else spoke. Class ended. I wondered what we had accomplished.

Given the constant distraction of mass media, the shortage of families sharing meals together, and the increased independence of young people today, many students have limited experience observing adults in their lives exchanging ideas in a thoughtful fashion. Some students come into our classes lacking the ability to participate in discussions with their peers. These important conversational and listening skills must be taught and practiced to prepare students for membership in the interdependent community of scientists in your classroom.

Why Discuss?

Though you may hold in some corner of your mind the caricature of a career scientist hunched alone over a microscope or hiding in a lab full of bubbling test tubes, the truth is that professional scientists do a lot of talking in a variety of settings. Scientists present their thinking to colleagues within their organizations at frequent meetings. At regional, national, and international conferences, global scientific communities with common interests come together to exchange ideas and learn about the work of peers. For professional scientists, meetings and conferences are opportunities to listen, ask questions, challenge colleagues' thinking, and synthesize new information with what they already understand. Much of this learning takes place through conversations in pairs, small groups, and large forums. These discussions are the petri dishes where thinking grows and evolves. Similarly, we can encourage and expand our students' thinking through structured, purposeful discussion of meaningful science.

Well-structured discussions

- promote thinking and reasoning,
- make science meaningful,
- promote community, and
- culminate in understanding.

How?

Discussions Promote Thinking

As participants in a discussion, students are expected to respond. Formulating one's ideas and stating them for the world to hear is an act of synthesis that requires careful thought. As one's ideas are made public, shared, and further discussed, thinking continues to evolve. Students are spurred on to draw their own conclusions from the community-stimulated reasoning process of a discussion (Reardon 2004).

Reading about stem cell research may present new scientific and ethical dilemmas to learners in your class. "I never really thought about that before," a student scientist might say. These topics may be tempting for a teen to gloss over in light of other more pressing considerations, yet when students are invited to discuss their thinking and opinions, the ensuing discussion brings the learning to life.

Discussions Make Science Meaningful

"Students need opportunities to explore the significance of science in their lives." This is first in the list of "Qualities of Best Practice in Science Teaching" presented by Zemelman, Daniels, and Hyde in their book *Best Practice* (2005). Discussion affords students the opportunity to do just that—make personal connections to ideas and issues, asking, "What does this mean to me?" and answering that very question. Through conversations, science is contextualized.

For example, after a unit of study on alternative energy sources, students can discuss the best strategy for meeting the energy needs of their own community. This discussion will need to integrate their content knowledge as well as an awareness of local resources and liabilities. Through their conversation, students will contextualize and synthesize their content understanding in personally meaningful ways.

Discussions Promote Community

Discussions invite a variety of perspectives. When we listen to the thinking of others, reflect on it, respond to it in respectful and thoughtful ways, we honor our colleagues and develop a deeper sense of our symbiosis as a community of learners.

Inviting student thinking about a controversial topic such as global population growth may elicit a broad range of opinions from those in favor of dramatic birth control measures to those concerned about the rights of the unborn. When we teach students to disagree and discuss their reasoning in a civil manner, we teach them the essential skills of participatory democracy.

Discussions Culminate in Understanding

Discussions present wonderful opportunities for students to air and reconsider preconceptions about a topic. Reflection time after a discussion allows students a chance to think about how their own thinking has evolved. These essential components of science learning—addressing preconceptions and time for metacognition—are featured in the book *How Students Learn Science in the Classroom* (Donovan and Bransford 2005).

After many a classroom discussion, I have spoken to students whose thinking changed over the course of our conversations. "I used to think that AIDS was about some other people very far away from me, but today I realized that my friends know people who have been affected by this disease. Their stories were intense. They made finding a cure seem more important to me."

These benefits—thinking, relevance, community building, and understanding—are gleaned when we hone our discussion topics and provide support to ensure that all students are engaged and learning throughout.

What Are We Supposed to Be Talking About?

There is just so much to discuss! We must start with a purpose, a generative topic, a conflict, or a dilemma. Discussion topics can link classroom science learning to contemporary, often unanswered, issues. Fruitful discussions can sprout from a number of seeds.

- *New Information:* What does the threat of an oil shortage mean for our future?
- *Divergent Data Sets:* In our experiments, why did we get different results for the same catapults?
- *Ethical Dilemmas:* Are the subsequent discoveries and inventions worth the cost of space exploration?
- *Case Studies:* Do human needs outweigh the social and environmental consequences of China's Three Gorges Dam?
- *Integrating Big Ideas:* How do humans affect the stability of groundwater systems?
- *Future Projections:* Is human population growth a problem?
- *Student Confusion or Concern:* Why, after Chernobyl, do we still have a nuclear power plant working close to our city?

In order for a discussion to be generative and thought provoking, we need to start with the right questions. One excellent resource for discussion topic ideas is Richard F. Brinkerhoff's *One Minute Readings* (1992). In this slim volume, he presents eighty issues with short descriptions, inviting students to seek the "best possible" solutions to dilemmas ranging from world population growth to nuclear power. These are wonderful models of generative topics for us to pursue with our students.

Integrating the Big Ideas

Many discussion topics are well suited to integrating the big ideas presented in Chapter 2: energy, evolution, patterns of change, scale and structure, stability, and systems and interactions. Invite students to connect these ideas to specific content by asking them to discuss along these lines:

- Which big idea do you think this topic best exemplifies and why?
- How does that big idea help you connect this learning to other science you understand?
- How could this topic be used to illustrate a particular big idea?
- Which big idea is most difficult to connect to this topic? Why?

Open-ended questions—those that cannot be answered with a simple "yes" or "no"—can start us out on the right foot. Also, we can avoid questions whose answer is a simple point of fact (such as "Why is the sky blue?") in favor of questions that expand

and invite thinking (such as "Would it be possible to make the sky another color? How?") Far-flung as a topic may be, by providing resources and building students' background knowledge before a discussion, we ensure that the conversations are grounded in factual science.

Form Follows Function

Every teacher has her own bag of tricks when it comes to discussion structures. Many of us use formats we got from someone else and then tweaked to suit our needs. Depending on the purpose and learning goal of the conversation, select the structure that will best set students up for a meaningful conversation about science.

You may find success starting the year with more frequent whole group and short, paired discussions where you retain control, can do some explicit modeling, and offer immediate feedback and critique. Then as students' skills develop, they will be ready for success in groups of four, six, and so forth.

In Figure 9.1 there are a few discussion formats that have worked well for my students; feel free to bend them to suit your needs.

The suggested formats above each have a different purpose and potential use in the context of a science class. Feel free to adapt these to suit your own needs, but certainly give students ample time to understand and practice with the format to ensure that their minds can focus during the discussion on the *science thinking and science content* rather than the rules of protocol.

Teaching Discussion Skills

Learning to participate positively in a discussion is a long-term, even lifelong, endeavor. Regardless of the format selected, students need to know how to play their roles in the conversation's success. The norms for discussion begin in the norms of our classroom community (see Chapter 5). Students need constant reminders as well as opportunities to reflect on their own participation and learning. While this practice and review does take some time, discussion skills are essential to the democratic process and well worth the investment of effort to teach and learn.

Thinking Before Talking

Some students do not easily engage in discussions simply because they need time to formulate something to say. Allow them this time. Before launching a conversation, ask everyone to think, write, or chat with a partner. This will prime the pump of learners' minds so that when the comments do start flying, they feel they have something to contribute. Also, do not hesitate to press the pause button on a conversation. If things get heated, stuck, or off-track, ask students again to think, write, or share—allowing them to reenter the discussion with new insight.

Thought Critique	
Purpose	Use one sample of student work or student thinking to spark discussion about an important topic.
Structure	Begin with a student sharing thinking aloud, or by giving copies of a piece of student work to all. Then invite conversation: "What questions do you have for Alicia? Did anyone think about it in another way? What do you appreciate about her thinking? What suggestions would you make?"
Ideal Use	During or after a learning activity to draw together the group's thinking.
Example	Midway through an investigation on genetic mutations, invite a student to share his thinking about the similarities and differences between a mutation and an adaptation. Ask other students to build on their classmate's thinking.

Role Play	
Purpose	Invite students to empathize with stakeholders' thoughts and feelings about a topic.
Structure	After stating the issue, assign specific roles to individuals or small groups. Give students time to research and consider the views of the role they are playing. During the whole group conversations, structure students' turns by offering an order for speakers and time limits for comments. You may also include time for questions and answers.
Ideal Use	Dissecting a complex dilemma with multiple stakeholders and perspectives.
Example	In exploring how to preserve habitat for prairie dogs amid rampant urban development, assign students to play the roles of builder, environmentalist, farmer, homeowner, horse rider, soccer player, mayor, hawk, prairie dog, and so forth.

Socratic Tickets	
Purpose	Structure discussion to ensure that all students have opportunities to speak their minds and hear each others' thinking about a controversial topic.
Structure	Each student gets, say, four tickets: two green, one yellow, and one red. In order to speak, a student needs to give up a ticket by tossing it into the middle of the circle. Pose a question and invite students to share their thinking. But students can only use a yellow ticket once everyone has used up their greens. A student can only use his red ticket after everyone has used up their yellows.
Ideal Use	Works great to give all learners air time during a discussion about a heated topic where students may hold contentious, opposing views.
Example	"Should the highway speed limit be reduced to improve traffic safety and conserve fuel?"

FIG. 9.1 *Discussion Formats for Specific Purposes* *(continues)*

Opinion Continuums	
Purpose	Students take and defend their stance on important issues.
Structure	This kinesthetic activity invites students to move about the room in response to a question or statement, and position themselves along a continuum between two (or more) positions—perhaps "Agree" or "Disagree"—in opposite corners. Once students have chosen where they stand, leader invites learners to stop and talk with the people near them about why they chose to move to that position. Also, students can be paired with peers who chose opposing views and be invited to share.
Ideal Use	This is a quick way to energize paired or small group conversation about several related topics.
Example	Statements could include: "Human life should be preserved at all costs." "Tax money should sponsor pharmaceutical research." "Health care should be available for free to everyone."

Numbered Heads Together (from the work of Spencer Kagan)	
Purpose	Create small group discussions where every student is accountable for talking and listening.
Structure	In table groups, assign each participant a number (1, 2, 3, 4 . . .). Invite discussion around a particular topic. After a few minutes of conversation time, call on all of the 2s, say, to share with the class a synthesis of their table's conversation. After a few minutes to discuss the next issue, invite perhaps the 4 from every table to represent their group's thinking. It is okay to call on the same numbers twice. Some teachers use a die to decide which number to call on next, just to demonstrate the randomness of their selection.
Ideal Use	Works well for generating thinking about issues or topics with which students are somewhat familiar; also can be used for review of factual information.
Example	"What is a solar system?" "Why is Pluto no longer considered a planet?" "What is the value of space exploration?" "Would you want to be an astronaut? Why or Why not?"

Last Word (McDonald, Mohr, Dichter, and McDonald 2003)	
Purpose	This discussion format deepens understanding of a text.
Structure	Works best in groups of eight or fewer. Each student needs an index card. On one side of the card, ask them to choose and copy a passage of the text that stood out as important to them. On the flip side, ask students to write about why they chose that sentence or passage. Once everyone has committed their selection and thinking to a note card, the discussion begins. The first student reads aloud the quote she chose from the reading, then each student in the circle gets an opportunity to share their own thinking on that passage. Once everyone else has shared, the first student gets "the last word," and reads from the back of her card about why she chose that quotation. Then the second student begins and shares similarly.
Ideal Use	This protocol serves best once everyone has had an opportunity to read and think about a shared text. Works better with science current events or news articles, rather than a textbook.
Example	After reading an essay from Richard Feynman's book *The Pleasure of Finding Things Out*, students select and discuss passages that interested them.

FIG. 9.1 *Discussion Formats for Specific Purposes (continued)*

REAL Discussion Skills

It may help to start offering participants some ground rules to set the tone and clarify expectations. Here are some guidelines for a REAL discussion, one that promotes thinking as a community endeavor.

- *Reference text.* Reference real data and sources in your conversation.
- *Engage.* Focus your eyes, ears, mind, and body on the conversation.
- *Acknowledge.* Respectfully think and talk about the ideas of others.
- *Learn.* Pay attention with an open mind; ask questions as needed.

Let's listen in as some students strive to practice these skills while discussing global warming:

> Six sophomores cluster together around a small table. Each has a copy of a graph documenting global temperatures for the past million years, and an article they just read about global warming. Their question is "What should we do about global warming?"
>
> "I don't get how they can figure out what the global temperature was like ten thousand years ago. How do they do that?" Louise asks.
>
> "Remember from the article we read? They use evidence from rock formations and fossils," Eduardo explains.
>
> "So, if these graphs are right, what's the big deal if the Earth is warming up again now? It keeps warming and cooling, warming and cooling," says Jordan, pointing at the graph.
>
> "You are right, Jordan, the Earth *has* warmed and cooled many times in the past, but don't you think humans are having a big effect on the current situation?" asks Eduardo.
>
> "Maybe, but even if humans are having an effect, it is still normal for it to warm up," Jordan answers.
>
> "*I* think it's normal if it happens *naturally*," says Ben, "but humans weren't even around during the last warming trend. No one was burning fossil fuels. I think all this pollution from cars and factories is making it a *lot* worse, a *lot* faster."
>
> "I never thought of it that way," Louise shares.
>
> "So, do you guys think we need to do something?" Justine prods.
>
> "Yah, but it's not fair. We weren't here for the Industrial Revolution and all to really mess things up," Ben shares.
>
> "But the question is, 'What should we do?'" Justine reminds the group.

In the above example, the students are modeling all four of the REAL discussion skills. Now let us look at those one at a time more closely.

Reference Text

Referencing text starts with being prepared for a discussion by completing the required reading or learning activity. As a discussion participant, connect your thinking and the thinking of others with your own data, research, or reading.

In the brief transcript above, you find many instances where students reference the texts and rely on accurate information to make their points—Eduardo refers to the article, Jordan points to the graph. By constantly referencing actual data—whether in a text, from their own experiments, or life experience—students ensure that the discussion is based in scientific reality rather than the territory of mere opinions.

Engage

Engagement is shown through body language as well as verbally. Engagement means facing and leaning in to your group, and meeting everyone at the table. Keep your hands free to take notes, and look at the person who is talking. Engagement also includes engaging with the topic, and keeping the conversation on track.

Although you cannot see the students' body language in the example above, their conversation demonstrates engagement: they remain focused on and engaged with the topic, and with one another, throughout.

Acknowledge

While you may feel very strongly about your opinion and be excited to share your thinking, start by making a comment on or connection to what was just said. Build on or talk about what has already been said, rather than simply tossing out your opinion.

Of the students above, Eduardo does a particularly good job modeling acknowledgment: he answers Louise's question, and then later responds to Jordan by name and prods the group's thinking by asking a question of his own.

Learn

The goal of a discussion is to advance the scientific thinking and reasoning of all participants. Feel confident to ask questions about areas of confusion. Be willing to let go of or modify your position after carefully considering the thinking of your peers.

Louise, in the above example, models learning by asking the question about historical temperature measurement techniques. Later she comments on Ben's explanation, saying "I never thought of it that way." By asking a question and opening her mind to new ideas, Louise embraces the goal of discussion: learning.

These four guidelines detailed above do not constitute an exhaustive list of requirements of a fabulous science discussion. They are a starting point; a short and memorable foursome that can be posted and referred to throughout the year as you train students to take increasing responsibility for their participation and learning in group discussions about science.

Figure 9.2 is a rubric based on these four aspects of discussion success. Consider sharing this (or your own version) with students to reinforce your expectations for their participation in fruitful science discussions. Students can assess themselves or peers, as well as receive teacher feedback on their participation using a rubric like this.

Developing Competence

To succeed with any discussion format, students need to understand, observe, practice, and reflect on their proficiency.

	1	3	5
		All of 1, plus...	*All of 3, plus...*
Reference	Has a copy of related text or data set	Read text and refers to it throughout discussion	Draws on accurate, related scientific knowledge to enrich conversation
Engagement	Looks at speaker	Sits still, calm and focused; takes turns talking	Keeps group focused on topic; documents thinking throughout discussion
Acknowledgment		Refers to peers and their thinking by name	Connects each comment to what was previously said
Learning	Understanding evolves through discussion	Asks questions	Can describe synthesis of new ideas with prior thinking

FIG. 9.2 *REAL Discussion Participation Rubric*

One year, I demonstrated my expectations for quality conversations by first reviewing discussion ground rules, then inviting students to present short skits to the class. I jotted down familiar scenarios and offered them for student groups to embellish and present: the person who doesn't stop talking, the student who does not speak, the member who is playing with his cell phone, the interrupter, the controller, the one who rushes things along, the one who cannot let go of an argument. We laughed hard at the extreme models of rudeness, disengagement, or self-absorption presented in the skits, but students still got the point.

Through the gradual release of responsibility (see Chapter 3), students can take increasing amounts of ownership for a discussion's success. Early in the year, you may model in demonstration groups. For this, some teachers use a fishbowl format—half the class circled up as engaged participants while the other half gathers around to listen from the outside of the circle. Members of the outside group observe, silently scripting parts of the conversation or making notes on rubrics or other structured organizers about participants' performance and contributions, as in Figure 9.3. Then the two groups talk about how things went and switch roles.

As students' skills develop through modeling and conversation, you may invite small groups to discuss topics for increasing amounts of time. The teacher should always monitor and visit with the groups as they meet—and each needs to have some means to document their conversation (see the Accountability and Assessment section).

Regardless of the group size or discussion format, the teacher must remain active throughout a discussion—mostly listening, but ready to supply the essential prompt, the burning question, or respond to an inappropriate comment in order to keep the conversation on track. Ideally, as students develop proficiency and self-direction, the teacher's role in the discussion will be reduced, but first we must get conversations going and keep them on the right track.

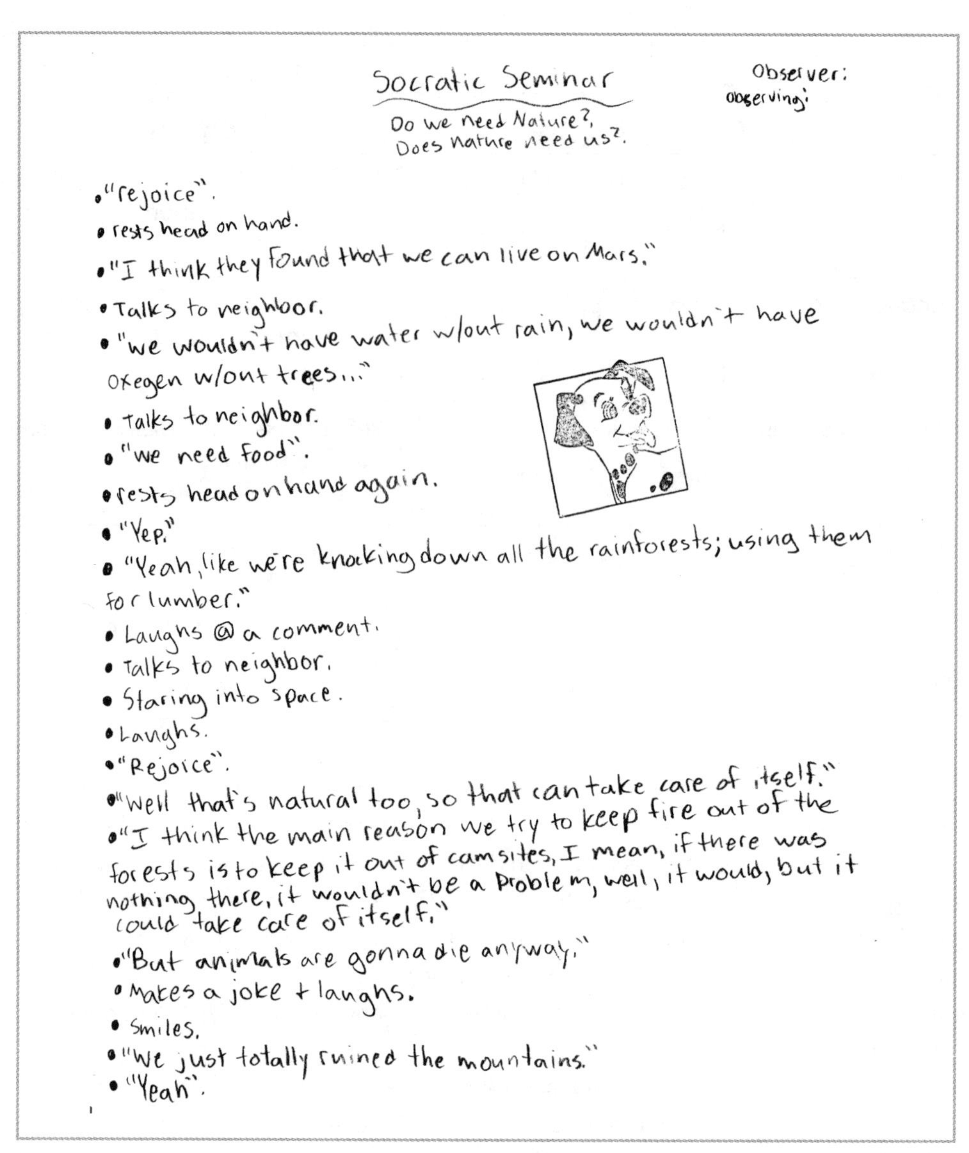

Socratic Seminar

Do we need Nature?,
Does nature need us?.

Observer:
observing:

- "rejoice".
- rests head on hand.
- "I think they found that we can live on Mars."
- Talks to neighbor.
- "we wouldn't have water w/out rain, we wouldn't have oxegen w/out trees..."
- talks to neighbor.
- "we need food".
- rests head on hand again.
- "Yep."
- "Yeah, like we're knocking down all the rainforests; using them for lumber."
- Laughs @ a comment.
- Talks to neighbor.
- Staring into space.
- Laughs.
- "Rejoice".
- "Well that's natural too, so that can take care of itself."
- "I think the main reason we try to keep fire out of the forests is to keep it out of camsites, I mean, if there was nothing there, it wouldn't be a Problem, well, it would, but it could take care of itself."
- "But animals are gonna die anyway."
- Makes a joke + laughs.
- Smiles.
- "We just totally ruined the mountains."
- "Yeah".

FIG. 9.3 *Student Observation Notes from a Fishbowl Discussion; the Writer Tracked the Participation of a Peer in the Inner Circle*

Accountability and Assessment

How can we know what students are *learning* from their conversations? I used to think that students were only engaged in a discussion if they were talking. While speaking *is* a sign of engagement, my own students taught me that some absorb information and think deeply without opening their mouths. While my goal has always been and continues to be that everyone should talk, I have learned to slow down in passing judgment on the silent participants.

Several ongoing assessment tools are well suited for use during discussions:

- listening in,
- inviting input, and
- inviting students to turn inward.

Listening In

As we move about the room leaning in to hear small group conversations, we can note students' understanding of a topic, and the agility with which they use scientific evidence and thinking to support a claim.

One year, my humanities teaching partner was studying the French Revolution with our students. We decided to assign the seventh- and eighth-grade students the roles of European scientists from the Middle Ages and Enlightenment eras and to put them on trial before the Pope and the King. I remember hovering over a group of students trying to make sense of Copernicus' heliocentric cosmology as they sifted through their research, preparing to publicly defend his views. Finally, a quiet boy chimed in, "Epicycles. That was his only mistake . . ." and he went on to explain.

His comment demonstrated a clear grasp of the content, though later in the group's presentation he left it to a team member to convey this same understanding. By listening in at regular intervals to each group, we can catch students demonstrating understanding.

Inviting Input

Another way to assess students amid conversations is to call on them directly during a large group discussion, or by entering a small group, turning to one participant, and inviting her thinking on the topic. As discussed in Chapters 5 and 8 it is important for all students to feel engaged and ready to share at all times. It is easy to call on an individual to contribute during a whole group discussion. You can also sit down and join in small group discussions, listen, and select students to draw out.

One masterful teacher, Steve, frequently used this approach while his students were engaged in small group discussions. He would pull up a chair and just wait, watch, and listen to see who was remaining quiet. Then he would ask very gently of that individual, "What do you think about what they are saying?" In this way, rather than quizzing anyone, he was merely inviting input. Over time, his students began to adapt the same approach, turning to quieter peers in their group and asking, "What do you think about what we are saying?"

As well as modeling positive participation, Steve's strategy allowed him to hear from a quieter student what she was thinking, understanding, and wondering as a result of the conversation surrounding her.

Turning Inward: Synthesis and Metacognition

After investing the time in a long discussion, role-play, or conversation, students benefit tremendously from the gift of silent time to gather their thoughts and assess their own growth in understanding (National Research Council 2005). The invitation to reflect could take many forms—a labeled pictograph of how their thinking has changed, a script of an imaginary interview with themselves, or a traditional narrative describing what they know now and how the group conversation helped their thinking to evolve, as shown in Figure 9.4 (also see Chapter 4 for more ideas). In addition to offering students this time to write, we teachers need to take time to read these artifacts in order to understand how discussions are—and are not—serving our purposes.

As well as reflecting on their learning about the content, students can also be invited and encouraged to reflect on the process—their participation as a member of a discussion group. Students can either self-assess or offer feedback to peers in their

> I think one of the main things I learned about arguments is that you have to be interested and have done your best, meaning to of worked hard to be able to do well. I think that because I noticed that the people who hadn't revised their arguments or supported their position couldn't have good arguments or counter arguments, so even if they were interested, they couldn't get in. The people who had worked hard, but weren't interested didn't care if they were involved or not so they mostly weren't. Before the debate I thought that you would just need one of these skills to do well, but now I'm thinking you mostly need both to do well. Like Auburn had some really good counters and arguments, but she wasn't that vocal or interested, so some points she could have made went unheard. Grant is a really good of example of using both, he was very interested and had done lots of research to support his position and he was very involved and did very well. I bet because he used both he will get a very good grade. I also learned you really need to listen to be able to be involved, even with those other two you won't do well if you don't listen.
>
> One ting that really challenged my position that I hadn't thought of was when people in my debate on the side said that we don't just use oil for transportation, that we also use it make other things, such as plastic. This almost made me change my position because it was so hard to argue against. On of the reasons that it was so strong is because we can defiantly find an alternative to gas, but there is really no reasonable substitute for plastic. We pretty much use plastic in our every day lives a lot so we basically depend on it. It made me think and wonder "Sure we have enough for transportation, but do we have enough to continue making plastic materials?" and I sort of thought to myself that we probably don't. Almost every one in my group agreed that eventually we will run out if we keep using as much as we are, or even much less then we will run out, the only thing is that I thought we would have stopped before that happened. The plastic production presented a new problem. Our plastic need will go up so soon we will still be using a lot of oil so it might run out if we don't find an alternative to plastic.

FIG. 9.4 *Student Reflection After Debating the Question, "Do we have enough oil?"*

group about their participation. By coming back to the norms of quality discussion, we reinforce for our students the importance of their participation in a culture of collaborative thinking.

In response to the prompt, "Describe your role in your group," one eighth grader wrote,

> Usually in a group I try to get everyone's ideas including mine, and I'm sort of the leader. I mean, I don't take charge and be the boss, but I try to make sure we get to everything.

This student demonstrates a high level of self-awareness about how she strives to serve the group by being a leader, but not a boss. It is through continuous modeling and conversations that students develop an understanding of what quality participation in conversations looks and sounds like.

To some science teachers, discussions seem like a time-consuming classroom activity with uncertain learning outcomes. In order to make discussions worth the time, we need to:

- select a generative topic,
- choose a discussion format suited to the learning goals,
- frame the discussion activity with a clear question and purpose,
- establish and model norms for participation, and
- devote time to synthesis and reflection after the conversation.

Amid the pressure for content coverage, it can be difficult to pause and discuss a topic in depth. But when we do take the time, we seize an important opening for students to develop original ideas and opinions about science topics and to link their learning to their own lives.

Here are some planning questions to help you design a discussion.

Quality Discussion: Teacher Planning Questions

What science do you hope students will learn from the conversation?

What format will you use?

How will you convey expectations for students' participation?

What questions will you pose?

How will you know what students learn from the discussion?

Dobetter Discussion

Ms. Dobetter is ready to integrate some of these ideas in planning a discussion for her class. Her ninth graders are midstream in an investigation about pendulums, and rather than using a written quiz to check their understanding, Ms. Dobetter elects to stage a discussion, hoping that students can move one another forward in their thinking.

What science do you hope students will learn from the conversation?

In this discussion, I would like to see the class synthesize their thinking about the nature of pendulums. In this way, I will get a sense of how far students have come in their investigations and for them to compare their data to peers', to orient themselves, figure out what they understand, and where they still have questions.

I guess my learning outcomes are more about the inquiry process, that students understand how data are used to draw explanations, that they see how we will address discrepancies with further trials.

What format will you use?

I always thought of this as just a discussion, but I guess you could call it a thought critique because we will be sharing and comparing our data and thinking about the nature of pendulums. I picture us talking together as one whole group.

How will you convey expectations for students' participation?

Now that it is January, students know pretty well what to expect, so I don't think I am going to do any big sort of modeling or explanation of norms, but I will refer to the REAL norms, posted in my classroom, as needed if we find ourselves off track. I think one of the best ways I can help them learn to respect one another is by respecting them and their thinking myself.

What questions will you pose?

I think I will start with reflection writing time and use the "What? So What? Now What?" format for that. Then, as I draw them together, I am thinking of asking, "What do you know for sure about the nature of pendulums?" and to get discussion going from there—one student sharing her thinking, and then inviting the class to comment. "Does everyone agree with Natasha? Who is thinking something different? Why? What other evidence do we need in order to be sure?" and so forth. My challenge will be not to affirm or debunk any of their ideas, but to allow them their time to talk them all through.

How will you know what students learn from the discussion?

After our whole group conversations, I will ask them to turn back to their initial writing (What? So What? Now What?), draw a line, and add another section: What do I know now? What am I wondering? What are the next investigations I would like to do along these lines? I will read all of their work before Monday, and it will serve as a good starting point for next week's work.

Ms. Dobetter's Constants Checklist

1. *Which feature of inquiry will I emphasize? How?*
This is definitely going to be a conversation about explanations based on evidence, the third feature. For every claim a student makes in the conversation, we will need evidence.

2. *What is the big idea, and how will I bring it to life?*
Patterns of change is the big idea: when we change a pendulum's length, the period changes in predictable ways. There is a pattern, but students' challenge will be to discover it.

3. *Which elements of the workshop model will I employ?*
Really, this is a small snippet of the bigger investigation, which was a workshop in itself. But the discussion will have some writing before and after, so we can call that a workshop as well.

4. *When and how will I assess students' content understanding and skill proficiency?*
Content understanding—the nature of a pendulum—will be assessed in their writing before and after our conversation, as well as by their final lab reports.

5. *How will students build and experience community through this learning?*
Talk about a community of learners—I love discussions like these where all of the students come to the table with their evidence, their understanding, and we get smarter together by looking at the collective data and figuring out what it means.

In the Swing

After working on a lab where students were designing their own experiments to investigate the nature of pendulums and find the patterns of change, Ms. Dobetter invited learners each to synthesize their thinking during silent writing time. She prompted them with three questions: *What* did you do? *So what* did you learn? *Now what* are you wondering?

After time to consider these individually, she called the group together for a discussion of their findings.

"So, what do we know about pendulums? Is there a pattern of change for their period?" Ms. Dobetter begins.

"Weight doesn't matter."

"What do you mean?" she probes the student's thinking.

"I mean, you can change the weight, add as many washers as you want, and the period does not change."

"Hmm," Ms. Dobetter resists the temptation to validate or invalidate this remark. "Do other people agree with Shannon that weight does not matter?"

"It didn't matter for us, but you do have to have some weight, like if there is no weight, the string won't even go."

"Okay, so Jaime is saying that we have to have some weight for a pendulum to be a pendulum, but back to Shannon's claim that weight doesn't matter. What are other people thinking?"

"I agree. It doesn't matter."

"But how can it not matter? We didn't test weight; we only tested length, but I think weight would have to matter because heavier things fall faster."

"Okay, heavier things fall faster. What do you all think?"

"No, I thought that too, but then when my group tried different weights, two washers, three washers, four washers, we did three trials of each with all the same string length, and the weight did not matter. I was really surprised."

"So, you agree with Shannon that weight does not matter." Ms. Dobetter clarified. "So raise your hand if you agree with Dr. Shannon that weight does not matter." Two-thirds of the class raises their hands. Ms. Dobetter creates a tally on the board and records how many express each opinion. "Raise your hands if you disagree, you are sure that weight *does* matter." Two hands go up. "Raise your hand if you are just not sure yet." Six hands. "And raise your hand if you have not yet raised your hand." One boy puts his digits in the air. "What are you thinking?" Ms. Dobetter asks him gently.

"I don't know yet."

"What did your data tell you?"

"That weight doesn't matter. But that doesn't seem right."

"Why not?"

"Well, I think we must have done something wrong. I think weight has to matter."

"Hmm. Weight has to matter. But your data does not tell you that."

"Same here," Juanita says. "I think like Cole that weight has to matter, but my data doesn't say so."

"So you are unconvinced. Hands up if you are unconvinced, if your data says one thing, but you still believe another." About half the class puts up their hands.

"Wow!" Ms. Dobetter acknowledges. "So what do we do now? What do professional scientists do when they are unsure of or do not believe their data?"

"More trials."

"Is that what we need to do?"

Some students nod. "Okay, so we are not all sure yet about how weight affects a pendulum. We will come back to that. What else? What other variables did you look at?" Ms. Dobetter continues the discussion to draw out students' thinking about string length, drop angle, and something they are calling "push," or the force with which the pendulum is dropped. Much of their data is inconclusive, but most students agree that length does matter (the shorter, the faster) and that drop angle does not. The students cannot agree whether "push" is a factor, but the group agrees that further research is needed along these lines. Although inconclusive, the discussion ends exactly as Ms. Dobetter had hoped—with more investigating to do.

Before excusing her students, Ms. Dobetter asks them to go back to their initial writing at the outset of the discussion, draw a line, and add three more questions: what they know now, what they are wondering, and what they would like to investigate next to clear up their confusion. As she shifts from discussion to silent writing, a palpable sense of dissonance hangs in the room; students want to know what *does* matter in controlling a pendulum. "Fantastic!" Ms. Dobetter is thinking. Confusion is fertile ground for learning.

So What?

In this discussion, Ms. Dobetter engaged her class as a community of scientists sharing their findings and developing explanations based on evidence. She did so by starting with a clear purpose, inviting students to record their thinking before the conversation, and then allowing them to respond to one another's thinking throughout the discussions. She resisted the temptation to explain away their confusion and instead allowed them to think like scientists and arrive at their own conclusions, with still more research to be done. In this way, the discussion served her learning goals for her physics students.

"Yah, but . . ."

- *"I don't think it is fair to put kids on the spot, like with the numbered heads together described in Figure 9.1."*

No one likes to be put on the spot. The great thing about numbered heads together is that kids have time to think and talk in their groups before anyone gets called on. I think this structure keeps everyone on their toes; they know they could be picked after any question, so students stay engaged and listening. If this format is uncomfortable to you, you could build in a "lifeline," an opportunity to call on a peer for support.

- *"My students just don't listen to each other."*

It is very frustrating to feel like students do not respect one another enough to listen. As soon as possible, they need to learn this life skill. They will learn from you through your consistently high expectations, modeling, and honest feedback. Start small, with short paired conversations of a few minutes. Ask students to report not their own thinking, but the thinking of their partner or the group. Slowly expand from there. Be relentless.

- *"My students just don't talk."*

How sad that after years of schooling some youngsters fall silent in our classrooms. This may be, in part, because we let them off the hook, call on the known talkers, or allow students to get out of sharing with a quick, "I don't know." Again, here is an opportunity to teach new norms of participation through consistent modeling and support. Celebrate students' good thinking whenever you can, and you will build back their self-confidence as thinkers and knowers in science class. Students deserve a voice.

- *"What if students make totally inappropriate, racist comments in a discussion, like saying that people in developing countries do not deserve protection from malaria?"*

Shocking as some students' opinions may be, the only way to address and help students outgrow those is to challenge them. Peers often pick up on morally inappropriate comments, though you also can feel justified to chime in, state an opinion, or ask a probing question rather than let an offensive comment stand alone. Rather than being silenced, students must understand *why* their comments are offensive and develop empathy for those they are hurting with their words.

For example, in response to a racist comment about the right to malaria vaccines, you might ask, "Does everyone agree?" or perhaps more pointedly, "If you were the Sudanese mother of a child dying of malaria, how would you respond to what was just said?"

- *"I don't have time to get into all of these issues. We have a lot of content to cover."*

What is content without real world application? Issues and dilemmas, controversies and paradoxes are what bring science to life for our students. When we seize these conversational opportunities, we help students to see that science is integral to their lives. This is worth our investment of time.

- *"I don't really feel comfortable raising controversial issues with my students. I am afraid of what might come of the conversation."*

Start small, with short, manageable conversations about fairly benign topics: Should insurance companies pay for corrective eye surgery? Should you be able to decide whether your home's energy is supplied by windmills or coal-burning power plants? With these, build students' understanding of the discussion norms you expect. From here, you could slowly expand the time allotted and the controversy level of the conversations. See where they take you.

CHAPTER 10

Reading

By providing students with engaging texts, workshop model instruction, explicit training with reading comprehension strategies, and tools for holding thinking, science teachers can enhance students' capacity to understand what they read.

Think Tank

- Why is reading important for scientists?
- What kinds of reading do I ask my students to do in science class?
- How do I support my students in making meaning of what they read?
- How do I know what students learn from their reading?

After a fifteen minute lecture introducing some key terms—ecosystem, producer, consumer, decomposer, carbon cycle, nitrogen cycle, and more—Ms. Benson assigns a reading task for the remainder of class. "Chapter 14: Ecology," she writes on the board, then explains, "When you are done reading, answer questions 1–18 from the end of the chapter. What is not completed in class can be done for homework." Seventh graders dig in their backpacks for thick life science books.

She returns to her desk as the students wordlessly get down to work. The minutes tick by in silence. At the end of class, only a smattering of learners are ready to turn in their assignment; most will come in the next day with their multiple choice answers scrawled onto binder paper.

Daunted by the text, Ursula spends most of the class fake reading—turning pages and spacing out. She is guessing that Tom will email the answers to their group of friends tonight. His cousin was in the class last year, and has given his science folder to

Tom. So Tom has the answers to just about everything. He and his pals are all getting As in science.

Reflection

What will Ursula learn from this reading assignment?

What suggestions would you offer her teacher?

The scenario described above is one example of how students develop their own strategies for survival in classes that require challenging content reading. Reading is difficult, especially for learners whose first language is other than English. Expecting students to read alone with no structure or support leaves many behind. If we hope our students will gain science content knowledge from the texts we offer them, we serve them best by explicitly integrating reading instruction within our science courses; in this chapter, I offer some insight into how.

Most of us expect students to read and understand important scientific information independently in order to achieve our courses' learning goals. An array of books on content-area reading, literacy in science, and science for literacy widely promote the critical relationship between reading instruction and content learning.

Reading science is difficult work, and many students need our support in order to get the most from the texts we offer them. We make the best use of reading for learning when we emphasize understanding and devote our energy to teaching students comprehension strategies—such as questioning, determining importance, and synthesizing—to help them make meaning of texts (Pearson 1983).

The Game of Reading

I myself grew up with the myth that reading was a race. Also, if I looked at every word on each page, that counted, and I had read that book. I did not understand the half of what I read, but I was very fast. I knew how to hunt for answers in a textbook chapter—how to locate boldface words, then copy their definitions. I knew that if the definition was not given in the same sentence as the boldface word, I could always turn to the glossary in the back of the book to get a meaning to write down. I knew that picture captions often contained special clues needed for answering the chapter questions. I was adept at this game called reading.

As a science teacher, I found that my students knew that same game. But when I asked them what a chapter meant to them, or how the new information related to their lives, no one had much to say. I realized that this was because I had not been asking learners to do much more than to play reading as the game I grew up playing, the one where you win by getting done first, with "right" answers on your paper. That game is not about making meaning, it is just about looking at the words. For my own teaching to be effective, for my students to be learning, I realized I had to teach a different reading game, one where you win by understanding ideas.

Enter my friend Jen Wood, a staff developer, who showed me that my students needed a *reason* to read, and something to *do* with what they had read. I played around with these ideas in my science classes for some time, with good results. Next, through my work with the Public Education & Business Coalition, I grew and deepened my own understanding of how we can harness the power of quality reading instruction to maximize science learning. This chapter is a synthesis of what I have learned and what I have taught.

What Is Reading, Really?

Reading is not just looking at words or hunting for answers. Reading is thinking and learning. To understand new information from a text, we need to have our brains hooked in and turned on to what the page before us is saying. In order to get learners playing this game of reading for understanding, we need to

- give students a purpose for their reading,
- select high-interest texts,
- explicitly teach comprehension strategies in conjunction with reading tasks, and
- offer students ways to hold their own thinking while reading.

Initially, these tasks might appear out of the realm of responsibility of a science teacher, but our students need our help. In order for the majority of learners to make sense of the complex written material we set before them, they need specific instruction and support. When we teach students to read—really read—for meaning, we empower them as scientists and learners for life. Let's look at how.

Purpose

Many times, we read a chapter in the text because it is the next chapter, or because it is the chapter about our current unit, or because it is what our partner across the hall is having her kids read. For our students, this may not be sufficient motivation to engage them. We need to dig deeper and develop a specific reason for each reading activity, and to convey that to the group effectively. Reading with purpose motivates students to make meaning of the often challenging scientific texts laid before them.

The purpose can be simple: we are reading this to build our background knowledge in order to write informed hypotheses tomorrow in our lab, or to participate in the discussion, or to develop research questions. Whatever the purpose is, linking the reading activity to other learning experiences helps students understand where they are headed, and motivates them to get on board. Readers need a purpose.

Choosing Texts

Science textbooks will likely always be a pricey staple in our schools. They come in all shapes and sizes, all densities and reading levels, and offer an overview of basic facts considered integral to a certain body of knowledge—earth science, physics, chemistry, and so forth. Since textbooks are designed to cover a broad range of topics within a discipline, they do not have the space to delve into the details and intricacies of each. Textbooks present predigested information, sifted and synthesized for easy access. These books are set up for students playing the old reading game, memorizing and copying. Traditional textbooks are not designed to support our students thinking as scientists engaged in genuine questioning, data gathering, and meaning making. For these reasons, it is important to introduce other reading materials to our students.

Either in addition to or aside from textbooks, we can offer our students reading material from a variety of sources. Consider reading with your classes

- original data, such as research from a *Science Daily* article about Hawaii's Mauna Loa volcano's recent changes;
- scientists' field journals, such as the published works of Charles Darwin;
- writing by scientists about science, such as Barbara Kingsolver's *Small Wonder*;
- newspaper articles about science-related topics found in your local paper or the *New York Times* science section;
- magazine articles from *National Geographic, The New Scientist, Popular Science*, or similar publications; or
- articles from professional journals such as *Nature*, or even *Lancet*.

While some of these sources may initially appear beyond the reading levels of our students, we can make these texts accessible either by revising the content, better supporting our students in accessing the material, or both.

Appropriate Reading Challenges

My colleague Jeff Cazier teaches science to an amazingly diverse population of students in one of Colorado's largest middle schools. He is adept at finding interesting nonfiction articles on the Internet that directly relate to what his students are studying. He shared with me a strategy for making adult-level reading accessible to his seventh-grade English language learners: after downloading an article, he cuts and pastes the text into an online readability calculator to assess the reading level, then edits the text to shorten sentences and replace difficult vocabulary words. He can then reassess the readability of the revised article until the level presents an appropriate challenge for his students.

One online resource for this sort of revision is www.standards-schmandards.com/exhibits/rix/index.php

Bringing these types of reading material to our students connects our classrooms to the real world. Primary sources are windows into the thinking of professional scientists. Original research documents present scientific data in its raw form. Current events put science learning in context. Magazine pieces present well written, in-depth narratives. These genres can serve to present or illuminate our content in meaningful, real-world ways for learners. Starting with a high-interest text—one well written and linked to current events, or students' lives and interests, or current events—can engage learners in a topic and drive them to want to understand. (See the Resources at the back of the book for some sources of high-interest science articles.) The use of primary and other sources of science reading material reinforces to our students that science is relevant and everywhere.

It is time consuming and frustrating to spend hours late into the night surfing the Internet for just the right article to introduce the next unit—which starts tomorrow. Rather than setting our sights on finding the perfect readings for each unit all semester, we can start small, find a few useful ones each year, and continue to keep our eyes open. Let family and friends know the types of reading material you are looking for, and they may just come across things you could use in your classes. Our students can be excellent researchers as well when we point them in the right direction. Over time, your collection of high-interest science texts will grow, and you will constantly be replenishing your stash.

Reading as Thinking

Once we and students know *why* they are reading and *what* they are reading, we need to help learners with *how* to make the most of their reading experiences. David Pearson (1983) uncovered a distinct set of seven strategies proficient readers use in all disciplines to make meaning while reading.

- *Monitoring for Meaning:* remaining self-aware, conscious of when you understand fully, and when you become confused by the text.
- *Background Knowledge:* connecting new information to what you already know.
- *Questioning:* posing questions before, during, or after reading; looking for answers in the text.
- *Inferring:* drawing conclusions based on your background knowledge plus the new information.
- *Sensory Imagery:* relating to the texts through personal memories of sights, sounds, smells, or other sensory experiences.
- *Determining Importance:* reading with purpose, identifying salient passages and information.
- *Synthesis:* combining new thinking with prior knowledge to deepen understanding.

While the initial research on these comprehension strategies was designed primarily to inform reading instruction, many of these thinking strategies described by Pearson are integral to the work of professional scientists. Figure 10.1 details how.

Pearson's comprehension strategies, then, are familiar territory to scientists. We can teach these strategies to science learners to support them in making meaning while reading new information in a variety of formats—texts, charts, illustrations, graphs, data tables, and so forth—as they study science. When explained, taught, and practiced, the strategies offer students a tangible way to engage in mental conversation with the text as they read. When learners' minds are active during reading, they come to understand what is on the pages much more deeply.

Depending on the text you have selected for your class, one strategy or another may be more or less appropriate to introduce and practice. In my work teaching reading to science learners and teachers, I have found the following strategies to be most broadly useful: background knowledge, questioning, determining importance, inferring, and synthesis.

You may select others to practice with your students as well. As science teachers, though, we must take seriously the responsibility of teaching students to understand complex science texts, even though we are not their English teachers. Otherwise, we leave them adrift and alone, unable to successfully navigate the sea of complexity that science readings can present. This can cripple their future confidence and opportunities as scientists and readers.

Thinking Strategy	How Scientists Use This Strategy
Monitoring for Meaning	• Scientists reflect on the validity of their hypotheses in light of new data. • If their new data don't fit their background knowledge, scientists assess the possibility of errors in the experiment. • Scientists repeat their investigations to ensure that their results are replicable. • Scientists consider how new discoveries impact existing theories.
Background Knowledge	• When planning an investigation, scientists begin with what they know. • Scientists build their background knowledge by reading the publications of other scientists, attending scientific meetings, and participating in peer reviews of their work. • Scientists formulate questions and hypotheses based on their background knowledge. • Scientists draw inferences based on their background knowledge.
Questioning	• Scientific inquiry is the systematic, reasoned process of investigating questions. • Scientists focus each investigation by posing specific, testable questions and designing experiments which can give definitive answers. • Scientists often pose new questions or modify their hypothesis after gathering new data.
Inferring	• Scientists develop hypotheses based on their inferences. • Scientists examine existing and new data and draw inferences to explain their observations.
Sensory Imagery	• Scientists make observations and gather qualitative data using their five senses. • Scientists record their qualitative observations with illustrations.
Determining Importance	• Scientists as researchers maintain their focus on a specific area of inquiry. • Scientists take data and carry out a statistical analysis to determine its significance. • When designing investigations, scientists determine the sequence of the steps to be taken in the process. • Scientists must demonstrate the significance of their research in order to obtain grant funding for their work. • Scientists try to communicate the importance of their work to the larger community and public.
Synthesizing Information	• Scientists analyze and interpret quantitative data using tables, charts, graphs, and diagrams. • Scientists draw conclusions from their data by synthesizing what they learned with what they already knew before an investigation. • When publishing their findings, scientists demonstrate and reference how their research is related to those who published earlier work.

FIG. 10.1 *Thinking Strategies in Science*

More on Comprehension Strategy Instruction

Our colleagues in the language arts department have been working hard for many years to teach these valuable comprehension strategies to readers. There are numerous resources available describing how content area teachers can integrate explicit comprehension strategy instruction to support student achievement. This chapter only provides an overview.

If you are interested in going into greater depth with this important work, I recommend:

Daniels, Harvey, and Steven Zemelman. 2004. *Subjects Matter.* Portsmouth, NH: Heinemann.

Keene, Ellin Oliver, and Susan Zimmermann. 2007. *Mosaic of Thought: The Power of Comprehension Strategy Instruction,* Second Edition. Portsmouth, NH: Heinemann.

Tovani, Cris. 2004. *Do I Really Have to Teach Reading?* Portland, ME: Stenhouse.

We can take the time to weave comprehension strategy instruction into all of our science classes. Students can practice within the context of science reading and science learning, so it is not as though we need to stop science class to do reading instruction. Providing direct instruction about a comprehension strategy before a science reading task makes the students' time doubly useful: students are learning the essential life skill of reading for meaning while also comprehending the science content we are striving to impart.

Workshop Model Comprehension Strategy Instruction

The workshop model, described in Chapter 3, is an essential structure for effective reading instruction in science. Below, we will look at how the "before, during, after" format can be used to teach and practice comprehension strategies as students make meaning of science texts.

Before Reading

Introduce and work on one strategy at a time, and spend plenty of time practicing each. In designing a minilesson introducing or emphasizing a strategy, include the following:

- examples of strategy use in a real-life context,
- an anchor chart,

- a system for documenting thinking, and
- plenty of modeling.

Strategies in Real Life

To start teaching students a new thinking strategy, I like to let learners know that this strategy is something they are already doing proficiently. Just as we are all scientists, we are all meaning-makers as well. So whichever strategy we may be working with, I look to share lots of examples of how that strategy is second nature to most of us.

Questioning, for example, is something adolescents do every day: Which side should I part my hair on? What is the purpose of life? How many calories are in that Yoplait? When will time end? How can I save the Earth? How can I get to sit by him on the bus without making it look like I want to sit by him? And so on. When we use examples from our own and our students' lives to illustrate the thinking strategies in action, we lower students' affective filters and give them confidence that these strategies are innate to their thinking already. Now we are just going to put that already proficient thinking to work in the context of a science reading task.

Anchor Charts

I learned about these from my elementary school teacher colleagues: an anchor chart is like a poster-sized, one-frame cartoon representing the strategy visually. Anchor charts are one tool for introducing and reinforcing thinking strategies.

For example, when explaining inferring, I may draw an anchor chart with a picture of an elephant visited by two blindfolded people. The people are each using their hands to gather information and draw inferences about the elephant. One person has the elephant's trunk around her waist and is grasping it. "It is very warm and friendly," says the bubble above her head. The next person is standing near the elephant's tail as it swats flies. The tail keeps smacking the person in the head. "It is angry and violent," that person is stating.

The observers are each drawing conclusions based on what they are experiencing, and, in this case, they are both wrong and both right at the same time. This is just one way that I could illustrate how inferring is about taking in new information through the lens of your background knowledge to arrive at original conclusions.

An anchor chart hanging in the classroom serves as a visual reminder for students as we discuss and practice a thinking strategy. Sometimes students can come up with their own—even more imaginative—images to represent a thinking strategy, and it is fun to have learners draw original anchor charts to exhibit their understanding of metacognition (see Figure 10.2 and Figure 10.3 to see anchor chart examples).

Once I have introduced a strategy with real-life examples and an anchor chart, I am ready to put it to work in the context of a science learning experience.

During Reading

After explaining and modeling a thinking strategy in several contexts, I need to model how that strategy looks and sounds as I read science.

FIG. 10.2 *Anchor Chart Depicting Synthesis*

FIG. 10.3 *Anchor Chart Depicting Questioning*

Think-Alouds

Thinking aloud is a wonderful way to model a comprehension strategy. Quite simply, a "think-aloud" means the teacher is reading out loud and stopping to talk about his thinking process and ideas while he reads. For think-alouds to be most effective, several things are needed.

- All students should have copies of the text the teacher is using.
- The teacher's copy of the text is visible to all students, ideally on an overhead projector or document camera.
- The teacher signals that he is reading by looking down at the text, then signals that he is thinking by looking up at the group.
- The teacher records thinking clearly and in good detail, on the text or a separate page.
- The teacher presents several different examples of reading and thinking.

For example, a teacher working with her students to read an article about stem cell research from the *Los Angeles Times* during a genetics unit would prepare by making one copy of the article for each student and also one copy on an overhead transparency (unless she has a document camera—even better). If they are practicing accessing their background knowledge while reading, their teacher would look for specific places in the text where she could highlight what she already knows about the topic. Then, as she stands in front of her students and reads the first paragraph aloud, she will pause and look up as she makes a connection to her background knowledge—a memory of her own thinking process in deciding not to preserve her own children's cord blood, perhaps. On the transparency, she will jot a margin note about her background knowledge, then continue reading.

Sometimes a teacher presents a think-aloud with the first few paragraphs of a text before asking students to read the rest independently. At other times, teachers find it useful to do a think-aloud with a separate text to model the strategy. Either is fine. The main point is that we need to model the thinking and documenting we would like students to do independently.

Anyone who has presented a think-aloud to students knows how challenging it can be for learners to keep quiet. When you start reading aloud a controversial article challenging students' preconceptions about the relationship between space and time, for example, they will be ready to chime in. Learners are having their own ideas while we are reading, and want to share those. This is where a think-together comes in: while the teacher retains leadership of the reading activity, he may read a sentence or two aloud, then ask students to share their thinking on the text. In this way, thinking is shared aloud together, while the teacher continues to document the ideas in the selected format. Most students benefit from observing several think-alouds and participating in a number of think-togethers with each new strategy in order to boost their ability to practice these strategies independently.

When students do begin their independent practice using a comprehension strategy, we need to be on hand conferring and checking for understanding: as students read the article, "Gluttony, Not Laziness, to Blame for Obesity," while practicing determining importance, our first conferring goal may be to check for understanding of the key concepts. Kneeling beside a reader, we may probe for understanding by asking, "What is gluttony? What is laziness? What is obesity? What do you think this article is trying to say? What kinds of evidence do you think the authors will use to make that point? What kinds of important information are you looking for as you read?" A reader's answers to these questions will help a teacher to assess and instruct the individual to ensure that he gets the most from the text.

Students need ongoing support and affirmation as they begin this work. Often, in talking with a student, we may find that she understands much more than she wrote down in her notes. At this point, it is important to emphasize the value of documenting thinking (see Chapters 3 and 4 for more details on conferring).

Documenting Thinking

While many proficient readers employ thinking strategies naturally in their own minds while reading, ask learners to document their strategy use in some way while they read. This makes students slow down and really think, rather than skim over the reading material. Some teachers use texts that the students can actually write on or in; others ask students to use sticky notes to record thoughts, or to document their ideas on separate graphic organizers, as in Figure 10.4.

There is no wrong way; the point is that students are using the strategy, thinking while reading, and recording that thinking in a tangible format that can be shared with peers and teachers. In *Subjects Matter*, Daniels and Zemelman present a broad range of excellent strategies for documenting thinking while reading, as does Cris Tovani in Chapter 6 of her 2004 book *Do I Really Have to Teach Reading?*

Once learners understand a strategy and have seen it in action, then turn them loose with a quality text to practice on their own, as one learner did in Figure 10.5. In the end, create time for students to reflect on how the strategy helped them to understand their science reading. This metacognition is one of the most important steps to success.

Title or website: ______

Purpose: What are the alternatives to gasoline that might curb oil consumption

Topic (Main Idea)	Details from the Text
Biodiesel	•It is renewible • made from oil in plants •It can be blened with peto or used by it's self • It is non-toxic • and it is biodogradeable • The problem with it is it is not widely avable
Compressed natural gas	Very clean burning • Gas engines can be very easily changed to run on it • but there is only one widey avable car that uses it • It is cheeper than gas • but pumps are hard to find and Tanks do not go as far
Electric cars	• run on Electricy • no emissians • and the power plants that fuel them use fossil fuels. So in a way they polut. To • only Hybird.
Ethanol	• can be used in gasoline engine • can be blanted with gas • also has E85 •
Fuel cell	runs of eletrochemical battery • The core source of energy is Hydrgen • which can be got out of water • But a cheep avable vistion will not be for a while
monthalol	• Clean burning and will mix with gas • has high octane
bio mass	• has to have more fuel than wood

p. 312a ~~339a~~ F.10-4 ~~15~~

FIG. 10.4 *Students Noted Important Information from a Text as They Investigated Alternatives to Oil*

What do you know about Whooping Cranes now?

* they're birds (with a big wingspan) → pretty big bird
* based on our targets they have some relationships with Denver
* might live in Nebraska → based on target
* they "Whoop!"
* birds eat fish
* Pollution on the platte
* Problem with Whooping cranes.
* the Whooping cranes Population is either increasing or decreasing.
* endangered?? * do they travel in flocks?
* 1940 — really low Population
* 1990 — started to pick up, more Whooping cranes! * how are they food-collecting?
* water birds? * where are the babies?
* maybe people were allowed to hunt them but laws stopped that.
* gone up so much that maybe they want to eat all the fish.
* up and down — due to hunting
* 2008 = 266 WC * theres different flocks
* 1940 = 22 WC * how many flocks are there?
* 22 and 15 cranes seems really, really low.

What I Read	Connections to Previous Texts
"Platte recovery Plan"	There is a problem on the Platte.
"Platte river problems With endangered Species."	The cranes could be the endangered species. In 1940 = 22 - thats low.
"The species are the endangered interior least tern, whooping crane . . ."	The Whooping cranes are endangered.
"In late 2006 the governors of Nebraska, colorado and Wyoming . . . signed the final program agreement."	The whooping cranes must live in Nebraska, Colorado and Wyoming if all three place's governors are involved.

FIG. 10.5 *Teacher Scaffolded Students' Thinking as They Made Connections Between This Text, Their Background Knowledge, and Other Readings*

Sample Strategy Instruction

Each teacher must develop for herself a means of conveying these strategies' value. Figure 10.6 presents some examples of how I have defined, explained, and modeled my favorite thinking strategies in the context of science learning. You can build on these to develop your own instructional plans for introducing and teaching these valuable comprehension strategies to support your science learners.

After Reading: Metacognition

Metacognition (or thinking about thinking) is an important part of the learning process. We need to ask students not only to document their thinking while reading, but then to do something with that thinking in order to solidify their understanding. Learners might share their written thinking with a partner, a group, the class; use it as a reference for a paper or test; sort it or sift it or connect it to other learning. In this way, harried students can appreciate the value of actually taking the time to write this stuff down.

For example, after individually reading an article about hybrid cars while practicing questioning, small groups of students could come together and share their questions: "Why are the batteries so big? Other than gasoline, are there other fuels that could power hybrids? What about just plugging them in?" With one another as resources,

Strategy	Background Knowledge
Definition	Using what we already know about a topic to help us make meaning. Drawing connections between the text and our own experiences in life, or with other texts.
Sample Real-Life Experiences	My daughter grew up visiting the ducks at the lake. One of her first words was, "Quack, quack." We went to California and saw seagulls. "Quack, quack!" she shouted with glee.
Anchor Chart	Drawing of a mind filled with information, with threads from the ideas in the mind connecting them to the pages of the text in hand.
Possible Format for Holding Thinking	Two column notes: What I read / What it reminds me of
Possible Use	During a weather unit, introduce background knowledge before reading a National Climactic Data Center article about Hurricane Katrina. Many students will have memories or personal connections to help them understand the magnitude of the storm.

Strategy	Questioning
Definition	Wondering while we read. Asking for the meaning, importance, or relationship between new information. Answers may or may not be found in the text; the point is to be thinking while reading.
Sample Real-Life Experiences	Every morning getting dressed: Does this match? Do these still fit? Where are my black socks? Am I going to be late?
Anchor Chart	A thinker holding up a book with a collection of questions floating above her head: Who? What? Why? Where? When? How?
Possible Format for Holding Thinking	Two columns: questions on the left, answers on the right. Add questions before, during, and after reading. Record answers found in the reading.
Possible Use	During an energy unit, prepare students to research renewable energy sources by brainstorming questions. While students read and work, they search for answers and add new questions.

Strategy	Determining Importance
Definition	Reading with purpose and sifting through the text for the important information that helps us attain that purpose.
Sample Real-Life Experience	"You are the bus driver. You drive downtown and pick up seven people, stop at the train station and pick up one more, drop off three. Head to the airport where you pick up five and drop off four. Who is the bus driver?"
Anchor Chart	A farmer jumping for joy after finding a needle in a haystack.
Possible Format for Holding Thinking	Three column notes: What I read / What it means (in my own words) / Why it is important
Possible Use	During a unit on treatment and prevention of communicable diseases, introduce "determining importance" before giving learners case studies to read and diagnose. This strategy will help student scientists consider what matters most in assessing a patient's needs.

FIG. 10.6 *Favorite Thinking Strategies for Science Learning* *(continues)*

Strategy	Inferring
Definition	Putting new information together with background knowledge to draw conclusions of our own.
Sample Real-Life Experience	My husband comes home from work singing, greets the family with big hugs, and is beaming; I infer that he had a terrific day.
Anchor Chart	Picture of a surfer riding waves, watched by three different people, each holding up a colored lens representing their background knowledge. One is thinking this is dangerous, another thinks it looks fun, a third thinks the beach is being invaded by aliens.
Possible Format for Holding Thinking	Two column notes; What I read / What I infer from the text
Possible Use	During a health unit, discuss and practice inferring before reading the data from a report on a clinical trial of a new medication for diabetes. After reading, ask students to infer the meaning of the data.

Strategy	Synthesis
Definition	Thinking about relationships and meaning, combining new ideas with background knowledge to create a web of understanding.
Sample Real-Life Experience	Baking a cake—the flour, eggs, and so forth look and taste totally different from the product you create when you mix it all together and put it in the oven.
Anchor Chart	Picture of a kettle of background knowledge into which new ideas are poured, stirred with the spoon of thinking, cooked on the fire of time to produce a delicious serving of understanding.
Possible Format for Holding Thinking	Concept mapping: List the important concepts from the reading. Create a web representing and explaining the relationships between those concepts.
Possible Use	During a unit on rocketry, introduce synthesis before asking students to read a series of articles about aerodynamics. After reading, ask students to synthesize what the articles, taken together, mean in terms of ideal rocket design.

FIG. 10.6 *Favorite Thinking Strategies for Science Learning (continued)*

they will likely find some answers and be able to narrow their collective questions to a short list of important ones. These could be shared with the class, answered if possible, or held onto until an explanation is found. In this way, students document, rather than gloss over, their confusion as they read; it becomes the fodder for further conversation as the class engages together in a collective project of meaning making.

In addition to wrapping up a reading activity by sharing thinking, it is also important to offer students an opportunity to be metacognitive about how the strategy helped them make meaning of what they read. In other words, we need to ask, "How did the strategy affect your experience as a reader? In what ways was it helpful to read with a purpose? Employ this strategy? Record your thinking? Share your thinking with others? How did this experience enhance your understanding of the text?"

When students have time to stop and see the value, how a strategy slowed them down and helped them to experience success as learners, they are more likely to hang onto the strategy, put it to good use the next day or week in the context of a course.

Assessment

After a reading experience, there are two important things to assess, content and process.

- Do students understand the content of the reading?
- Are students proficient with the comprehension strategy we have been practicing?

To answer the first question about what sense students are making of the text, we can look to a variety of quick assessment tools including conferring, exit tickets, quick quizzes, and future tasks that require students to apply knowledge from their reading.

Students' proficiency with the comprehension strategy is assessed through their understanding of the text, but also can be addressed independently. Surveys, interviews, conferring, and written reflections can invite students to consider how the strategy is working for them. Questions might include the following:

- How would you define this strategy in your own words?
- How do you use this strategy in your daily life?
- How do you use the strategy as a reader?
- How does strategy use affect your experience as a reader?
- What do you think you need in order to be a better reader?

When we encourage students to step way back and look at their experience as a learner in these ways, we empower them to find out what works for them and to make changes, to grow as learners.

Putting It All Together

What does this really look like, a thinking strategy layered into a science unit? The sample unit overview in Figure 10.7 illustrates how the comprehension strategy of background knowledge can be integrated throughout a unit on density for an eighth-grade science class.

This sample unit illustrates the importance of introducing and revisiting a thinking strategy over the course of time with a range of material. With practice and reflection, comprehension strategies are a powerful tool to assist learners in reaching our course's science learning goals.

While you may not think of yourself as a reading teacher, integrating direct instruction of comprehension strategies into your science course will directly benefit your students as science learners. They will build skill and confidence in their ability to make meaning of complex science texts. You will find an abundance of reading material now

Learning Targets

- Students will understand how density is an example of the big idea, stability.
- Students will understand the concept of density and be able to apply it in problem-solving situations.
- Students will understand that density is a relationship between mass and volume.
- Students will understand how density is relevant in the context of our daily lives.
- Students will become proficient at using the comprehension strategy of background knowledge to aid their comprehension of texts, diagrams, problems, demonstrations, and lab activities.

Day	Activity	Gradual Release of Comprehension Strategy
1	Preassessment	Written preassessment draws out students' background knowledge about density. After individual work time, class shares and charts what we already know.
2–3	Oil slick	Students work in small groups to separate oil from water using an array of tools. Before they start the task, we will brainstorm as a class what strategies might work best.
4–5	*Exxon Valdez* article (Grade 6 reading level)	Teacher introduces the idea of background knowledge with an explanation and anchor chart. Then leads the class in a think-aloud as we read together the magazine article "*Exxon Valdez:* The Big Spill." Teacher encourages students to draw on background knowledge built during yesterday's activity. After reading the article, students draw concept maps explaining and connecting a list of key words relating to density. Metacognition: Ask students how background knowledge gained from the oil slick activity helped them understand text.
6–7	Read Ch. 7 "Density" from physical science text (Grade 7 reading level)	In a think-aloud, teacher models two-column notes about background knowledge and connections as one reads. Students read along in the text, then continue reading and note taking independently.
8	Density column model	Teacher presents a density column and asks students to draw on their background knowledge to explain what they see. Students work individually, then in pairs to develop explanations. Teacher confers. To debrief, teacher leads class discussion emphasizing students' use of prior knowledge to support their explanations.
9–11	Read "Ice Floats, So Do Boats" from *Science Snackbook* (Grade 8 reading level)	Teacher begins lesson by eliciting students' background knowledge about what floating has to do with density. Then, teacher models two column notes about background knowledge again, but only for two paragraphs of the text. Students work in small groups, each group creating two-column notes on an overhead transparency. Groups share their notes about connections and background knowledge at the overhead. Teacher gives feedback to each group, looking for particularly meaningful and helpful connections to highlight. Students write short reflections on how they used background knowledge to boost comprehension and why it is helpful to them.

FIG. 10.7 *Sample Unit Plan: Density (with emphasis on background knowledge)*

(continues)

12–13	Activity: Create a density column	Students work in pairs to create density columns. Prior to distributing materials, teacher will assess each pair's comprehension of the written design parameters.
14	Read "A Famous Bath" from *Handbook to the Universe* (high school reading level)	Teacher elicits students' background knowledge about Archimedes, then briefly models note taking. Students work in pairs to create two-column notes about their background knowledge. Teacher confers with pairs during work time. Pairs report favorite connections to the whole class.
15	The algebra of density	Teacher introduces the equation for density (first seen in the reading Days 6 and 7) and models how students can solve density problems mathematically. Sample problems.
16–18	Density lab	Students weigh and find the volume of various objects, then calculate their densities. Debrief of lab links mathematical understanding of density to conceptual understanding. Students complete written lab reports.
19	Final strategy practice: *New York Times* article on oil spill cleanup technology (adult reading level)	Students read the article independently using two column notes on background knowledge. Teacher confers with students individually about their use of the strategy. Students take turns modeling their thinking by each doing a think-aloud of one paragraph of the text at the overhead. Homework: Write an explanation of background knowledge and how it helps readers comprehend texts.
19	Final assessment: Density problem solving	Students work individually to demonstrate their understanding of density by solving practical and theoretical problems, both hands-on and text based.

FIG. 10.7 *Sample Unit Plan: Density (with emphasis on background knowledge) (continued)*

accessible to help connect classroom learning to the wider world. In order to teach comprehension strategies effectively, you need to

- prepare for reading instruction by selecting high-interest texts and an appropriate comprehension strategy;
- explain, demonstrate, and invite students to practice the strategy; and
- encourage metacognition and awareness of how comprehension strategies enhance investment and understanding.

Here are some questions to help you plan quality workshop model comprehension strategy instruction.

Reading: Teacher Planning Questions

What is my learning goal for this unit?

How will I use reading to support students in achieving that learning goal?

What will students read?

Which comprehension strategy will I teach and practice throughout this unit? Why?

How do I use that thinking strategy in my own life? What examples can I give students as I introduce the thinking strategy?

What are the ways I can ask students to document their thinking while they are reading and practicing this thinking strategy?

How will I assess learners' proficiency with this thinking strategy?

Dobetter Reading

Ms. Dobetter is ready to look at revising how she incorporates reading into her seventh-grade earth science class. In the past, she has relied merely on the textbook for reading material and has expected all of her students to know how to get information from it independently. This year, she is going to look for some high-interest texts and experiment with teaching a comprehension strategy. Let's see how it goes.

What is my learning goal for this unit?

The unit is on plate tectonics. I want students to understand that the surface of the Earth is constantly changing, yet in predictable ways. I want to emphasize the big idea, patterns of change. Learners should understand how plate tectonics affect our lives by way of volcanos, earthquakes, mountain building, and other large-scale geologic phenomena.

How will I use reading to support students in achieving that learning goal?

I usually just use reading to practice vocabulary and build background knowledge for the classroom activities. I also like all of the timelines, charts, and pictures in the textbook. I suppose this time I could have them read the text with a more specific purpose, such as being able to really explain how plate tectonics relate to our lives. I also need to ask learners to do something with what they read—write about it, discuss it, share it so that it really sticks, and is not just like a separate homework task I usually assign that we do not talk about in class.

What will students read?

I usually have them read three chapters in the book—"The History of Plate Tectonics," "The Mechanism of Plate Tectonics," and "Plate Boundaries." They are pretty dry chapters, but with lots of illustrations. Maybe I can spice it up this time by finding a few related articles on the Internet that would pique their interest. I know seventh graders are all pretty curious about natural disasters, so maybe I could kick off the unit with some true newspaper stories about earthquakes and volcanos, then back into the topics from there. I would still like to use the textbook because it contains all of the main ideas and vocabulary, but I think some current event–type stories would bring the unit a bit closer to home for my students. I will look on some of the sources suggested in the Resources list.

Which thinking strategy will I teach and practice throughout this unit? Why?

I have not done comprehension strategy instruction in my science classes before, so I want to start with something that feels comfortable to me. Background knowledge feels like the most straightforward, but I am not sure how much background knowledge or personal experience my kids will have about plate tectonics or even volcanos. So now I am thinking about questioning. Everyone knows how to do that, and that is really what scientific inquiry is all about: questions.

How do I use that thinking strategy in my own life? What examples can I give students as I introduce the comprehension strategy?

I feel like I am constantly asking questions, both as a teacher and a learner. As a teacher, I notice myself asking, "How can I make this unit or activity better? Do my students really understand?" and questions like that. As a learner, I am constantly inquiring, wondering, curious about the world and all things in it: "How can we use wind power to reduce ozone depletion? Who will be our next president? Why does cheese become moldy?" These are real life examples of some of the questions I have thought about just this morning, not to mention the more mundane like, "What should I eat for breakfast? Is it going to rain?"

When I introduce the strategy for reading, I will give examples of how I am often asking questions before, during, or after reading a newspaper article: the title gets me thinking and wondering, facts from the text make me curious, when I am finished reading, I often want to know more. These are some of the examples I can offer.

What are the ways I can ask students to document their thinking while they are reading and practicing this thinking strategy?

Well, questioning should be fairly straightforward to most of my students. I am sure they can come up with a lot of questions as they read, so I have a few different ideas of how to document those. One idea I have is to have students keep a question log and list their questions before and during the unit, then take time at regular intervals to let them check if we have answered any of their questions, and write those answers down. But more specifically, while we read I would like them to use sticky notes to write questions in the textbook; when we read articles, I will let them write directly on the photocopies and record any questions they have. Then we will definitely need to make time to go back and answer them, the ones that we can.

How will I assess learners' proficiency with this thinking strategy?

That is a good question. On the one hand, I can see myself counting the number of questions the students develop, but I don't think that is the only thing. I also want to see the depth of their questions. For example, are they really thinking hard, or just tossing questions out for the sake of questioning. I think we will have to spend some time discussing what makes a "good" question. I can show them Bloom's taxonomy and talk about the kinds of higher-order thinking we should strive for when questioning.

Another thing I am wondering is what about answering the questions, where that fits in, whether I need to expect them to find the answers to everything they ask.

Ms. Dobetter's Constants Checklist

1. *Which feature of inquiry will I emphasize? How?*
With questioning as the comprehension strategy, this unit will be most closely linked to that first essential feature, engaging in scientifically oriented questions. I think most of their questions as they try to understand the text will be scientific.

2. *What is the big idea, and how will I bring it to life?*
Patterns of change will come to life through the reading and other activities of the plate tectonics unit. I need to work hard to keep that big idea alive, though, by referring to it at frequent intervals and asking students to reflect on how their learning applies to it.

3. *Which elements of the workshop model will I employ?*
I will definitely wrap the workshop model around all of my reading instruction.

4. *When and how will I assess students' content understanding and skill proficiency?*
Students will be assessed in a lot of different ways—through conferring, through their small group conversations, and based on their individual written questions and reflections.

5. *How will students build and experience community through this learning?*
We will do a lot of paired conversations and whole group discussions as we practice this strategy. Through these experiences, students will participate in a community striving to make meaning together of new information.

Questioning Plate Tectonics

Introducing Questioning

Before kicking off her plate tectonics unit, Ms. Dobetter decides to orient her students to a new thinking strategy, questioning. "We are all constantly wondering about things—from social to scientific—all the time," she starts. She describes her morning getting ready for school and all the questions she asked herself: "When I got downstairs for breakfast and grabbed for the cereal, there was only Shredded Wheat left, and I wondered, 'What happened to all the Honey Bunches of Oats?' After breakfast, I thought about lunch, 'Will I have time to go out to lunch, or do I need to pack it?' As I decided between my thin fleece jacket and my warm coat, I was asking myself, 'Is it going to be cold today?' Some of my questions were answered—my cousin visiting from Chicago admitted to eating all the good cereal. I realized that I never have time to go out to lunch, so decided to pack one, and then I looked on the Internet and checked the weather.

"As I arrived at school, I wondered about more things: 'Why can't I get here any earlier?' 'What is wrong with the copier?' 'Where shall I take my cousin, who is visiting this week?' Some of those questions are still unanswered. Some are important, some are not, but nonetheless, when I stop and listen to the chatter of my own mind, I realize that I am asking questions all the time."

Ms. Dobetter then asks students to each take out a piece of paper and write down any question—any at all—that they have wondered about since getting up this morning. After several minutes of silent work time, she asks students to each look back over their list and answer which of their questions got answered through the course of the day, which were not yet answered, and which may never be answered. She invites students to share examples of each and records them in three columns on the board:

Questions Answered	Questions Not Yet Answered	Questions Unlikely to Be Answered (Ever)
• What's for breakfast? • Where is my iPod? • Why won't our car start? • How long is my brother going to be in the shower?	• What are we going to do in science today? • Is it going to rain? • When is Ciara's next album coming out?	• Why does she hate me? • Will infinity ever end? • Who stole my cell phone? • If we all stop driving our cars today, can we end global warming?

Ms. Dobetter uses these lists to point out how there are different types of questions, and that we each live with a great deal of uncertainty every day. "Our minds are full of unanswered—or as yet unanswered—questions. Similarly, scientists are also constantly asking questions, and throughout this unit, we—as student scientists—are going to practice our questioning skills." She introduces an anchor chart restating familiar question words, and asks students to notice themselves questioning for the rest of the day.

The second half of the class Ms. Dobetter devotes to preassessment of the unit learning goals. Students create concept maps synthesizing what they know about how the unit's key terms—continental drift, crust, mantle, plate boundaries, magma, and so on—relate to one another.

Practicing

The next day, students enter Ms. Dobetter's darkened room. Her projector shines on the anchor chart listing question words in bright colors: Why? How? Where? What? If? When? She begins class by reminding students that they are all natural questioners, and that today they are going to put those abilities to work as scientists—geologists. Ms. Dobetter has selected a number of slides of geologic events. Before sharing those with students, she explains that for each slide, she would like them to generate as many questions as possible in their notebooks. The show begins: lava oozing underwater, Mt. St. Helens, Mt. Surtsey, Mt. Fuji, Kilauea, Crater Lake . . . Ms. Dobetter pauses at each slide for several minutes to give students time to think and write. The room is awash with questions, none of them as yet answered.

After the slide show, Ms. Dobetter asks the students which of the slides (1–10) they are most interested in discussing. The class votes and selects slide five (Grimsvotn, Iceland), which Ms. Dobetter flashed on the board again for all to see. Then she invites questions, which they shoot rapid-fire as Ms. Dobetter records them on the board. Answering none, she affirms the group's curiosity and invites them back tomorrow for more before the bell rings.

Modeling While Reading

Now that Ms. Dobetter's learners experienced asking questions as they view photographs, she is ready to introduce the comprehension strategy of questioning while reading a text. When the students arrive, she piques their interest by reminding them of the recent tragedy in the news, then passes out the article. She has selected a recent newspaper piece about a cataclysmic earthquake in Mexico City; she flicks a transparency of the article onto the overhead and begins her think aloud. Ms. Dobetter refers to the anchor chart and describes how she will be recording questions in the margin as she reads. She proceeds to do so on the transparency as students follow along on their own page.

After reading three paragraphs and jotting five questions, Ms. Dobetter pauses and asks students to notice what kinds of questions she is asking: they are thoughtful science questions, probing for meaning in the piece. She is *not* asking questions like, "Why do we have to read this?" she points out. Ms. Dobetter asks the students what questions they have about the strategy before they proceed on their own. All seem ready to give it a try, and so she asks learners to read and think in silence.

Learners Use the Thinking Strategy While Reading

As the students work, Ms. Dobetter circulates and confers with them. She pauses to notice questions students are recording in the margins of the page, celebrating insightful ones by reading them aloud to the class. After sufficient work time has passed, Ms. Dobetter calls the students back together and asks them to think about where they would find the answers to their questions: In this text? Where? Students pair up and analyze their questions, sorting them into categories based on how they think each could be answered. Then, by way of closure, she asks each student to write for a few minutes about one of their questions that *was* answered today in their reading. Ms. Dobetter's students leave the room curious, some irritated by how much they still want to know and understand about earthquakes.

The next day, Ms. Dobetter has a story of a different sort of natural disaster caused by geologic forces: the explosion of Mt. St. Helens. While this volcano erupted before her students were born, several of them have heard of the event, and she invites all to join her in a think-together as they begin to read the article, her at the overhead, students with copies at their tables. As she reads aloud, she pauses, asks the students for their questions, and records those on her transparency. This collective activity gives Ms. Dobetter another opportunity to discuss how good questions should represent higher-order thinking:

- *Analysis:* Why did Mt. St. Helens explode, while Mt. Fuji only smolders?
- *Synthesis:* If change takes place in a predictable pattern, what will happen next to Mt. St. Helens?
- *Evaluation:* Why couldn't scientists have prevented this disaster?

After reading the first page together, Ms. Dobetter releases the class to finish the reading independently, continuing to record their questions.

As they get down to work, one girl complains that stopping to write questions is really slowing her down. Ms. Dobetter asks the rest of the group if they agree. Several do. As a remedy, Ms. Dobetter suggests they self-edit: instead of writing every last question—now that they are experienced questioners—record only those that seem most pressing, at least a handful per page. This feels like a reasonable compromise to the naysayers in the group. This article is longer, and few students finish reading it before the lunch bell sounds. Ms. Dobetter asks them to finish reading—and to finish questioning—for homework.

Metacognition

Friday, their fifth day on questioning, Ms. Dobetter decides that it is time to introduce metacognition. She begins class with a "quick write": How is this strategy—questioning—helping me to understand the texts? Students write their answers before sharing them in pairs. Since they have had think time, Ms. Dobetter draws names from her hat and calls on individuals to share their answers:

> "Questioning really slowed me down, but that was because I wanted to know what the article said to see if my questions were being answered."
>
> "I realized that I always do questioning while I read. This time I just had to write the questions down."
>
> "There were a lot of words in the articles that were new to me, and instead of just skipping over them, I made them into questions. I looked some of them up."
>
> "Questioning is just like what scientists do when they are trying to understand something. Questioning while reading these articles made me want to know more about geology."

Ms. Dobetter's geology unit continues: she weaves the questioning strategy into every aspect of their work. Students use questioning while reading from the text, and also when they are pursuing their culminating project analyzing earthquake data from the San Andreas Fault: their task is to predict an earthquake, and so their questions are about which conditions indicate that one is expected. Frequently, Ms. Dobetter pauses to celebrate questions and laud the virtue of this strategy as an important skill for thinking in science—as well as all other content areas.

While not all of her students' questions are answered at the end of the unit, Ms. Dobetter is not disappointed. She managed to get these kids more curious about plate tectonics than any class before them. Their curiosity drove them to learn more than she had ever hoped about volcanos, earthquakes, and other geologic phenomenon. And there is no question about that.

So What?

By explicitly teaching a comprehension strategy within a science unit, Ms. Dobetter built students' thinking skills while helping them make sense of important content. While it did take an investment of time to explain and model questioning at the outset of the unit, that investment paid off. Students were able to use the strategy again and again to engage with visual media, current events articles, and the textbook. Questioning gave students' minds something to focus on while they were taking in new information. The results in terms of student engagement and student learning were noteworthy.

"Yah, but . . ."

- *"I am not the English teacher."*

Anyone teaching in an English speaking country is an English teacher. In fact, research shows that students learn more new words in freshman biology than in a first year foreign language course (Williams 1992). In order to succeed in our classes, students must learn vocabulary and the skills of reading, writing, and thinking like scientists.

For best results, we can ask our English teacher colleagues to share their rubrics, strategies, and other tools so that the students make connections between our classes and see that language skills are imperative for success across the curriculum.

- *"Who has time for strategy instruction; we have to get to the content!"*

While strategy instruction may appear to take time away from science learning in the first analysis, it will actually enhance everything you do in class thereafter. With these tools, they will be better equipped to understand the science content of your course, which will help them to engage more fully as learners, so comprehension strategy instruction is well worth the effort and investment. Thinking strategies are lifelong skills that will serve our students throughout their learning careers. In five or ten years, your pupils may not remember the difference between a strike-slip and oblique-slip faults, but they are likely to remember the value of questioning—and other thinking strategies as tools to keep their minds turned on.

CHAPTER 11

Projects

Teachers can design accessible, engaging projects demonstrating students' understanding of big ideas and important science content.

Think Tank

- Why do I (or don't I) use project-based learning in my classes?
- What sorts of projects do I ask my students to do?
- How do I ensure that projects facilitate and demonstrate student understanding?
- How do I convey my expectations for quality work on projects?

Mr. Monroe had spent an entire period explaining the astronomy research project to his ninth-grade earth science class. He gave them two whole weeks to work on it at home, and accommodatingly extended the due date to after Presidents' Day weekend for the benefit of students who claimed they needed more time. By the Tuesday the posters were due, 60 percent of Mr. Monroe's students turned something in; of those, only a handful looked as though they could earn beyond a C on the rubric he'd typed up over the weekend. Some stragglers seemed to have confused "due" with "do" and brought their work in a day or so late, but these extra days did not seem to have boosted the quality of their products whatsoever.

When the students stood up to present their tri-fold presentation boards, Mr. Monroe found himself even more disappointed. When asked about the future of our sun, Lexi, whose research was about star life cycles, shrugged her shoulders. Crystal's poster included a timeline of astronomical discoveries downloaded and printed directly from the Internet; she could not explain what it was or what it meant. Rubin's poster included spectacular photos by NASA, but he did not label them or know what any of them represented. Despite two weeks of work time, most students appeared to have absorbed an infinitesimal amount of information about astronomy.

Frustrated, Mr. Monroe decides to throw in the towel on project-based learning altogether. He just cannot see the students getting anything out of it. Despite his best intentions to create an open-ended learning opportunity for his classes, the students squandered their time and resources. Mr. Monroe is thinking that projects are a waste of time.

Reflection

Why, given so much time to work, do students seem to have learned so little?

What suggestions would you have for their teacher?

While the initial idea of Mr. Monroe's project seems well conceived, the students in the example above fell short of creating products that demonstrated understanding. Lack of skills, structure, or support may have been the cause of their shortcomings on the project.

If we plan for students to invest precious learning time in in-depth projects, we must engage them, design the tasks carefully, and offer frequent opportunities for instruction and conferring throughout work time to ensure that all accomplish the task successfully.

Well-Designed Projects Are Worth the Time

"Projects" encompass a wide range of long-range learning tasks we structure for our students; they may include original experiments, scientific research, model building, story writing, poster making, performances, video creation, and much more. Some projects may be completed entirely at home, others during class time, or any mix of the two. Successful project-based learning can present a number of challenges for science teachers, as Mr. Monroe and many of us know firsthand. Yet when designed and conducted well, projects can be highly engaging, differentiated, meaningful learning experiences for all of our students. Well-planned projects have the potential to:

- make learning purposeful and meaningful,
- promote universal success, and
- simplify teacher planning.

Projects Make Learning Purposeful and Meaningful

Many learners become engaged in new ways when their learning is integral to the work of completing a large-scale task. In *Teaching Science for Social Justice*, researcher Angela Calabrese Barton documents the far-reaching positive impact of involving homeless and disenfranchised youth in project-based after-school science programs, where they have designed and constructed large-scale projects including furniture and community gardens (Barton 2003). While our classroom-based tasks may not be as extensive, students can nevertheless benefit from the authentic learning and personal empowerment integral to completing a large-scale task.

Projects Promote Universal Success

As master teacher Ron Berger describes in his book *A Culture of Quality*, project-based learning creates room for all students to work at their own level and at their own pace with the support of their classmates and the guidance of their teacher:

> The project must therefore be structured to make it impossible for individuals to fail or fall behind. Through continual conferences, critique sessions, and peer and teacher support, student progress is sustained and assessed at all points during the creation process. (Berger 1996)

Projects invite multiple opportunities for differentiation; while the outcome of the project may not look the same for all, each student is offered opportunities to learn. For example, each of your students could work on predicting the population growth rate of different species based on birth rates, habitat encroachment, and other limiting factors; some students may look at just one generation, while others may be capable of projecting well into the future. Still, all experience differentiated instruction targeted toward a common learning goal.

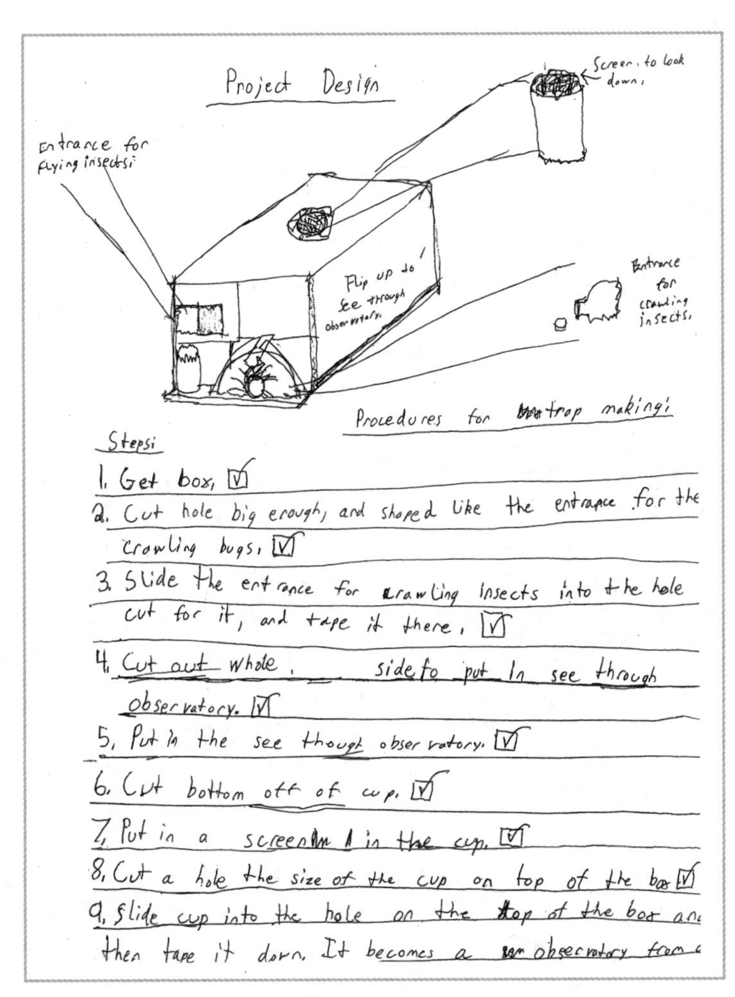

FIG. 11.1 *A Student Designs and Plans the Construction of an Insect Trap*

Projects Simplify Teacher Planning

As one savvy teacher explained in favor of projects, "It is like building a house. When you are building a house, you don't go to work every day and wonder what to do next; you look at what you did yesterday, and it is pretty clear what needs to happen today." The daily work of planning becomes straightforward for the responsive teacher: minilessons target the learning, and work time creates opportunities for teachers to confer with each individual or team. When well designed, with clear learning goals in mind, projects create ideal opportunities for the implementation of the workshop model.

If your students are designing and building solar cars, for example, the long-range nature of the task itself will light the way each day. Your planning is guided by the simple question: what will my students need to know in order to successfully take the next step?

An initial investment of planning time is required to create a wonderful project, but once things are rolling, the teacher's job becomes one of coach rather than conductor. Learners come to class focused, ready to continue work on their project. They leave class thinking about the next steps and come in the next day ready to get back to work (see Figure 11.1). Well-designed projects are surely worth the effort and time, yet the art of project design requires careful thought; project work is fraught with potential pitfalls worthy of our attention.

Project Pitfalls

Teaching through projects—whether posters, plays, or PowerPoint presentations—can be complex and problematic. In many ways, the virtues of project-based learning are themselves the dilemmas of this learning modality.

Projects are open-ended. Some students use these opportunities to let their imaginations soar, impressing us with their creativity and cognition. Others may find themselves overwhelmed when faced with an open-ended task. A kite could be designed in a million ways, for example, but the burden of creating one may cause students to struggle aimlessly, needing a better understanding of what quality work on a finished product would look like. Our challenge is to provide models and examples to guide *all* learners in channeling their creativity.

Projects are hands-on. Many students love kinesthetic work; in the case of many projects, this is the hook that engages the learners. Students who have been waiting all year to use the microscopes will be inherently engaged by the chance to draw a meiosis flipbook. However, hands-on work can be nothing more than that—a way to keep hands busy. Our challenge is to find ways through projects to turn minds on and achieve intentional content learning goals.

Projects take a lot of time. A week or two on one specific task allows time for students to delve into and understand the work thoroughly. An originally designed mousetrap car cannot be built in just one class period. For some, though, this long-term endeavor may offer too much time to get lost or procrastinate. Our challenge is to break tasks into smaller steps and provide scaffolding along the way.

Projects are often completed in groups. Depending on their experiences working in groups, many students grow to either love or hate cooperative learning. While all students may have roles in a play about Tesla, one individual may snatch the opportunity to write the script herself. As teachers judging only the product of a group's work, it is difficult to assess who learned what through the experience. Our challenge is to create systems for individual accountability and assessment during and after the project.

Projects are inherited. In some schools or districts, students have heard about the cell project, the food chain diorama, the egg drop, the spaghetti bridge, and so on since kindergarten. Traditions can be a source of inspiration, yet tradition alone is not reason enough to conduct projects. Our challenge is to ensure that each inherited project is pursued based on its virtues as a standards-based learning experience.

In order to address these dilemmas of project-based learning, we as teachers must take time to clarify the purpose and learning goals of each project, then plan a process to lead our students from here to there. As you read on in this chapter, think of your own classroom and that one project—the marble roller coaster, the egg osmometer, the rocket building unit—that you only wish you did not have to ever teach the same way again. Here is your chance to make a change.

Designing Projects

Five virtues are essential to all well-designed projects. These conveniently match up with the five vowels, taken in reverse order. Just as vowels are the essential building blocks of virtually every word, the five vowels can remind us of five essential components of quality projects.

Ideal projects will

U: target student Understanding;

O: culminate in a visible product or Outcome;

I: illustrate Important big ideas through specific science content;

E: be Engaging; and

A: make learning Accessible.

Let us now take a look at each of these vowels one at a time.

Understanding

The understanding goals for the project must be identified specifically at the outset, and learners, ideally, would be unable to complete the project work without that understanding. In other words, understanding is implicit in the task you set for your students. For example, one cannot debate the virtues of solar energy versus wind power without understanding both. Yet one *could* create a model of a solar panel without *necessarily* comprehending how it works. It is this difference we must consider carefully. Understanding can be assessed in a separate oral assessment or presentation, but ideally it is implicit in the project design and work process. It is the thoughtful teacher who can ensure that the understanding goals remain at the forefront throughout project design and project work. (See Chapter 2 for more on understanding goals.)

When understanding is clearly defined and targeted throughout project work, we avoid the potential pitfall of a project being too open-ended.

Outcome

With specific learning targets in mind, teachers can carefully select an appropriate product or outcome suited to the content. The options are endless. One useful strategy for selecting the outcome is to start with the understanding goals, and then ask, "If my students really understood X, what would they be able to do?" or "How could they best demonstrate their understanding?"

Figure 11.2 contains a small collection of familiar project outcomes; as you read them, take a moment to circle the products you feel would serve as the highest-quality demonstrations of understanding.

As a science teacher, I favor projects that require original thinking and creativity, rather than those that simply suffice with regurgitation of information. This condition is not necessarily a result of the product selection, but more of the product requirements. In other words, if your students are creating a museum exhibit, it must be clear to them that everything in the exhibit should be their original work, not copied or downloaded from elsewhere.

Certain products—board games, debates, persuasive letters (as in Figure 11.3), skits, songs, and Venn diagrams—are harder to plagiarize than the more ordinary brochure, demonstration, or poster. We must always be explicit in our expectations about original work.

Important

Of course, you would not have identified your understanding goals were they not related to important big ideas of science. It is imperative that your students see this connection and the importance as well. Just because a particular project we may have done in the past—designing a periscope, for example, is fun and interesting—does not necessarily mean it is connected to significant scientific ideas unless we make it so for our students.

We must ask ourselves: What is so important about this? What is building a periscope about? "Systems and interactions," how mirrors convey an image around a corner to your eye? Or about how scientists developed technology to assist them in observing the world? Once we articulate that importance for ourselves, we must convey it to students so that they see the relevance and meaning of this small project in the context of the bigger picture of science. The importance of the project must be reinforced

Performance	Written	Visual
Debate	Brochure	Board game
Demonstration	Children's book	Diagram
Game show	Essay	Diorama
Interpretive dance	Flip book	Drawing
Newscast	Graph	Model
PowerPoint slide show	Graphic novel	Museum exhibit
Skit	Persuasive letter	Painting
Song	Poem	Poster
Video	Venn diagram	Puzzle

FIG. 11.2 *Possible Demonstrations of Understanding*

May 28, 2008

The Honorable John McCain
Unite States Senate
Russell Office Building, Room 241
Washington, DC 20510

Dear Senator McCain:

This spring my 7th and 8th grade science class has been studying climate change and what we can do about it. We started out by looking at data of CO_2 and temperature. Then we looked at the different kinds of energy the sun emits, and how that energy affects our earth. After that we studied the carbon cycle, and how the industry and human actions of today might affect it. This led us to the subject of how to work on the problem of global warming. We looked at what the nations of the world can do to work towards a solution, and in particular we looked at the Kyoto Protocol as one solution.

I think that global climate change is a serious issue, and from your statement in the Los Angeles Times, "Global warming is a serious threat", I am inferring that you do too. But, I would like to state my opinion about the Kyoto Protocol. Although there are pieces of the plan that I like, there are a lot of major flaws in the plan. When you are elected to office, I would like to see you reject the Kyoto Protocol, or sign it ONLY if some major changes are made to it. The first flaw that I would like to see fixed is a point that you brought up before, as in the video on your campaign site where you state "...if we could get China and India into it, then the United States should seriously consider-on our own terms-joining with **every other** nation in the world to reduce greenhouse gasses." I think that this is one of the biggest problems in the Kyoto Protocol. The Wall Street Journal points out that the Kyoto Protocol **does not** include 9 nations out of the top 20 CO_2. The fact that these countries are not included compromises the ability that our nation has to help the environment, because if some nations work towards a cleaner future, while others do not, than our strife is pointless. A second issue that the Kyoto Protocol presents is that it compromises our abilities to profit in the global economy. For example, if we are required to buy new technology for our factories, then the factories in under-developed or developing countries will now have a cheaper product that they can make because they don't need to buy the special carbon-limiting technology for their factories. The Wall Street Journal stated that the Kyoto Protocol "penalizes the growth of energy efficient nations while rewarding those [countries] emitting much greater quantities of noxious gasses. So, what I am trying to convey is that not only developed countries need to be involved in our efforts to fight climate change, so that we are all on an even playing field. You said yourself that, "[Fighting global warming] has got to be a global effort." A final reason that the Kyoto Protocol's present terms would not work for the United States in that it demands too much, while returning too little. About.com printed the fact that the US would have to spend 400 billion dollars, and lay off 4.9 million people just to meet the Kyoto targets. Although the cost itself is bad, especially as our nation becomes more and more in debt, but also, the amount of workers that would have to be fired is unacceptable. Our unemployment rate is already 5%, and we would see a considerable spike in that percentage if we were to lay off this many people. It would also we morally irresponsible to do so. So, as you can see, it would simply not work to sign the Kyoto Protocol.

As the amount of damage on our environment is increases, and the prospect of an irreversible global climate change looms in the distance, we are in dire need of a solution to global warming. But, I think that the Kyoto Protocol is not the only path to an answer, and is fact, the wrong answer. As one of the leading nations in "green" technology, I think we could continue to research solutions, and to strive towards a cleaner country, and ultimately cleaner world for our generation, and the generations to come.

Good luck,

Daniel Hartman-Strawn

FIG. 11.3 *As a Culminating Project, Studnts Wrote Letters to National Leaders About the Kyoto Protocol*

throughout project work so that a student working on the product understands the bigger picture and could explain to any visitor what this undertaking is really about.

With Importance as a filter, we can avoid the pitfall of adopting an inherited project that does not have inherent value as a learning experience.

Engaging

Our project ought to be interesting for all styles of learners. By their very nature, projects tend to be engaging; they are a step outside the ordinary and invite students to lend some creativity to the task. Still, teachers can formulate projects in a variety of ways to make them even more engaging.

- *Audience.* Invite or create a special, outside audience for the products—a neighboring class, parents, experts in the field, administrators, or school lunchroom staff. With this audience in mind, students can refine their work and hone their ability to explain the science content appropriately.
- *Choice.* Some teachers offer a range of choices of product in an effort to engage students. In some classrooms, this works well. In other instances, when students have too many choices at once—a poster, a model, a comic book, a board game, a video, a PowerPoint presentation, or a speech—the learners may be unfamiliar with the formats or quality expectations for each without an explicit model and instructions. Limit the choice to a short menu of similar presentation formats: for example, invite students to create a newscast, a puppet show, or a play. With all students working on similarly styled presentations, a teacher can present useful information about what quality looks like in oral reporting, for example.
- *Controversy.* For young teens, topics that entail some element of controversy, opinion forming, and side taking can definitely get their juices flowing. One year when teaching genetics to eighth graders, rather than starting off with the mundane memorization of the differences between mitosis and meiosis, I started with a question: should we clone humans? En route to developing their own answers to this question, students learned the rudiments of cell division and genetic recombination, yet all with a view to answering an important ethical question for themselves. Even my most reluctant learners were motivated to present their views and back them with scientific evidence. Introducing related controversies as central to the content, not sidebar issues, contextualizes the science that students are learning and hooks their minds and hearts.
- *Materials.* Sometimes students get involved in the work simply because the materials they are working with are interesting. When we can furnish our labs with real science equipment—a beaker rather than a glass jar—students feel they are being taken seriously. Sometimes glassware and other science supplies can be acquired secondhand from universities or professional laboratories that frequently obtain new equipment.

Accessible

Not only does the task need to be accessible, but more importantly the *learning* should be made accessible through the task. With projects, the workshop model becomes a crucial tool for instruction and access. For example, building a paper boat that can bear maximum weight presents a challenge for both a fourth grader and a fourth-year university student. Depending on the structure and expectations for thinking before, during, and after working on the task, the same project can be designed as a suitable challenge for students at different levels.

As teachers, we must search far and wide for project ideas that make content learning accessible to the wide range of learners in our classes. Differentiation need not mean that students are expected to create different products. It can mean that all students are expected to achieve the same understanding goals, perhaps with differing outcomes, and will require differentiated instruction to get there (Tomlinson and McTighe 2006). This is inclusion in the truest sense.

These five points can guide our revision of familiar projects, or help us to formulate new ones. Project plans that fit this description—clear Understanding goals, defined

Outcome, illustrate Important ideas and content, Engaging, and Accessible—when well-conducted, have great potential to maximize student learning.

Project Transformations

Sometimes transforming a project is just a matter of taking the same product—Mr. Monroe's astronomy posters, for example—and layering workshop model instruction throughout the work time. In this way, all students are scaffolded to higher levels of success. Within the structure of the workshop, targeted instruction supports individuals' success, and expectations of quality work can be conveyed incrementally. In this way, we can use the workshop structure to transform our good ideas into rich learning tasks.

At other times, the product itself, not just the learning process, may require an overhaul. In my experience, some of the most creative ideas for new projects come about when groups of teachers sit together and courageously brainstorm: What do we want learners to understand? What could they do to represent that understanding?

When we take the time to analyze our existing projects through the lens of our five vowels—Understanding, Outcome, Importance, Engagement, and Accessibility—we can reframe our projects as true invitations to and demonstrations of learning. Below are a few examples of typical projects that teachers have adjusted in order to create pro-

Goal	Typical Project	Enhanced Project
Understand how volcanos work	Draw a poster of a volcano; label the parts	Create a model of a system designed to reduce the possibility of a volcanic eruption
Understand what creates weather	Create a mobile with pictures and definitions of different types of clouds	Design an imaginary continent; explain and justify its weather system patterns
Understand optical systems	Use a kit and follow directions to build a telescope	Design and create an original telescope
Understand atomic structure	Make a three-dimensional model of an atom of a specific element	
Understand point and nonpoint sources of pollution	Research a local pollution source, and write a newspaper article about it	
Understand planetary motion and how eclipses occur	Create a flip book showing the process of an eclipse	
Understand the taxonomy of living things		
(Your original idea here)		

FIG. 11.4 *Practice Project Transformations*

found opportunities for student thinking and understanding. In these examples, the teachers continued to target the same big ideas and understanding goals, yet creatively transformed the projects to create deeper opportunities for student thinking. The partially completed chart in Figure 11.4 invites you to consider a few more project transformations, and to explore some of your own creative ideas by filling in the empty boxes.

In some of the examples above, you may look at the enhanced projects and think, "That is too difficult!" True, some of these enhanced projects are a lot more difficult than their predecessors, but the good news is that we have the workshop model in our back pocket as a tool to break even complex projects into shorter stages with coaching along the way.

Over the course of a project-based learning experience, we can scaffold students' success by breaking the end product down into specific steps, offering targeted instruction each step of the way. For example, if our understanding goal is that sixth-grade students can explain threats to local water quality and our outcome is that they each write a persuasive letter to a local politician about water issues in our community, we can make the project accessible by breaking it into smaller steps. Students will need to

- identify threats to our local water quality,
- gather data to assess the severity of these threats,
- brainstorm and research solutions to address their concerns, and
- learn to summarize data and opinions in the form of a persuasive letter.

If left to their own devices, few sixth graders I know could succeed at this task. Yet with workshop model instruction, we can target our minilessons to address each of the steps within the project, confer with individuals during work time, and create opportunities for students to share and gather feedback on their work each step of the way.

With this sort of support and guidance, even our most reluctant learners can experience success with a long-range science project. It is amazing where our students can go when we set our sights high and offer them well-planned support all through the learning process!

Working Together

I remember when I was in college, and on the first day of an environmental science class our professor put us together in groups of ten to study sections of a local watershed. We were all shocked, not by the task but by the structure: how were we supposed to work together with a huge group of people we had just met to complete a semester-long project? Later our professor confessed his rationale: if we are to solve the world's environmental problems, the most important thing is that we learn to work together. And we did.

Project work in groups presents challenges to many of us, and our students alike. For ideas on how to support learners' success in collaborative learning, see Chapter 5.

	1	3	5
		All of 1, plus . . .	*All of 3, plus . . .*
Depth and Quality of Research			
Use of Time	• Works on project during class • Attends class discussions	• Completes task in the time provided • Focuses during class, small group, and paired conversations	• Makes excellent use of all independent work time • Participates thoughtfully in all class discussions and peer critiques
Quality and Variety of Resources	• Uses sources for research • Integrates peer and teacher feedback	• Seeks websites, books, and current journals for information on the topic	• Exhaustive research uncovers most important facets of the topic
Science Content Understanding	• Aware of the topic of study	• Understands the main science idea addressed through this activity • Understands relevance of this topic to his or her own life	• Clearly understands stated science learning goals • Contextualizes learning from this investigation within the field of science
Product/Presentation			
Communication	• Serves as evidence of work on project	• Documents important learning about topic • Completed on time	• Provides audience with a clear, complete, and comprehensive understanding of all student's related work and learning
Craftsmanship	• Created by the student	• Demonstrates effort and care	• Professional quality

FIG. 11.5 *Generic Science Project Rubric*

Assessment

Project-based learning can be challenging to assess. Students can demonstrate understanding through a finished product, as well as through the process of creating it. We serve students best by sharing expectations for quality work, as well as our rubrics and assessment tools, up front. Assessment data can be gathered over the course of students' work time on the task. Figure 11.5 is a generic project rubric developed over my years of striving to get it right.

Projects can be a highly engaging learning tasks when well designed with clear goals and specific products based on important science content. Project-based learning can be accessible to all with the support of workshop model instruction. Think through the UOIEAs to get started.

Projects: Teacher Planning Questions

U: What do I hope all students will Understand after completing this learning experience?

O: What will the Outcome—or product—be?

I: What is really Important about the science we are learning?

E: How can I Engage all of my students through this task?

A: In what ways can I make the understanding goals of this project Accessible to all learners?

How will I use the workshop model to scaffold students' success with this project?

Dobetter Projects

Ms. Dobetter traditionally asked her students to create labeled models of typical animal cells, including all organelles. The seventh graders always came in with gorgeous work: brightly colored modeling clay with toothpicks and typewritten labels, glittery Styrofoam carvings with calligraphy signs, gelatin and marshmallow creations labeled with icing, and so on. Each year, the students became increasingly creative in their displays, and given all the time they had clearly invested in these cells, Ms. Dobetter found herself unable to give anything but As to the majority of the class.

She realized, though, through an uncomfortable discussion with her instructional coach, that this central pillar in her cell unit was really just a copying task. Little understanding was conveyed through this process or product. Bravely, in collaboration with colleagues, she redesigned the project into something more delicious than any gelatin cell she had ever seen.

U: What do I hope all students will understand after completing this learning experience?

Well, I want them to understand about cells and about organelles—what they do, how they work together, how the cell is like a little system and all the parts have a job, a microcosm of our own bodies. I can't believe it took me this long to realize that all those gelatin molds were not getting us there. Those kids could make fantastic looking models, three-dimensional representations of the picture in the book, and I would give them an A for their hard work, but they really didn't learn anything at all except how to mold gelatin . . . so what could I have them do instead that would really force them to get it?

O: What will the outcome—or product—be?

I don't know. I really don't. What could they make or do?

(*Ms. Dobetter had to think about this for a long time. After many days and ongoing conversations with colleagues and friends, here is what she came up with.*)

Okay, I've got it! We are gonna play "Organelle Survivor," a jigsaw activity. Students will be organized into "cell groups" of six. Each student in each cell group will be assigned an organelle—nucleus, cell membrane, endoplasmic reticulum, and so on.

Then the organelles (one from each cell) will gather in expert groups—all the ribosomes together in one group, all the mitochondria together in another, and so on. In those expert groups, the students will research the roles and responsibilities of their own organelle, preparing to return to their cell and make the case for themselves as essential to the cell's survival. When all the organelles are reunited with their original cell groups, they will be charged to discuss everyone's role, and "vote" an organelle out! Just like that TV show! Students will have to know their stuff because they are fighting for their own survival!

I: What is really important about the science we are learning?

This is about interdependence, about how cells are living systems; we are living systems, we rely on our living Earth to feed us. The big idea I would like students to understand through this project is stability, how it is maintained through interdependence. And students will not only study that interdependence but experience it as members of their jigsaw learning groups. Oh, I am really excited! It is like a play within a play!

E: How can I engage all of my students through this task?

Well, I am going to assign everyone a role, and they will be held accountable through the structure of the task. Because if they are the only ribosome representative in their cell, they have to make darn good use of the research time in the jigsaw group so that they can come back and know their stuff. As I introduce the project, I think I will really take time to emphasize how each person's job is unique. Students need to be here every day participating, or the project will simply flop! I hope to engage them with that—the feeling that they are each needed.

Also, I think the competitive stuff will engage some of them, the threat of being "voted out." For some, that will be a big motivator—to "win" and keep their place in the cell. For others, it may be intimidating, so I am not sure how much I want to play it up. We'll see.

A: In what ways can I make the learning goals of this project accessible to all learners?

I know I've got to break it down, break it down, break it down, and show them. Some kids will get hold of the resources and just run with it, but I am thinking I need to give them lots of graphic organizers, checkpoints, and note catching tools to make this work. I will definitely be conferring with each person, making sure they know their stuff before we leave the expert groups. That will be really important.

I am feeling kind of nervous, actually. I am really putting a lot on the kids. If they don't do their part, this whole project will totally flop. But I guess that is what responsibility for learning means.

How will you use the workshop model to scaffold students' success with this project?

I am seeing it as one big workshop with lots of daily workshops inside it. We will start the whole project with a minilesson about the purpose, and end the project with sharing and reflection, but then each day will also be a workshop with a purposeful minilesson targeted to that facet of the task, then work time with conferring, and some opportunities to reflect.

Ms. Dobetter's Constants Checklist

1. *Which feature of inquiry will I emphasize? How?*

This project will really be about learners connecting explanations to scientific knowledge. They will be using their own research to justify their position as an organelle in the cell.

2. *What is the big idea, and how will I bring it to life?*

I think the big idea will emerge over the course of cell groups' discussions about who to "vote out." They will have to be asking the question, "How can we maintain our stability?"

3. *Which elements of the workshop model will I employ?*

All of them. Every day. Lots of conferring.

4. *When and how will I assess students' content understanding and skill proficiency?*

There will be opportunities for assessment throughout their research and work time, but really their thinking will come out the best during their discussions in their cell groups. I will ask students to reflect on and write about what they come to understand through these.

5. *How will students build and experience community through this learning?*

Well, they will experience both the positive interdependence and support of their expert groups and the competition between organelles of their cell groups. I think as long as we can keep the conversations all based on science content understanding, even the "competition" can be about building understanding.

Organelle "Survivor"

Knowing she wants to teach the cell unit differently this year, Ms. Dobetter leafs through her old binder from last year in search of appropriate activities to kick things off. What she finds is a fading collection of dry articles, word searches, crosswords, and coloring tasks. She decides to recycle them all and start fresh, start with thinking. She visits the downtown public library and checks out every book at every level that has a section on cells. She returns to her classroom with a huge tub of material, ranging from college textbooks to primary picture books. Then she checks out her department's microscopes for the first day of the unit, and digs through the supply closet to find slides of a variety of cells so that everyone can look at a few different ones. Somehow she feels prepared and totally unprepared all at once.

The first day of the unit, Ms. Dobetter gets to school early and sets up the microscopes, one for each pair of students. She stands outside her classroom and greets her students with instructions that they leave their backpacks in the back of the room and take only a pen or pencil to their desks. *Before* work time, during her minilesson, Ms. Dobetter quickly reviews what the group already knows about how to use microscopes, then passes out the slides.

During work time, learners take turns looking through the microscopes and drawing what they see on the blank paper she provides. As they get started, she hears an array of interjections including "Eeeh!" "Ugh!" and "Wow!" She circulates and assists with microscope management, but declines to answer content questions. Instead, she encourages her students to write their questions down. After a few minutes, she asks learners to pass their slides along, so that everyone gets to look at a variety. Students continue to share and exchange slides throughout the work time.

After about fifteen minutes of work time to look and draw and question, Ms. Dobetter asks the students some questions in a think-pair-share format: What do you notice? What do you wonder? Then she gathers the findings of the whole group on the board. Many students do know that they have been looking at cells, but they still have a lot of interesting questions: "Why are they so different?" "What are the bumps?" "What are the dots?" "Do our cells look like that?" "Where is the DNA?" "How does it grow into a whole animal?" "What is a stem cell?" "Can we do this again tomorrow?"

Ms. Dobetter ends class with the sad news that they will not do this again tomorrow, but that instead they will become the cells themselves. What does she mean? Well, they will just have to come back in the morning to find out!

On day two, Ms. Dobetter presents their group project: as students enter, each pulls a small slip of paper from a hat. The letter and number on their paper randomly assign learners to working groups. They are told to sit at the table that corresponds to their number. Students find their places in groups of six at the newly clustered tables. Ms. Dobetter had resisted the temptation to engineer the groups and just let the kids pick their group assignment as they entered. Once all are seated, she implores them to hang onto their number and letter; they will need it later. Next, Ms. Dobetter directs the learners' attention to the task sheets "Welcome to 'Organelle Survivor'" already piled in the center of their tables. Students scramble to get their hands on one.

Welcome to "Organelle Survivor"!

You have just joined your cell.
Each of you represents an "organelle" inside this cell.
In this game, your job is to learn all that you can about yourself.
You will need to explain and defend your importance.
Before getting started on your organelle research, work with your cell-mates to answer these background questions:
What is a cell?
What do cells do?
What are organelles?

With a brief minilesson, Ms. Dobetter introduces the project, then directs students to get started working with one another using the books piled in the middle of their tables as resources. Students flip through books, discussing, scrawling answers on paper. After just a few minutes—not quite enough time for everyone to finish—Ms. Dobetter calls for attention and explains that the learners will soon be moving into their expert group for the next phase of the project. She refers everyone back to their slip of paper with a letter and a number, explaining that their number is their cell group (where they are now) but their letter represents their organelle expert group. Ms. Dobetter flashes a

My Organelle: ______________________________

Sketch a cell; draw and label your organelle inside it.

What does your organelle do?

Why is this important?

FIG. 11.6 *Organelle Project Note Catcher*

hand-written page under the document camera, and the key to what the letters mean is projected onto the screen at the front of the room:

C: Cell membrane

E: Endoplasmic reticulum

G: Golgi apparatus

M: Mitochondrion

N: Nucleus

R: Ribosome

She then directs everyone to rearrange themselves at new tables to meet with their expert groups. Students shuffle and get settled as Ms. Dobetter flashes another page under the document camera, a copy of the note catcher on the back of their task sheet, presented here as Figure 11.6.

Ms. Dobetter instructs the expert groups to share their answers to the questions on the first side of the task sheet, then flip it over to answer the organelle research questions. She refers students to the resources on their tables, then wastes no time in getting moving around the classroom herself, conferring with her budding biologists as they embark on their research. Time passes quickly.

A few minutes before the bell, Ms. Dobetter wraps up the day's work time. She stops all talking and asks students to look over their own notes, ensuring that all the details they learned this day are recorded there. Then she asks them to flip their papers over and record their answers to one question on the back: Where will I begin tomorrow? She slides between the groups gathering the task sheets and excusing students from class. That evening, she spends time skimming each of their notes, mostly jotting prompting questions in the margins—"What does this mean?" "Why is this important?" "How does this compare to . . . ?" She notices room for further explanation in many of their answers.

On the third day of the project, Ms. Dobetter elects to start class with a minilesson designed to deepen learners' background knowledge about how cells function. Based on their questions from the previous day, she and her students create a glossary of important terminology related to cells. During work time, learners rejoin their expert groups, get their notes back, and are encouraged to extend their written explanations with their new learning from today's minilesson. Next their job is to prepare to move to their cell groups and talk about their organelles. She has prepared a graphic organizer (Figure 11.7) for all to use as they listen and learn from their organelle peers.

Now reunited with their original cell groups, students share what they each learned about their organelles. All are feverishly taking notes, knowing that this information is the fodder for their upcoming debate. When one organelle is not explained in sufficient detail, peers prompt that student to explain further so that all can understand the roles each plays. After this work time with their cells, students close their learning by looking over their notes and recording on an exit ticket, "What will you need to know in order to decide which organelle should be voted out?" Learners write quietly. After the classes leave for the day, Ms. Dobetter gathers the students' exit ticket questions and records them on chart paper: What is a protein? What are amino acids? Once the cell is formed, why does it need a nucleus?

Ms. Dobetter begins class with these questions on day four: she asks students to discuss the questions with their expert groups and to decide which are most important to answer. During work time, learners look to their books and research materials as resources, and Ms. Dobetter does her best to maintain a stance as coach—conferring with each group, rather than slipping into becoming the expert who answers all of the questions.

Organelle	What does it do?	Why is this important?
Nucleus		
Endoplasmic reticulum		
Ribosome		
Cell membrane		
Golgi apparatus		
Mitochondria		

FIG. 11.7 *Organelle Notes*

The Workshop Model and Project-Based Learning

In this learning sequence, you see Ms. Dobetter use the workshop model on two levels—the daily level and the project level.

On a daily basis, she frames students' work time with an introductory minilesson. Some of these include direct instruction about content. On other days, she is simply reminding students of what came before and where they are headed, then offering instructions for work time. During daily work time, she confers and supports students in their work, then closes each class with an opportunity for all learners to gather their learning and thinking for the day. During some class sessions, she uses a "catch and release" structure, switching back and forth several times between whole group instruction and small group or individual work time (Bennett 2008).

In addition to the daily workshops, there is a workshop that encompasses the entire scope of the project: she begins with a minilesson familiarizing her students with the world of cells by examining specimens under microscopes. The bulk of project work time is invested in the "Organelle Survivor" research and discussion, and the project closes with reflection and assessment on the final days.

This example illustrates how workshops within workshops can anchor and promote student learning by breaking long-range tasks into smaller steps, and maintaining a strong focus and clear expectations throughout.

After some time on the questions, Ms. Dobetter changes the subject slightly and asks each expert group to stop and rank the organelles in order of importance. Heated discussion ensues. Ms. Dobetter closes class with more individual writing time. Two questions are on the board: Which organelle is least valuable? Why? Students think this through silently; as Ms. Dobetter notices them finishing their thinking, she collects papers and excuses the group, reminding them that tomorrow is the day that their cells will actually decide who survives (see Figure 11.8).

The air is abuzz with excitement on the fifth day of the project. Students take their seats in cell groups and listen to instructions: they will each have a turn to speak, going around the circle. They may not interrupt one another, but only need listen carefully. The goal is to arrive at a consensus. The question they are to answer is "Which organelle can we do without? Why?" After a few minutes of required silence allowing students to gather their thoughts, Ms. Dobetter asks the cells to get started. While they share their thinking, she circulates with a clipboard, recording particularly astute or interesting comments on a transparency.

"I am thinking we don't need the nucleus, because we are already constructed. We do not have to reproduce, so we can ditch the nucleus and go on autopilot."

"I don't think we have to have the endoplasmic reticulum. It just holds the ribosomes. They could just float freely in the cytoplasm, and I think it would work alright."

After time for each individual to state a case, Ms. Dobetter asks each cell to tally its members' opinions, then invites students to go around their cell again, each taking another turn to talk and respond to the first round. She encourages learners to continue

Day 1: Microscope activity; notice and wonder	Day 2: Form cell groups; begin expert group research	Day 3: Report to cell groups; develop research questions	Day 4: Research in expert groups
Day 5: Survivor discussions	Day 6: Reflection writing	Day 7: Quiz	

FIG. 11.8 *Organelle Survivor Project Calendar*

this round-robin of sharing until everyone feels they have had a chance to say what they are thinking. Some students find this structure frustrating, but Ms. Dobetter implores them to stick with it in a spirit of democracy. Time is running short. "You have to decide now," she says. "If you don't have consensus, just vote." She forces an opinion from each team, then asks a recorder to document their group's reasoning. Tempers are heated; voices are loud. The bell rings. Ms. Dobetter collects decisions at the door.

By the next day, the tension in the room has dissipated, though she can still see some sour faces and dissenting voices. Today Ms. Dobetter has rearranged the chairs into rows again, inviting students to leave behind the group identities of the week.

This day is a day of reflection. Five questions are on the board. Students work quietly to record their thinking:

What is a cell?

What is an organelle?

Which organelle did your group decide to vote out? Why?

What do you think will happen to your cell without that organelle?

After allowing appropriate writing time, Ms. Dobetter invites the group to talk more about their experience of this project. First, she takes a poll and finds out which organelles were deemed unnecessary. After some discussion about the rationale for these decisions, she asks, "Was it hard to decide who to vote off? Why?" Students share the difficulties they encountered with the task; some call it "rigged." Ms. Dobetter feigns curiosity and listens with interest as her students explain the interdependent nature of living cells. "Hmm," she says, "so really we can't get rid of anyone?"

"Quiz tomorrow!" she ends class by reminding the learners that the next day they will be assessed individually for their knowledge about organelles. This quiz, along with Ms. Dobetter's participation notes and students' daily writing tasks, will form their grade for this project.

Ms. Dobetter sits typing up a simple quiz on organelle structure and function for the next day. Rather than asking students simply to define the organelles, she asks them synthesis questions:

Which organelles could we live without? Why?

Describe how the organelles work together to keep a cell alive.

How are cells an example of the big idea, stability?

She exhales heavily, confident that her learners have already met the most important learning goals of this project. She leaves school that afternoon grateful that not a box of gelatin was spilled in her class this year in the name of science learning.

So What?

How does Ms. Dobetter's "Survivor" project compare to the cell models her classes had constructed in the past? In Figure 11.9, let us take a look again at our five vowels.

Ms. Dobetter's new project engages more students more deeply and thereby meets understanding goals more effectively. Through this example, Ms. Dobetter models for us the courage to rethink an existing project in the name of student understanding. She also demonstrates that a great project idea is not sufficient. Daily work time must be structured and supervised; learning must be guided each step of the way to ensure that the process is accessible and successful. For a brilliant task to meet its full potential, it must be coupled with high-quality workshop model instruction every step of the way.

"Yah, but . . ."

- *"We have no time for projects in my classes."*

Many teachers do find their semesters so packed with content to cover that no time is left for projects. At the same time, it may be worth considering the virtues of packing together several learning goals into one project. In working on the organelle project de-

	Cell Model Project	**Organelle "Survivor"**
Understanding	Understanding may or may not be derived from this task.	Understanding is created through participation, and is required for participation.
Outcome	Students create posters.	Students engage in research, then a discussion and decision making process.
Important	In this project, students are learning the roles of the organelles.	In this project, students are learning how each cell is an interdependent system. Cells are one example of the big idea, stability.
Engaging	Some students enjoy artistic creations such as models, and would have been highly engaged in this task.	Some students enjoy competition discussion and debate, and would appreciate the creativity inherent in this project.
Accessible	Students worked individually and approached this project at their own comfort level.	Knowledge is socially constructed in both stages of the jigsaw. Students are challenged by peers to deepen their understanding.

FIG. 11.9 *Vowel Analysis of the Cell Poster Versus Organelle Survivor*

scribed above, Ms. Dobetter's students developed an understanding of the work of cells—as well as of living systems, and of the bigger idea of interdependence. While the project did consume almost two weeks of work time, much learning was accomplished in the process.

- *"Our school has no money to buy supplies for projects."*

While most every school I have ever visited feels some level of want, this need not rule out the possibility of creating engaging projects with students. We can find many supplies by scavenging recyclable materials or shopping at the dollar store. Often, if parents know in advance the sorts of things we may need during the year, they can help by keeping their eyes open for those materials.

- *"Some of my students bring in work that I am sure their parents did for them."*

Our students could do a lot worse than to have parents who want to help them with their science projects. Still, whoever does the work does the learning, so it is important that students do take on the tasks themselves. To this end, we can be proactive in explaining our expectations to students and parents, and require that work be completed in class to the extent possible. In the event that a student does bring in a project that appears not to have been her own creation, what remains important is what she learned; we can use oral or other assessments to ascertain how much each individual understands.

- *"I don't have any ideas."*

It is hard to think of new, great ideas for projects. It is helpful to talk with other teachers at your school, at conferences, wherever you get the opportunity. Ask them to share the best projects they have going. You can also ask friends and relatives about any science projects they remember from their own school days—often these are interesting jumping off points for new ideas. National Science Teachers' Association (NSTA) publications and other online resources offer clearinghouses for idea sharing among teachers. Above all, I think, it is important to use the planning questions above and think each project through in order to make it your own. The first time you conduct a new project with your students, it might not turn out perfectly, but that is your first step in the ongoing refinement of the project design process. You will get there.

CHAPTER 12

Activities

Teachers can refine even the briefest learning activities by establishing a clear purpose, closely linked to the unit's learning goals, and ensuring that students will be thinking like scientists throughout the task.

Think Tank

- How do I choose activities for my class?
- How do I use activities in my class?

The class is boisterous, some students seated around tables, others bobbing about the room. Two different tasks appear to be taking place: some groups are huddled over posters, while others' desks are strewn with photocopied word searches hiding unit vocabulary. All the activities relate to the seed cycle. The teacher is conferring with one group, while the rest of the class carries on.

At one table of apparent word searchers, everyone is talking about tonight's dance. After a few minutes of trying to make sense of the scene, I cannot help myself. "What are you supposed to be doing?" I ask the girls.

One, whose hair is done with great care, replies with a blank look, "Nothing."

"What is this?" I poke at the paper on the table.

"Oh. We already finished our poster," she gestures to the wall. "So we're supposed to do that."

"What was your poster about?"

"Seeds."

"What did you learn from it?"

"Nothing." The scrawled poster, a rough sketch of the cross section of a flower, is labeled and some of the terms are defined. The word search is blank. "What happens if you don't do this?" I ask, pointing to the paper.

"Nothing." She turns back to her friends' conversation.

Reflection

Why does this student keep using the word "nothing" to describe her work?

How could these activities better serve students in their learning?

The activities in the class described above did not seem to evoke student thinking. The first is a copying exercise where learners are asked to work in a group to replicate a textbook diagram on bigger paper. The other is a simple hunt for spelling words in a cluster of jumbled letters. Students could complete both of these tasks with very little thinking about or understanding of the actual seed cycle. Further, students do not seem to feel accountable for their learning, or for completing quality work. These activities, time-fillers at best, need revision in order to be worthy tasks promoting student thinking and learning.

Classroom activities serve the gamut of purposes and address the diverse learning styles of all of our students. In order to make best use of activities in class, we must design for and facilitate thinking throughout.

What Is an Activity?

For my purposes in this book, I use the term "activity" as a catchall category for everything that is not a reading, lecture, discussion, demo, lab, project, or fieldwork. Many teachers integrate various short, one-period instructional activities into each unit. These may be drawn from the textbook, the workbook, a resource book, the Internet, the file cabinet, the teacher across the hall, or one's own imagination. They represent the gamut of creativity. Activities often involve manipulatives, art supplies, and group interaction. Activities are often designed to be "fun."

Many sources offer these types of small science tasks. Yet it is our duty as conscientious consumers of curriculum to ensure that the activities we select make good use of our students' minds.

Keeping thirty-plus teenagers safe, focused, and learning hour after hour is one of the toughest jobs I have ever done. In my early years as a teacher, I sometimes settled for the first two goals—safe and perhaps focused—and worried less about the goal of actual *learning*. It was just too much for me some days. At times, I resorted to filler activities photocopied from a book or downloaded from the Internet. These, at least, provided some essential quiet time in class allowing me to confer and visit with individuals while the other students "worked."

Once I realized how much time and paper were being wasted in my room, I got into the habit of tweaking and adjusting activities found elsewhere in order to ensure that these tasks met my intended learning goals. I did not have to start from scratch—although, at times, I would.

Effective learning activities, I found, have three distinguishing features: They

- have a clear purpose,
- are directly tied to and supportive of the big ideas and the unit's learning goals, and
- require students to engage as scientific thinkers.

Let us look at the range of possible activities and see how these three guiding principles can help us to refine some tasks.

Types of Activities

Based on my experience observing in many science classrooms, most activities I see can be divided into some general categories.

- *Exploratory:* Students use or examine specimens and tools, often for the first time, with the goal of becoming familiar with them.
- *Vocabulary Building:* Students practice important unit terminology.
- *Data Collection:* Students record observations.
- *Data Analysis:* Students read or analyze data tables, graphs, maps, charts, or other information.
- *Presenting Information:* Students color or create posters, drawings, models, or other representations of scientific phenomena.
- *Content Review:* Students play games such as Bingo or Jeopardy based on science content.
- *Media Consumption:* Students watch video or DVD presentations, or research topics on the Internet.

Activities in these categories offer a broad range of effectiveness in terms of getting students thinking well about important science content. For example, imagine being asked to read and answer a set of simple multiple-choice questions about a given graph, as opposed to being asked to create an original graph representing a data set. Or consider the difference between practicing vocabulary by completing a crossword puzzle in which the clues are textbook definitions, versus creating a concept map relating important terms to one another. Activities can range from evocative to downright boring. Let's shoot for the former.

The Role of Activities

Activities can be powerful tools able to carry across or reinforce an important concept or idea. For example, from a real-life model accurately draw a monocot flower; from life, draw a dicot flower; then, create a Venn diagram comparing the two. Activities can also be aimless in terms of science learning. For example, color in a drawing of a flower.

The best activities increase student engagement and reinforce important content in meaningful ways. Such activities usually are not situated on a worksheet. Excellent activities are purposeful, meaningful learning endeavors inviting students to develop and demonstrate understanding.

Knowledge	Comprehension	Application	Analysis	Synthesis	Evaluation
Define Label List Name State Write	Describe Explain Illustrate Paraphrase	Apply Compute Construct Demonstrate Solve Use	Analyze Categorize Compare Contrast Separate	Create Design Develop Hypothesize Invent	Critique Judge Justify Recommend

FIG. 12.1 *Bloom's Taxonomy (adapted from the work of Benjamin Bloom)*

Thinking and Understanding

The goal of any activity is getting and keeping students thinking as scientists about the content learning targets of the unit. In planning for thinking, we could turn to the five essential features of inquiry (see Chapter 1) for some good ideas about the kinds of work activities we could ask students to do. Bloom's Taxonomy (also described in Chapter 1) offers a broad overview of thinking skills to consider integrating, as shown in Figure 12.1.

Which of these sorts of thinking do you believe promote understanding? The types of thinking toward the right side of this chart are considered "higher order," requiring increased intellectual energy and producing greater gains in understanding. These, then, are the sorts of thinking we would ideally ask our students to do more of the time. Surprisingly, the terms toward the left of the list seem to constitute much of what students are asked to do in school: define, describe, label. No wonder they need our help developing their confidence and skills as scientific thinkers!

In his meta-analysis, *Classroom Instruction That Works,* Robert Marzano (2001) and his colleagues identify a list of the nine most effective approaches to supporting student learning. Marzano's list includes

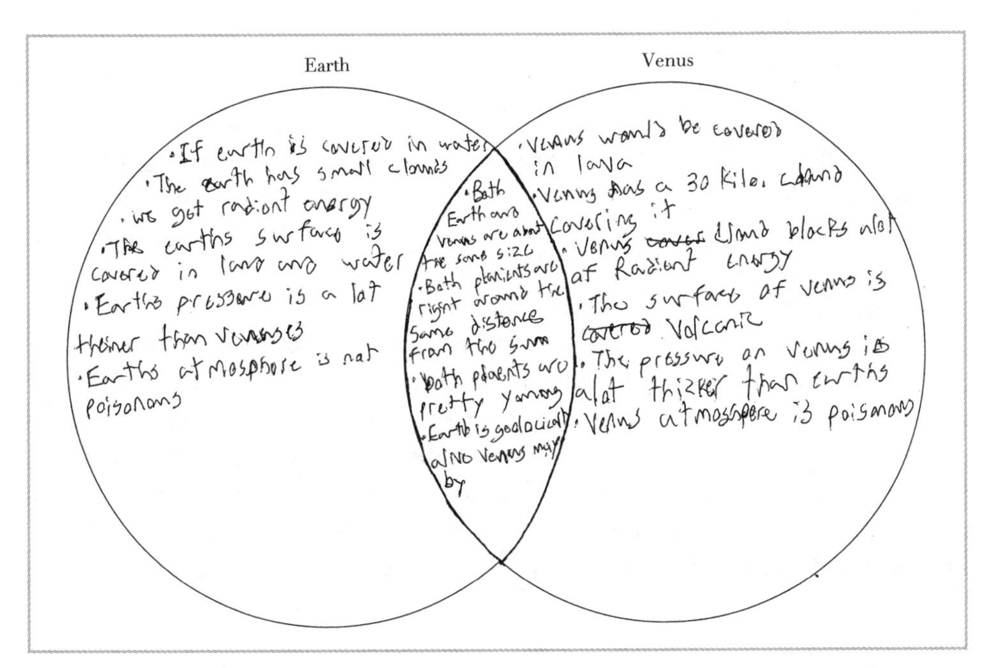

FIG. 12.2 *Venn Diagram Comparing the Earth to Venus*

- identifying similarities and differences,
- summarizing and note taking, and
- nonlinguistic representations.

These three types of tasks can be incorporated into a variety of activities: Rather than defining terms, students can compare them with a Venn diagram (as seen in Figure 12.2). Rather than answering questions about a graph, students could summarize what it means. Rather than labeling a schematic of an engine, students could draw pictographs representing the function of each part. When we strive to integrate Marzano's research and Bloom's taxonomy into our task designs, ideas for revision abound.

Ideal Activities

Let us look at some common activities and find opportunities to transform them into more thought-provoking ones.

Exploratory

Teachers often use exploratory activities at the beginning of the year (or a unit). We may invite students to explore new tools (lenses, magnets, or measuring devices, for example) or materials (specimens, artifacts, or images, for example). Whatever we are exploring, the purpose of exploration ought to be *understanding*.

A standard exploratory activity might be found on a worksheet: a class being introduced to microscopes is asked to read a short text and then label the parts on a diagram; a group beginning a study life cycles is asked to cut out numbered pictures representing each stage, then glue those in order on construction paper. In these standard exploratory activities, the learners are one step removed from the actual tool or specimens; meanwhile, the thinking skills required are limited to labeling and sorting.

A quick and easy fix for both of the tasks described above would be to

- give the students real materials to work with—a microscope, a set of preserved specimens—and
- give students a thinking task to do while looking.

For example, learners could be asked to create a Venn diagram comparing a dissecting microscope to a reflecting one. In order to do this, yes, the students will need to learn the names of the parts and their jobs in making the instruments work, but the next step is utilizing that information—the comparison.

Alternately, students could be asked to do some noticing and wondering about how the microscope functions. Or students could read and learn about microscopes in order to write a user's guide to this tool. Students could even study simple microscopes and then, based on their understanding, invent ways of making a more powerful, more effective one. All of these tasks accomplish the same purpose of understanding the microscope, but each asks the student to do more than label and memorize—to first understand, and then do something with that understanding. These are just some possibilities in terms of making exploratory activities more thought provoking.

Activities and the Workshop Model

Even for a short learning task, students benefit when we introduce them to their work with the workshop model. As described in Chapter 3, we need to give students a learning purpose for their work, engage their minds in the topic, and model the thinking we expect them to do independently. During the activity, we support learners by conferring and encouraging their progress. To close even a brief task, it is beneficial to pause and ask the group to reflect on how they did and what they learned.

Vocabulary Building

Science introduces and requires students to know vast numbers of new terms. Mentioned in Chapter 10, students enrolled in a typical first year college biology course are expected to learn more new words than a learner taking a first year of foreign language (Williams 1992)! Students *do* need support in grappling with all of the new words they encounter in our science classes.

Vocabulary tasks are helpful supports throughout a learning sequence. Standard vocabulary tasks may include finding and defining boldface words from a chapter, solving a crossword puzzle, or locating terms in a word search grid. These activities expose students to the words and their definitions in a few different formats, but do not ask learners to engage with this information in deeply meaningful ways that require understanding.

In order to empower students to make meaning of science words, some savvy teachers introduce students early on to the Greek and Latin roots of many science terms. All year long, students can draw on their understanding of these prefixes, suffixes, and root words in order to decipher such terms as *chronology*—from the term *chronos* meaning "time," and the suffix *-ology* meaning "study of."

To this end, students can build their own glossaries of science terms and keep these charts with them all year long. A glossary might include the root word itself, the meaning in words and pictures, examples and definitions of science words that include this root, and possibly space for common words—not only in English, but also in other languages students know—utilizing this root. Each learner can maintain a four- or five-column chart with these sections in the back of her binder, referring and adding to it throughout her studies. This structure, modeled in Figure 12.3, can go a long way toward empowering students as meaning-makers throughout their future work in the vocabulary-laden field of science.

In addition to maintaining a chart of root words, students can develop similar tables to record vocabulary from a specific unit. A unit vocabulary chart might include columns for the term, the root words found in that term, the definition in the student's own words (perhaps in the student's first language, as well as English), a nonlinguistic representation of the term, and an example (as depicted in Figure 12.4).

In addition to these recording systems requiring original thinking and multiple representations of meaning, teachers can invite students to practice and use unit vocabulary in meaningful ways. When studying minerals, learners could write and share a

Root	Definition in Words	Definition in a Picture	Sample Science Words	Sample Common Words
chronos	time		chronometer chronological	chronic
-ology	study of		biology geology	phrasology sociology

FIG. 12.3 *Sample Root Words List*

Term	Roots	Meaning	Picture	Example
abiotic	a = not bio = alive	non-living		a rock
terrestrial	terra = earth ial = related to	having to do with Earth		terrestrial plants live on land, not water

FIG. 12.4 *Sample Unit Vocabulary Chart*

children's story by explaining important terms, perhaps with illustrations. To practice meanings, students could make and play cards: each term written on one card, a player picks two, and explains what they have to do with one another. To investigate the relationships between important terms, students could design concept maps (see Chapter 4). Opening up ongoing conversations about new words and their meanings with a classroom "word wall" gives students ownership of this knowledge. In all of these tasks, students are engaging their minds with the content in meaningful ways.

Data Collection

Data collection is an important skill for working scientists. The second essential feature of inquiry asks us to give priority to evidence—data. Scientists' observations are the bases of their hypotheses, theories, and conclusions. Through classroom activities, students can learn about the range of data collection strategies, including understanding the meaning of various units of measure; reading instruments to gather quantitative data; creating systems to record and organize data; employing their senses (but not tasting or smelling!) and then finding appropriate descriptive words to document qualitative data; and drawing a specimen accurately from life.

Ideally, data collection takes place within the context of a lab—but, at times, data collection tasks stand alone within a unit. Many common data-related activities include playing games to learn to use measuring tools. I admit that I conducted a version of the "Metric Olympics" for several years running, but eventually recognized that I was missing opportunities to weave data collection into authentic content learning experiences. Practice measurement and data collection within the context of your studies, not as a separate unit on the process of science.

When you do have occasion to ask your students to collect data based on a demonstration or observation experience, engage them more deeply as scientists in understanding data and data collection. Invite learners to hone their observational skills by drawing life drawings of their own. When feasible, rather than providing an organizational structure for data collection, train learners to devise their own data tables, to make meaning of data for themselves in a way that makes sense to them.

Data Analysis

Data analysis is an important science skill and one that standardized test writers seem to love to assess: interpreting data tables and reading graphs. Often classroom tasks inviting students to practice their data analysis skills are akin to those presented on standardized exams: Based on this bar graph, in which year did Quito, Ecuador, experience the greatest rainfall? Based on this line plot, how much taller did the tomato plant grow in the third week? Based on this box and whisker plot, what is the mean birth rate of sub-Saharan African countries?

Students do need to learn to read and understand graphs in order to develop explanations based on evidence, as described in the third essential feature of inquiry. This sort of true data analysis takes place when we ask and teach students to really *analyze*, not just read, the data related to your current unit of study.

For example, a teacher introducing a unit on human population dynamics might select a few of the unique graphs from Joni Seager's 2004 *New State of the Earth Atlas* and ask students to interpret them by

- looking for trends,
- making predictions,
- proposing alternate representations of the data,
- developing questions based on the data, or
- synthesizing the stories a series of graphs tell.

These types of analysis tasks—different from simply reading graphs and charts—invite students to think as scientists about scientific evidence. Data analysis can be a wonderful entry point into a unit, getting students thinking about the facts of the topic. Or data analysis may be an appropriate end point, a chance for students to apply what they learned about a topic to a concrete data set. Even anyplace in between, data analysis tasks are worthy thinking practice when we ensure that thinking is integral.

Presenting Information

Usually toward the end of a unit, instructors may invite students to demonstrate content knowledge creatively. Presentation formats include

- posters,
- drawings,
- skits,
- comic strips,
- narrative writing, and
- model building.

Most of these creative tasks fit into the category of Projects (see Chapter 11), but sometimes with brief activities we ask students to present information. How can we ensure thinking is integral to the task?

- Rather than asking learners to draw a schematic of a refrigerator based on the diagram in the book, let them design and create a better refrigerator, and justify the improvements.
- Rather than asking learners to build and label a clay model of a dip slip fault based on the sketch in the textbook, let them design a ride that will demonstrate to the rider what it would actually feel like to experience the movement as a dip slip fault shifts.

These are just a few ideas of creative ways for students to present what they know. The difference is that these tasks ask students to, rather than simply reiterate information, understand and create something original based on their knowledge. In revising the informational presentations we assign, consider especially the kinds of thinking the task requires of students.

Content Review

Most teachers feel we owe it to our students to let them know what will be on each test and to give learners an opportunity to review at the end of a unit. Typical review activities can take many forms—filling out a question sheet similar to the questions on the test, or perhaps playing Bingo based on unit vocabulary (each student writes the terms in the boxes on his 5 x 5 card, and the teacher reads definitions instead of numbers).

Review activities can be about synthesis, though, rather than simply recall.

- By way of reviewing, teachers can invite students to develop concept maps illustrating how all of the unit's important terminology relates.
- A game of "Pictionary" encourages student artists to develop nonlinguistic representations or concepts and terms while guessers rack their brains to make meaning of their peers' work.

Students may be able to develop review games of their own, yet they are served best when these learning tasks ask them to practice meaning making, ensuring that learners are able to transfer knowledge to new, novel situations.

Media Consumption

A vast number of sources provide media products designed to teach science: DVDs, films, downloadable slide shows, computer simulations, virtual dissections, podcasts, websites, and more! If we are not careful, our students can become simply an audience for science content.

Some teachers work hard to design Web quests requiring students to hone their research skills; others carefully preview videos and design detailed viewing questions to help students follow along and record information as they watch. Media consumption in the classroom is seductive; electronically delivered content is alluring, and the classroom work of the teacher is reduced when a virtual expert takes the helm. Let us approach media with care and caution, using it as a tool for understanding and not a replacement for student thinking.

Media in the classroom can promote thinking in a variety of ways:

- students can watch and then summarize films in their own words;
- learners can be trained as critical consumers, able to discuss what a film did or did not do well, and how it might be revised to more effectively deliver information;
- in researching on the Internet, students can practice their skills at determining importance as they locate information that truly answers their research questions.

As well as being thoughtful consumers of media, learners can create their own. Projects might include producing slide shows, films, websites, or other electronic means of sharing what they understand. Criteria for quality media productions can be based on students' own experience as media consumers in science class and elsewhere (for more on projects, see Chapter 11).

Whenever classroom activities involve media, we must find ways to make students active thinkers about, rather than a passive audience for, science.

Matching Activities to Learning Targets

This list of ideas could go on and on. But what you really need is an activity that suits your content and students. You have two choices—use (or revise) someone else's idea, or create your own.

Revising Activities

If you are too busy to spend time thinking up your own, original, well-tuned activities for every single week of the school year, good news: no need! You can turn to a wealth of resource books and online sources for ready tasks. Yet as you embrace activities authored by others, approach these with a selective eye and openness to revising as needed: you want activities that are purposeful, connected to big ideas, and minds-on.

For example, let's say you hopped on the Internet and downloaded several tasks related to the hydrologic cycle. How can you pick and choose, modify or merge them into a meaningful, manageable mental task culminating in content mastery? Ask yourself these questions:

- What is the purpose?
- What kinds of thinking are students asked to do?
- What kind of product results?
- How does that product demonstrate understanding?

Answers to these questions are occasions to revise or rethink or recycle the material in order to develop something worthy of your students' fine minds. Perhaps parts of the activity are worth hanging onto while others need changes. Use all the good ideas you can find, and build from them.

Consider this example. One year, in a nifty library book, I found a sundial design: all you had to do was photocopy the page and cut out and assemble the parts to create a sundial. "What a terrific idea!" I thought. But where was the student thinking in cutting and pasting? I decided to take their idea and make it my own—students would design and create their own sundials. No pattern. No hint. I would just let them figure it out based on their background knowledge and an experimental process. To me, this seemed like a terrific new version of the library book task because learners would be involved from the design stage, creating from their own imaginations and prior knowledge a system to use the sun's movement across the sky to count the hours of the day. More on this later.

Inventing Activities

Now if you do have the time and heart to make up your own activities from scratch, I salute you! Here are some starting points to walk you through the planning process.

- What do I want students to understand?
- What kinds of thinking will lead to that understanding?
- What sort of activity will require that thinking?
- What products will they create?
- How will that product demonstrate understanding?

Whether revising or creating, consider what you want students to understand, to think about in order to reach that understanding, as well as what they will create to demonstrate their understanding. Once you have those basics decided, you are ready to plan your instruction around the activity.

Planning for Success

Remember the sundial task I described earlier? No one succeeded! Why? They did not have enough information, and neither did I, about how to make a sundial work! Here is a great example of a good idea gone bad.

What could I have done differently? One thing I have learned is that if you are going to ask students to create or do something novel, it is important to try it yourself first, even if you never show it to anyone or tell them you did it. Walking through the process of the task yourself shows you the challenges and pitfalls your students will have to overcome to succeed.

Once you know the stumbling blocks and what students will need, use the workshop model to set learners up for success (see Chapter 3). Even though your activity may use just a portion of a class period, a well-thought out minilesson before the work time will make the difference for some students between success and time squandered. This may mean sharing a model of a finished product, doing a think-aloud about how you would approach the task, or describing what you want the work time to look like. These few minutes of frontloading can ensure much greater student success. Conferring during work time will seal the deal.

Assessment

If you only gave learners thirty minutes to work on an activity, do you want to spend several hours grading it? Probably not! Here are some ideas for briefly assessing and giving feedback.

- Invite students to self-assess.
- Have students share and evaluate one another's work.
- Note points or assessments on a clipboard as you walk around during work time.
- Assess based only on one portion of the product.
- Orally assess students' understanding during work time.
- Create a quick quiz to assess the understanding goal after the activity.

Most important, though, is that in even a short activity, students must know the purpose—the learning goal—from the outset and therefore be motivated to make good use of their time. The task may not even have to "count" in terms of points in a grade book, but everything counts as a means to student learning.

Regardless of what sorts of activities we are planning for our students, we need to select those that will purposefully advance students' thinking about and understanding of the unit's learning targets. Here are some planning questions to support your efforts to this end.

Activity Design: Teacher Planning Questions

What is the purpose of the activity?

What do students need to think about and learn through this experience?

What do I already have?

What might need to be improved?

How need I revise it?

How will I set students up for success?

What evidence of understanding will be assessed?

Dobetter Activities

Ms. Dobetter has been hanging onto a favorite activity for years: atom model mobiles constructed of sugary cereal over the course of two class periods. It is a standard every autumn as she introduces the rudiments of chemistry to her sixth-grade general science class. This year, she decides to see whether it could be revised to be a more effective stepping-stone to students' understanding of scale and structure, a big idea. She starts by looking over the teacher planning questions.

What is the purpose of the activity?

I want students to understand all of the information contained in a periodic table entry, like what atomic number, weight, mass, electron configuration, symbol and so forth—what they all mean. Atoms are a great example of the big idea, scale and structure, and I want to do a better job of driving that home with this task.

What do students need to think about and learn through this experience?

Well, in the past, they did not need to think about much. There was a lot of—really—copying. What I would like students to actually think about is how and why the periodic table is important, and why it is organized as it is. I want students to learn to read the periodic table, but more importantly to value the scientific thinking behind its design.

What do I already have?

Well, for years, we have been doing this thing with hangers and construction paper and Fruit Loops where the students create mobiles to represent their element from the periodic table. You know, the Fruit Loops are the subatomic particles, and the kids make a nucleus and all of the shells, and then we get to hang them from the ceiling tiles. They always seem to really like it, very hands-on.

What might need to be improved?

I think I need to revise it to make it more about thinking, and less about copying. Really, they are just creating a three-dimensional model of a two-dimensional periodic table entry. Not a lot of higher-order thinking skills required there.

How need I revise it?

Well, maybe making a model of an atom is not so helpful. Maybe they could be doing something different to meet this same goal of understanding a periodic table entry. Let me look back at Bloom's Taxonomy . . . maybe instead I could have them really study the organization of the periodic table as a whole and then suggest alternate representations of it. To do so would require an understanding of all of the information contained in a periodic table entry, and then some.

How will I set students up for success?

I think I will need to explain, define all the terms—*symbol, atomic number, atomic mass, electron configuration*, and so on—and show how they are usually organized in the table. Then perhaps I will give students time to do some noticing and wondering about the table, engage in a conversation, and answer questions before I ask them to justify why it is as it is.

What evidence of understanding will be assessed?

I think by reading their justifications or alternate proposals, I will be able to get a good sense of what they understand. I do have 150 students, so I think I will just skim their work quickly. This may not be as fun as the Fruit Loops project, but I always felt bad about wasting all that cereal and glue anyhow.

Ms. Dobetter's Constants Checklist

1. *Which feature of inquiry will I emphasize? How?*
Explanations based on evidence. Students will be looking at the periodic table and developing alternative structures. They will need to explain those, and to justify them with evidence.

2. *What is the big idea, and how will I bring it to life?*
Scale and structure, both the table and the elements themselves. I think students will be looking closely and thinking about the structures of each in order to do this task well.

3. *Which elements of the workshop model will I employ?*
I think I need to set students up for success by offering sufficient instruction at the outset and conferring throughout work time.

4. *When and how will I assess students' content understanding and skill proficiency?*
Their final products, as well as my notes from our conversations, will serve as the assessments for this activity.

5. *How will students build and experience community through this learning?*
They will be working in small groups on the task, and we will share with the whole. I want to encourage them to think creatively, literally outside the box, and to celebrate their peers' good thinking as well.

Periodic Reasoning

Ms. Dobetter turns to the page in her planner where she had jotted "Atomic Mobiles" and erases those words. In their place, she writes, "Periodic Reasoning," and jots her new plan for the class.

When the day comes, she starts the class off with a frightening story about dihydrogen monoxide, the hidden scourge that can kill and injure us all if we do not beware. After a few minutes weaving her tale, she writes the name of the hazardous substance on the board and waits until a few smarty pants students figure out she is talking about water. She uses this story to help set the purpose, emphasize the importance of understanding the elements.

Next, she passes around a single periodic table entry (oxygen) blown up to fill a full sheet of paper. She gives a copy to each student and also has a version copied onto chart paper, which she hangs at the front of the room. "What is this?" she begins. Some students know, and some do not. Launching from the class' background knowledge about atoms, subatomic particles, and their properties, Ms. Dobetter explains the shorthand information contained in this rectangle in a short presentation. She asks the students to pair up and quickly quiz one another to ensure that no confusion lingers about this basic information before moving on. After answering a few clarifying questions, Ms. Dobetter grabs another set of handouts: color copies of the periodic table.

She asks for silence as students take these in. Then, to ensure learners transferred their understanding from the minilesson, she asks them each to point to a symbol and then calls on a few students to share examples. Next she asks them to each find an atomic mass, again calling on students—knowing that if they do not read her a number with several decimal places, in most cases, they are pointing to the wrong thing. She carries on with a quick review to be sure they are all together on this page, then explains the task:

"Scientist Dmitri Mendeleev developed a periodic table like this one about 150 years ago. In looking at it closely, I think you will understand why he set it up the way he did. So your first job is to write a brief summary of how this periodic table is organized and why. After that, your next task is to develop your own, alternate way of organizing this same information; justify how and why your system works. . . . What questions do you have?"

"Can we work with a partner?"

"I would like you to do the first part, summarizing the format of this table, on your own. Then, once I see that you have that done, you could choose to work with a partner or in a small group to make your own version."

Many students are now looking down, studying the page as fodder for their summaries, wanting to complete that step so that they are able to move to the more creative thinking task. Ms. Dobetter circulates, chats with a few who are sometimes slow to start, and ensures they understand the activity. After a few minutes, hands begin to reach toward fluorescent lights, a request for Ms. Dobetter to check their work.

Circulating, she reviews written summaries, asks probing questions as needed, and encourages more detail or clarity if necessary: "Tell me what you are thinking. Why does that make sense? Is that the only way you have considered? How did you decide?" While visiting with students, she makes quick notes on her clipboard of their understanding; this is her assessment strategy for the day. Soon more than half of the class is clustered together brainstorming and considering how else the periodic table could be organized. As they puzzle, Ms. Dobetter visits with the students still working on their summaries, ensuring they understand and are able to complete the task.

A group calls her over. "Can we cut this up," one student asks, waving the original periodic table in the air, "to make ours?"

"What is your plan?"

"We think we could put the elements in order based on their phases."

"Okay, let's see how that looks" Ms. Dobetter replies. "Max, can you get out the scissors, glue sticks, and some construction paper?" A boy nods and heads to the supply closet.

Soon most groups have decided to follow their lead, not only designing a new idea for organizing the periodic table but also cutting up the old one to use the entries in a new order. Scissors, paper, and glue are put to work as students rethink how and why we organize the elements.

After issuing a five-minute warning, Ms. Dobetter calls work time to a close and gives students just a few minutes to clean up before it is time to share. Some complain of not being done yet; Ms. Dobetter jokes that scientists are never done thinking, so they are in the right class.

Groups volunteer to share their new ideas. Students' new tables are organized by phase, alphabetically by symbols, clustered by electron configuration, and based on chemical properties. The work might not have changed Mendeleev's mind, but Ms. Dobetter is delighted with the ways that her students worked together as scientists to make new meaning for themselves.

As a quick final assessment, Ms. Dobetter asks students to each write a letter to Mendeleev describing the structure of their own unique table and why it makes sense.

No one asked her what happened to the mobiles.

So What?

Ms. Dobetter's courage to reexamine a familiar, successful, hands-on activity allowed her to realize that, while fun, the task was not encouraging her students' scientific thinking. Back at the drawing board with a clear purpose and learning targets, she was able to develop a more minds-on task that, while challenging, supported her students in understanding the content more deeply. Supported in their work with workshop model instruction, students in her class puzzled as scientists to make sense of the characteristics and relationships between the elemental building blocks of the universe.

"Yah, but . . ."

- *"Some of these sound more like projects than activities."*

True, as we reevaluate our activities in hopes of making them richer, they can also become more complex and time consuming. So we must pick and choose. What are our learning goals? How will we reach them? Which activities or projects give us the greatest leverage toward those? Fewer, deeper tasks, rather than a smorgasbord of activities, may serve your students better.

- *"My students love all of the cutting and pasting and creative work we do in science."*

Revising activities does not mean putting away the scissors and glue, as illustrated by Ms. Dobetter's example above. In planning high quality activities, though, our focus needs to be on what students' minds—rather than their hands—are going to be doing.

- *"Our kits are full of activities, all planned out."*

Kits can be a wonderful resource; they vary in the kinds of student thinking they require. You can use the questions in this chapter to review the learning activities in your kits and decide which of them promote higher-order thinking, which to revise, and which to skip entirely. As long as you are effectively driving at the prescribed learning goals of the kit, making modifications should not upset the apple cart.

CHAPTER 13

Fieldwork

With careful planning and clearly identified learning goals linked to thinking tasks before, during, and after an outing, teachers can transform typical field trips into opportunities for students to conduct fieldwork like that of professional scientists.

Think Tank

- Why leave the building?
- How do I focus learning during fieldwork?
- How do I connect learning in the field to learning in the classroom?

Last fall, a fascinating hands-on engineering exhibit came to our local science museum. One day, visiting the museum with my own children, I found the area packed by a throng of middle schoolers and managed to pick up several copies of their assignment sheet left behind on the floor between the life-sized foam catenary arch construction kit and the air-powered rocket launchpad. The teacher-generated handout was designed to guide students' experience in the exhibit. Here is what the crumpled, yellow sheet asked students to do.

> Try to answer the questions below:
>
> Name three kinds of bridges.
>
> Why is the Millennium Bridge a cable bridge?
>
> What do the Golden Gate and the Royal Gorge Bridges have in common?

What did a Denver engineering company do in Singapore?

List two ways the sun's energy can be used.

Name one thing Engineers without Borders does and where.

What is the center of gravity for an airplane?

What allows an airplane to fly?

The students left their handouts behind and were busy constructing towers and rockets, creating boats and bridges, testing aerodynamics and friction by engaging in the hands-on activities of the exhibit.

Reflection

Was this field trip worthwhile?

How did the teacher support opportunities for student thinking?

How will the teacher know what students learned at the museum?

I laud this teacher's good effort to structure students' experience visiting the exhibit, yet her intended task was lost on the learners. Instead of searching the room for facts, they elected to engage in the work of the exhibit. Students might have done a better job documenting their learning during this fieldwork experience if they had been asked different *kinds* of questions.

Many teachers dread the travail of taking students away from school for a day. So much preparation is involved that the task can feel overwhelming. So when we do get up the gumption to take our students on the road, it is worth every ounce of effort to ensure that the experience is not only an exciting change of pace from the classroom routine, but also an authentic, organized experience of thinking and learning. How can we make fieldwork *work*?

Why Field*work*?

The term *fieldwork,* by definition, reflects the work of professional scientists. Fieldwork involves on-site collection of raw data to be studied and analyzed. Fieldwork is a purposeful visit, intimately tied to important research. Distinct from a field *trip,* which is a mere outing, field*work* involves detailed research and planning, thinking and reflection. How can we create the same for our science learners?

Many of us who have had the courage to take students outside of school walls for a broader experience of inquiry have had the misfortune of watching our vision of a day-long learning experience shrink into an hour of mild engagement. Alternately, we have witnessed the frustration of planning for students to accomplish one thing while out on the trip and then watching them, instead, get distracted by another topic entirely—nail polish, perhaps. These disappointments once led me to wonder if it is worth the effort.

In fact, many concerns could deter us from planning fieldwork: cost, distance, risk, the challenge of organizing transportation, complex school policies regarding outings, the difficulty of recruiting chaperones, issues around school schedules and class coverage, and the chore of getting students to return signed permission slips. All of these, though, can be overcome, and these difficulties will pale once students and teachers together enjoy the experience of engaging in learning in the field.

For many convincing reasons, I encourage you to go ahead and call the bus. According to research by Braund and Reiss, well-designed fieldwork can supplement classroom learning in the following ways:

- extend authentic, practical work;
- improve students' integration of concepts;
- offer access to rare materials;
- stimulate further learning;
- promote collaboration and responsibility for learning. (Braund and Reiss 2006)

After many years striving to get fieldwork right for my students, I am convinced that these experiences serve as touchstones for learners farther into the future than we may ever know.

Fieldwork Promotes Community and Culture

One of the best things about leaving the school building with students is that the new environment shifts relationships. We have opportunities to chat with colleagues and learners alike while in transit, during lunch, and while waiting for the bus. These casual conversations are a golden opportunity for us as teachers to develop our own understanding of the people in our community without the time pressures of an ordinary school day.

Additionally, fieldwork creates opportunities for students to relate to one another in new ways: together away from the familiar environment, students' interdependence increases. If learners are not traveling or working in their familiar groups during their fieldwork experience, students are pressed to stretch their wings. These are some of the fringe benefits of fieldwork.

Extending Our Classrooms

I actually began my teaching career far away from a classroom. I worked for a summer adventure program, then taught in a school-based life lab science project before realizing that in order to do what I wanted to do, I needed to go back to school and become a "real" teacher. But those early years working with youth outdoors showed me the power of learning in real-life settings.

My first "real" teaching job was in an Expeditionary Learning (EL) school. The EL school design promotes interdisciplinary studies connected to the world outside of the classroom. Our school owned its own vans, and administrators encouraged teachers to take our students out—not on field *trips* but on field*work,* experiences away from the building that mirrored the work of experts in our areas of study.

This was a fortunate beginning for me. In my first few years in the classroom, I took students on more fieldwork than most educators are able to organize over the course of a career. My colleagues and I figured out a few things that any teacher, whether in an EL school or not, can do to make good use of the world as an extension of her classroom.

Fossil Follies

But the first time I took my middle school students to our local science museum, I was sure they were going to enjoy a titillating afternoon reading every placard and label in the entire dinosaur exhibit. Young Tony was the first one to awaken me from my dream: about fifteen minutes after we arrived, he found me ogling over some apatosaurus bones and asked whether he and his chums could go outside and play football yet.

I was crestfallen. Here we were in an expansive collection of prehistoric artifacts, and all that my seventh-grade boys wanted to do was go out to the park and chase a ball? How could it be? Well, actually, I had not given them anything much better to do! I had not given them anything in particular to think about or any reason to slow down. By the time they found me, they assured me that they had "seen everything."

The next time I took students to the museum, I thought I would be much more savvy: in advance of the field trip, I visited the museum and created a scavenger hunt–type activity for the students. On that trip, learners were more engaged, running back and forth with their pencils and clipboards madly copying from museum signage. Even when we sat down for lunch, they were still talking about who had number seven and where they had found the answer to number nineteen. I was delighted. But soon, it became clear that, busy as they were with their clipboards and pencils, learners retained little knowledge and virtually no understanding of the big ideas about evolution presented in the exhibit. Where had I gone wrong?

Linking Fieldwork to Classroom Learning

As with all learning experiences, fieldwork requires careful planning—clear learning goals and an assessment that requires thinking and demonstrates true understanding.

The very best thing you can do to ensure a quality fieldwork experience is to select fieldwork that supports important content learning goals. Ideally, you would be able to take your students to see a roadcut featuring noticeable rock layers while studying the rock cycle; this outing would be scheduled naturally within the learning cycle of the unit, with related studies and conversations in the classroom before and after the visit.

Alternately, your local museum may be hosting an internationally acclaimed exhibition on human anatomy, and so you might be able to insert a few weeks of study about the body systems in order to make the most of this learning opportunity for your life science students; this way, again, the fieldwork is connected to the classroom curriculum.

Doomed, though, are the field trips with no connection to what is going on at school; while these outings offer students some fresh air and a change of scene, learning opportunities, sadly, are missed. Learning goals, rather than convenience or tradition, need to drive fieldwork selection. As long as you are going to go through all of this trouble, make it worth your while!

Planning for Learning

The workshop model (see Chapter 3) can help us think about how to set students up for success on fieldwork.

- Before the trip, students need to understand the purpose, become interested in the task, and see the thinking work of the trip modeled.
- During fieldwork, students need support to engage and continue working with the teacher through coaching and conferring.
- After the outing, learners need structure to reflect on and make meaning of what they did and learned while away from the building. In this way, the fieldwork can be the text or the task enveloped in a standard workshop experience.

Before

As you begin to plan, consider the big idea and learning outcome, think about what you expect students to do during their fieldwork, and then ask yourself, "What will they need to know and be able to do beforehand in order to make this trip a success?" Take the time to prepare by modeling the thinking skills and a system for recording thinking expected during the outing. Perhaps learners will need to see how to take field notes or record data. Maybe they need you to model interviewing skills or measurement techniques. Whatever the task you've planned, utilize the workshop model to teach necessary skills, ensuring that students are well prepared.

During

On site, set learners up for success by reviewing their task, grouping them in a way that makes sense, and staying involved in their work. Find ways to keep everyone as active and engaged as possible: if you only have five meter sticks, and everyone needs a turn with one, have another task or tool on hand for students to work with while waiting. The group size needs to suit the task, not the available tools, as described in Chapter 5.

Support learners by continuing to confer while they work, even if this means walking distances between them or moving back and forth between groups. Whenever possible, recruit enough chaperones that you yourself as the trip leader do not need to be in charge of a small group. This way, you are free to oversee the outing, move between teams of students, and ensure that everyone is learning.

After

Once back at school, link learning in the field to your classroom experiences. Create follow-up activities to gather students' data, share thinking, and assess students' comprehension of the stated learning goal. These may include presenting research, discussing findings, developing new questions, or synthesizing fieldwork learning with prior classroom experience. One excellent assessment of student understanding of fieldwork learning goals is their ability to apply the particular evidence, examples, or experiences in the field to the broader concepts studied in the classroom. If a learner can say, "We saw the prairie dogs in their natural habitat, and how the airport construction will be encroaching on their land. This is an example of how urban development disrupts ecosystems, an example of the big idea of systems and interactions," we know that the point was made.

Where to Go

Do you remember your own experiences of field trips or fieldwork as a student? Where did you go? What did you learn?

Every part of the country offers unique opportunities for learning outside of classrooms. Many schools plan tried-and-true outings students anticipate from year to year. These may include local museums, zoos, libraries, or science centers. In addition to the obvious, you also might consider visiting some less-frequented fieldwork venues.

Life Sciences: wildlife habitats, wetlands, animal shelters or rescue centers, nursing homes, restaurants, preschools, health centers, university research labs, farms, food production factories, wildlife preserves, national forests, native plant restoration sites, insect research centers (see Figure 13.1), or even your school grounds.

Earth and Space Science: fields or forests, local geologic sites (faults, craters, roadcuts, rock formations, volcanic evidence), mines, local construction sites, water and sanitation plants, landfills, the public works department, planetariums, telescopes, university geology labs, broadcast meteorologists, space centers, rivers, lakes, wetlands, waterways, hollows, valleys, or the highest point of land around.

Physical Science: parking lots, sledding hills, airports, bridges, tall or unique buildings, printing presses, vehicle manufacturing plants, food packaging plants, pharmaceutical companies, university research labs, software companies, poison control centers, race courses, amusement parks, or anyplace else you can think of where students can witness science in action.

This is just a partial list of possibilities. As you walk through your days, look for evidence of science, and consider what your students might be able to learn at the nail

FIG. 13.1 *Baboon Spider*

salon or the baseball field. Perhaps you could make it worth a trip. I was always happily surprised by how cordial professional adults can be at, say, the sewage treatment plant, when I called wanting to bring a group of students to learn about what they do.

Working with Experts

The great thing about visiting with experts is that they know so very much about the topic. The challenge is to help experts share what they know in ways that are appropriate and accessible for students.

Depending on your expert, this may not be of concern, but I suggest talking with your expert before a visit, clarifying your learning goals with her, and brainstorming with her some ways (such as those below) she can engage students as thinkers, rather than just listeners, while you are together.

- Have students come with questions for the expert.
- Ask the expert to walk students through his own thinking process solving an important problem.
- Invite the expert to present to the students some real-world problems or dilemmas related to her work, and to get their input.
- Encourage students to write or ask questions that they think of during the visit.

When to Go

Fieldwork can serve as a springboard into a learning experience, a culminating activity wrapping up a unit of study, or anything in between. The bottom line, though, in selecting a destination is ensuring that it aligns seamlessly with your course's learning goals and assures that you make the most of students' time while away from school.

Scheduling fieldwork can present a huge challenge, so it may be necessary to adjust classroom work to ensure that the fieldwork connects well to current studies. We waste time and energy when we release a herd of students to run through the zoo with no real reason to slow down. Fieldwork must begin and end in the classroom, so be sure to time your outing in such a way that allows for a sandwich of related classroom experience before and afterward.

What to Do

You have selected a terrific site because you know just how much students can learn there. Now you need to stretch beyond the scavenger hunt to create deep thinking activities for students while in the field. Consider the work a professional scientist would do at this site.

Engage in Scientifically Oriented Questions	Give Priority to Evidence	Develop Explanations Based on Evidence
• conduct experiments • develop research questions • interview an expert • investigate careers • test equipment	• count • collect specimens • document observations in field notebooks • draw • gather samples • measure • take photographs	• graph • make inferences • note similarities and differences • sort data

FIG. 13.2 *Some Ideas for What to Do During Fieldwork*

A scientist would arrive with a research question, a specific goal for his or her learning on-site. Take the time to clarify for your class the learning goal of the outing. You may have many to choose from and much to gain from visiting that venue, but you must narrow the focus and choose just one or two.

For example, we could visit a bridge to study measurement, observe geologic features, demonstrate an egg drop container, or examine engineering structures—all of them worthy! It is our duty to choose one or two measurable learning goals related to our coursework, and then to design the students' responsibilities on-site to target that understanding.

Given the learning goal, we can choose from a range of possible activities to serve that purpose on-site. Think about the essential features of inquiry (see Chapter 1) and which of those a student could experience at this site. Figure 13.2 presents a few of the myriad possibilities of what students could do.

Several of the possibilities suggested in Figure 13.2 could be folded together into one fieldwork experience. For example, while visiting a local fossil dig, my students could draw and write in their science notebooks, interview experts, and also take photographs.

In order to ensure students' successful use of time in the field, it is essential that we prepare them for the outing and follow-up on their learning once back at school.

Logistical Planning for Fabulous Fieldwork

One of the difficulties of developing quality fieldwork is that few teachers can afford or are permitted to take students out more than once or twice a year, so they never get near as much practice facilitating these outings as they do leading text-based discussions.

Fieldwork is best shared, so engage colleagues in the planning process, and invite their good thinking both before and after the trip to find ways to improve for next time.

Here are some friendly suggestions on the logistical considerations for orchestrating quality fieldwork.

- *Research.* Choose the best site to meet your learning goals. Consider distance, cost, and the practicalities of your group size before proposing this outing.
- *Get approval.* Find out your school's procedures for organizing a field trip and follow them. Some schools have forms that must be submitted and signed by

several parties. While you are in their office getting signatures, invite school administrators to chaperone.

- *Book the venue.* Some sites have limited openings available for groups, visitors, and tours. Scholarship or reduced admission rates may be available if you register early. As soon as you know where you want to take students, book it.
- *Develop a budget.* If not yet required to do so in the approval stage, develop a budget that includes the cost of transportation, student and chaperone admissions, equipment, and any other expenses associated with the outing. If you are heading to a site unaccustomed to visitors that does not charge a fee, consider taking a small gift to your hosts. Your school or district may have funds available to cover some field trip costs—ask. If the cost may be prohibitive for some families to cover, consider grant writing or fundraising options with your students.
- *Find transportation.* It may be possible to reach the site on foot, via public transportation, in school buses, or in private vehicles (if your school's regulations permit parents and staff to drive students).
- *Recruit chaperones.* In addition to recruiting parents to accompany your group, consider inviting school administrative staff, student teachers (even if they work in another classroom or department), PERAs, specialists, or other volunteers. Clear all chaperones (or drivers) with your administrator.
- *Preview site.* Imagine your students on-site. Find out what, if any, learning materials the destination offers for students. Anticipate safety concerns, picture ideal group size, and identify group meeting areas.
- *Medical preparation.* Know the medical condition of all students and adults in your party. Arrange to take a first-aid kit; your school may have a special one for just this purpose.
- *Gather permissions.* Copy and collect signed permission forms. Make the forms due at least a week before the trip to avoid the last-minute drama of a student unable to participate because of a forgotten form.
- *Train chaperones.* Ideally students will be so well prepared and so keen to engage that they will not require adult prompting while in the field, but just in case this is not the case, it is best to communicate to your chaperones a clear sense of the plan and provide them with some coaching strategies so that they can intervene and support students, rather than just follow a group of unfocused adolescents through the museum.
- *Preview the day with students.* Let them know the schedule of the day, your expectations for their thinking and learning, behavior expectations, and consequences for misbehavior. Talk about what *not* to bring, and that all school rules still apply while on this outing. Ensure that all students understand what they need to bring back with them as evidence of their fieldwork, and how those artifacts will be integral to your next learning steps in class.
- *Plan contingencies with your students.* Give them each your cell phone number or a school number to call in case of being separated from the group. I used to go so far as to have kids write this on their hands. Designate an emergency meeting area.
- *Enjoy!*

√	Task	Notes
	Research and Select a Venue	
	Get Approval (keep copies of all forms submitted)	Approved by: Date:
	Book Venue	Contact Person: Contact Number:
	Budget	Transportation: Admissions: Other:
	Transportation Plan	
	Recruit Chaperones	(Keep list of names and contact info on a separate sheet)
	Preview Site	Learning Resources Offered: Safety Concerns: Meeting Area: Other:
	Review Students' Medical Forms	(Bring copies of information about any students with significant medical conditions)
	Get First-Aid Kit	
	Gather Permission Slips	
	Train Chaperones	Date: Time:
	Prep Students	Emergency Contact Number for Students:
	Enjoy!	

FIG. 13.3 *Fieldwork Logistical Planning Checklist*

Figure 13.3 presents the information in a checklist. You could make a photocopy of it and use it to guide the planning of your students' next wonderful out-of-school learning experience.

Fieldwork, like any instructional approach, takes practice. Going back to the same place year after year allows a teacher the opportunity to build comfort and familiarity with the venue, as well as to hone the on-site learning task. Every time you go, it will be easier and better. As you design and prepare for your outing, here are some questions to think about.

Designing Fieldwork: Teacher Planning Questions

What is the learning goal of the fieldwork?

Where will we go?

What will students do and think about while there?

Before the trip, how can I best prepare students for success?

Once back at school, how will we follow up on the fieldwork experience?

Dobetter Fieldwork

In her usual spirit, Ms. Dobetter decides to brave revising her school's standard eighth-grade zoo field trip to see how much science learning she can pack into the day. Let's see what happens.

What is the learning goal of the fieldwork?

This trip will be part of our unit on adaptations. Our purpose will be to look at animals and how they are adapted to their environments. So I guess the learning goal will be to observe and understand some specific examples of the concepts we are discussing in class, especially convergent and divergent evolution. That is our big idea, evolution.

Where will we go?

Well, actually, the eighth grade always goes to the zoo. That is where we are planning to go again this year, but I have to make it better. Usually, the kids just run around and get into kettle corn fights and annoy the zoo staff.

What will students do and think about while there?

I want them to do some work looking really closely at the animals and their adaptations. I think I will have them select two species and create life drawings of them. The two should be related in that they are either an example of convergent or divergent evolution.

Life drawing, I have found, requires students to look very closely at something, every detail, and to really observe like scientists. Then I will ask them to make a Venn diagram of those two animals' similarities and differences. I will refer them to our general list from class of all different types of adaptations.

Before the trip, how can I best prepare students for success?

Most importantly, I will need to teach them what a life drawing is and build their confidence. I know a lot of students don't have the patience for this. I will show them some examples from early naturalists' notebooks—Darwin's, probably. We will practice in class, drawing pinecones or something.

Also, we will need to revisit how to create a Venn diagram. Perhaps we can practice that around a familiar topic, like cats and dogs, and talk about features to consider, such as habitat, diet, reproduction, and so on.

Logistically, I need to remember to bring clipboards. Kids do much better work when they have a hard surface to write on.

Ms. Dobetter's Constants Checklist

1. *Which feature of inquiry will I emphasize? How?*
I think we will be looking for evidence and explanations based on evidence as we consider convergent and divergent evolution.

2. *What is the big idea, and how will I bring it to life?*
Evolution is the big idea. We have been talking a lot about this topic, so I think students understand it well and will use the concepts correctly.

3. *Which elements of the workshop model will I employ?*
We will definitely have work to do before the trip, practicing the skills needed to attain success at the zoo. Then, when we get back, there will be sharing, reflection, and assessment. The zoo visit itself will be like the "work time."

4. *When and how will I assess students' content understanding and skill proficiency?*
The work they bring back with them, their drawings and Venn diagrams, will be the basis for assessment.

5. *How will students build and experience community through this learning?*
Traveling and exploring together always builds community. Also, once back at school, students will share their work and receive feedback from peers.

Once back at school, how will we follow up on the fieldwork experience?

Students will definitely be responsible for bringing their work back to the class. We will hang it in the room and do a gallery walk, where they give each other written feedback on their products. That way, they will all benefit from seeing one another's examples. Maybe we could even assemble all of the drawings and diagrams into some sort of a display in the hallway or class book to share. I will think more about the final audience, but their work will definitely be peer critiqued and graded. Their final assessment for this unit will ask them to explain examples of both convergent and divergent evolution, so they will need to be ready with their own as well as with some other examples.

In some ways, Ms. Dobetter feels fortunate that the zoo trip is a staple of the eighth-grade curriculum: she does not have to research a site, lobby for approval, or request special funding. Her whole teaching team is going, so they won't have any coverage issues. The trip is already a tradition.

The downside of the tradition is that her students are expecting to get to do what their older brothers and sisters have been doing for years: running past the animals, crowding at the snack bars, and hovering in the gift shop deciding whether or not to part with their spending money. Ms. Dobetter has decided that this aspect of the tradition needs to change.

Before

At a team meeting, she presents her idea that the zoo trip be more connected, this year, to students' work in life science. She explains the adaptations unit in brief and describes to her colleagues the zoo tasks she has planned. They look a little shocked. "How are you going to get *them* to do *that*?" a social studies teacher balks.

"*I'm* not. *We* are," she says, and proceeds to lay out her plan. Many teachers nod as she describes how she will start with classroom-based studies of adaptations, evolution, and life drawing; organizing students into small interest groups led by trained chaperones on-site; and following up with classroom sharing and assessment. Her colleagues know that the zoo trip has not lived up to its learning potential for many years, yet this departure sounds to them like a lot of work. She assures them that it may well be, but that it will be worth the effort.

Ms. Dobetter plans all of the logistics and gets all the forms organized a week before the outing. All ten chaperones turn up for their training, and she appreciates their kind attention as she explains her students' recent studies in science class, presents models of what their zoo task could look like, and offers suggestions for guiding students to success. In addition to distributing copies of logistical information—student lists, the day's schedule, and emergency procedures—Ms. Dobetter has also made copies of the students' task sheet and some chaperone prompts, questions for her fellow trip leaders to ask students who appear stumped or are slacking off on their work. The questions include:

- What are you supposed to be learning about today?
- How will this task help you?
- What is it that you *do* understand about what you are supposed to be doing? What are you confused about?
- What do you think your teacher/parent would say if she saw this (work/behavior)?
- How could you make it better?

While more than half of the chaperones are teachers, Ms. Dobetter knows from experience that even teachers can be shy about getting involved in students' learning outside of their own content area, so she implores all to take ownership of this outing as a learning success.

In class the weeks before the zoo trip, Ms. Dobetter delves into the work of Darwin: students study and critique his line drawings, and practice their own hand at the same. Ms. Dobetter reviews students' understanding of adaptations through an activity designed to remind them of their own uniqueness: they attempt normal tasks like tying shoes, eating, and walking up stairs without such things as opposable thumbs, eyes, and bendable knees (respectively). Ms. Dobetter uses this task to underline the idea that we are each adapted to our environment (or, in the case of humans, our environment is sometimes adapted to us). In connecting their understanding of adaptations and Darwin's work to the zoo plan, Ms. Dobetter introduces the concepts of convergent and divergent evolution and asks students in small groups to brainstorm examples of each.

The day before their departure, Ms. Dobetter models for students their work at the zoo. They have four tasks: two line drawings, each of a different animal; a Venn diagram comparing the adaptations each of those two animals possesses; and an explanation of whether those two animals illustrate convergent or divergent evolution, and why.

In addition to describing the tasks, Ms. Dobetter has created a model of each (based on animals they will not be seeing at the zoo—a whale and a piranha). She shares these models with her students and asks them to critique her work based on a rubric provided. While her models are of high quality, she intentionally does not give her students ideal samples, hoping that in her work they will be able to see room for improvement. She closes class with an exit ticket question, "Describe what you need to do and learn at the zoo tomorrow." In reading these over, she grows in confidence that her students will make good use of the fossil fuels expended to transport them across town.

During

Thursday, the day of the outing, students gather in the auditorium for a review of the plan and tasks. The principal visits with the students to review behavioral expectations on the bus and at the zoo. Ms. Dobetter answers the few questions that arise before directing all to the parking lot.

Once at the zoo, students disperse into their small groups. Each group has a map and needs to decide which areas of the zoo they will visit. Students in each group are not all expected to draw the same animals, but they do need to pick animals in the same vicinity so that their chaperone can visit with each of them while they work. As groups head out, Ms. Dobetter jots notes on where each is headed so that she can find and confer with each.

Ms. Dobetter sighs a great sigh once the entry area is clear and all the groups have set off with their clipboards, pencils, and paper. She pauses to admire the polar bears before tracking down the first of ten groups. She is delighted to find students hunched over their work, straining to see and capture small details of animal anatomy. While not every student is a budding da Vinci, her peeks at their papers indicate that she succeeded in conveying to them the rudiments of life drawing. Ms. Dobetter spends her day circling the zoo at a saunter, conferring with students, chatting with chaperones, and appreciating the focus and good thinking she sees.

Students do end up with time to peruse the exhibits and hover in the gift shop after their work is done, but in all the mood is quite different. Students today came to the zoo as scientists, rather than tourists. Even the zoo staff notices and comments as much.

After

Back at school the next day, Friday, Ms. Dobetter asks students to pair and share their work with a partner who was not in their zoo group. Students look at their rubrics together and give feedback to one another on their finished products. Much of class time is devoted to revision; students' work will be posted Monday for peers to see and learn from, so this is their chance to finalize, revise, and improve.

In closing the day and the week, Ms. Dobetter asks students to take a few minutes to reflect on their learning as follows:

1. What did you learn from your work at the zoo?
2. How was *this* zoo trip different from other visits you have made there?
3. What suggestions do you have for making the zoo fieldwork even better next year?

Over the weekend, Ms. Dobetter flips through their reflections. She finds their answers to number three most interesting; she had braced herself for students to recommend less work and more play time, but actually few students commented to that effect. Instead they said that they would have liked more time to draw, that they would have enjoyed taking paints, and that they wish the spider monkeys could have held still. Their responses suggested that the learners themselves were won over by this shift from field trip to field*work*.

So What?

With the support of her team, Ms. Dobetter significantly structured a traditionally lax outing and created a positive learning experience for her student scientists. While this trip required a significant investment of energy to organize, the rewards included increased student learning, improved student behavior, and colleagues who are rethinking other school outings.

"Yah, but . . ."

- *"My colleagues will never agree to letting me take students out. It is too disruptive to the schedule."*

One of the pitfalls of the comprehensive high school, and other large schools, is the interdependence of the schedule. Coverage can be difficult to negotiate, but consider the following options: rather than getting a sub for yourself while you are away, distribute the students from the classes you are leaving behind to several other teachers' rooms with good work to do. Or give your remaining students research to do, and get the librarian or computer specialist involved in hosting learners. Imposing on colleagues can be tough, but if you need to do this for the sake of student learning, find a way to make it up to them.

- *"I teach 180 students. There is no way I can take them all out at once."*

You don't need to take everyone the same day! Maybe you can make two trips a week for two weeks, and that way ensure that all students enjoy the opportunity without overwhelming yourself. The logistics will take some organizing; if this is not your forte, find a colleague whose it is.

With this approach, the fieldwork experience will fall at different points in the unit for different classes, so your classroom instruction will have to be adjusted accordingly, but this is surmountable.

- *"We have no money for this kind of thing."*

Fieldwork can be expensive, but it need not be. If cost is an issue, consider taking short, free trips close to your school. Or if you do want to visit costly venues, ask for scholarships, discounts, or other group deals. Students may be able to bring money or fundraise (see Chapter 5 for information on *DonorsChoose.org*, a potential funding source).

Once school personnel and community members see that your fieldwork is intimately linked to learning, you may find you receive more support than ever before.

Conclusion

We are counting on you. Your students are counting on you. Your school is counting on you. Your community, your country, and our world. We are all counting on you. The future of our Earth is *truly* in the hands of our teachers. We need to educate a generation of empowered and creative problem solvers prepared to outdo the Rocket Boys, ready to dig deep and find solutions to the pressing crises of our day. This is no time to fall short of the mark.

Start today:

- Believe in the innate capacity of every student scientist who enters your classroom.
- Maintain and model high standards for scientific thinking and understanding.
- Support every student in achieving those standards with workshop model instruction and assessment for learning.

How?

My hope is that the information and examples in this book prepare and inspire you to dig a little deeper. As you get started on this journey, I suggest several things.

- Pick one thing to work on at a time. Even though it may be just one small thing, it is likely to have a domino effect and influence many aspects of your teaching.
- Find colleagues who share your interest in improving science instruction. Meet regularly to support one another: visit one another's classrooms, plan together, create an action research group, study a professional text.
- Keep the faith. Trust your students. Trust yourself.

Change takes time. Celebrate even your small successes, and build on those.

"Yah, but," you may still say, and you would not be alone. I had the opportunity to attend an education roundtable discussion held in conjunction with the 2008 Democratic National Convention taking place in my city. I listened as national leaders in the field discussed the need for improvement in our public schools. Low standards, poorly designed tests, funding shortages, ill-prepared teachers, bureaucracy, lack of parent involvement, changing student populations, shortages of classroom technology—all of these were cited as impediments to progress. You may see these concerns in your school as well.

In spite of all of these, the truth remains that each of us has an opportunity to positively impact the lives of our students. Take heart in the words of our 44th President, Barack Obama:

> We know that from the moment our children step into a classroom, the single most important factor in determining their achievement is not the color of their skin or where they come from; it's not who their parents are or how much money they have. It's who their teacher is. It's the man or woman who stays past the last bell and spends their own money on books and supplies. It's people like my sister who go beyond the call of duty because she believes that's what makes the extra difference. And it does. (Obama 2007)

Every day you teach is a gift to our children. Thank you for your good work. Do what you can. Do better.

Yet each of us has the power to control our own attitudes and behavior. We do not need anyone's permission to take our students seriously as scientists. They deserve it.

Do what you can. Do better.

Resources

I made this list imagining that I could give you one milk crate full of books to tote throughout your teaching adventures. This list is by no means an exhaustive collection of everything you ought to get your hands on, but these are some cornerstones to help you build an exemplary teaching practice.

General Best Practice

Hill, Jane D., and Kathleen M. Flynn. 2006. *Classroom Instruction That Works for English Language Learners.* Alexandria, VA: Association for Supervision and Curriculum Development.

This is a practical guide to integrating research-based, best-practice instruction serving linguistically diverse students.

Marzano, Robert J., Debra Pickering, and Jane E. Pollack. 2001. *Classroom Instruction That Works: Research-Based Strategies for Increasing Student Achievement.* Alexandria, VA: Association for Supervision and Curriculum Development.

Clear explanations and practical guides for implementing research-based, effective instructional practices for all content areas.

Tomlinson, Carol Ann, and Jay McTighe. 2006. *Integrating Differentiated Instruction and Understanding by Design.* Alexandria, VA: Association for Supervision and Curriculum Development.

Presents a framework for planning, teaching for understanding, and assessment in diverse classrooms.

Wiggins, Grant, and Jay McTighe. 2005. *Understanding by Design: The Expanded Second Edition*. Alexandria, VA: Association for Supervision and Curriculum Development.

This book is a terrific toolkit for planning high-quality, in-depth studies that culminate in student understanding.

Wolk, Steven. 2002. *Being Good: Rethinking Classroom Management and Student Discipline*. Portsmouth, NH: Heinemann.

This book reinforces and offers practical suggestions related to many of the ideas presented in Chapter 5 about creating community in your classroom.

Wormeli, Rick. 2006. *Fair Isn't Always Equal: Assessing and Grading in the Differentiated Classroom.* Portland, ME: Stenhouse.

Practical and insightful guide to differentiation, from planning to grading and assessment.

Science-Specific Teacher Resources

American Association for the Advancement of Science. 1990. *Science for All Americans.* New York: Oxford University Press.

This text gives a detailed and thorough overview of the content of science and illustrates how different disciplines interconnect and overlap.

Brinkerhoff, Richard F. 1992. *One Minute Readings: Issues in Science, Technology, and Society.* New York: Addison-Wesley.

These brief readings serve as wonderful starting points for discussions relating science content studies to social and ethical issues.

Fathman, Ann K., and David T. Crowther. 2006. *Science for English Language Learners.* Arlington, VA: National Science Teachers'Association Press.

Presents useful, practical strategies to support students of all language backgrounds in science success.

National Research Council. 2000. *Inquiry and the National Science Education Standards.* Washington, DC: National Academy Press.

This primer offers material for teachers, coaches, and administrators ready to pursue inquiry-based instruction.

National Research Council. 2005. *How Students Learn Science in the Classroom.* Washington, DC: National Academy Press.

Edited volume demonstrates how to address students' preconceptions, model inquiry, and use metacognition to advance science learning.

Discipline-Specific Favorites

Depending upon what science content areas you teach, here are just a couple of things you might add to your collection of resources.

Biology

British Broadcasting Corporation. 2006. *Planet Earth.* Narrated by Sir David Attenborough. DVD.A BBC–Discovery Channel Co-production. BBC Warner.

Five DVDs of incredible footage depicting interactions between the unique species in all biomes on Earth.

Kingsolver, Barbara. 2002. *Small Wonder: Essays.* New York: HarperCollins.

A biologist and novelist, Kingsolver explains and reflects on the wonder of nature in practical and meaningful ways.

Sis, Peter. 2003. *The Tree of Life.* New York: Farrar, Straus and Giroux.

Beautifully illustrated, magically detailed biography of Charles Darwin for young readers.

Chemistry

American Chemical Society. 2006. *Chemistry in the Community*, Fifth edition. New York: Bedford, Freeman & Worth.

High school level textbook and curriculum on conceptual chemistry designed to link chemistry to societal, environmental, and health issues.

Lehrer, Tom. [1959] 1990. "The Elements." *An Evening Wasted with Tom Lehrer*. Audio CD. Reprise/Wea.

Humorist puts the names of the chemical elements to the tune of "Major General's Song" from *The Pirates of Penzance.*

Earth Science

Bryson, Bill. 2003. *A Short History of Nearly Everything.* New York: Broadway Books.

An accessible survey of Earth's history from the Big Bang to the modern day. Includes forays into chemistry and physics, as well as a range of geology topics.

Johnson, Kirk, and Ray Troll. 2007. *Cruisin' the Fossil Freeway: An Epoch Tale of a Scientist and an Artist on the Ultimate 5,000 Mile Paleo Roadtrip.* Golden, CO: Fulcrum Publishing.

A wonderful and unique illustrated adventure through the geologic and prehistoric riches of the western United States.

Environmental Studies

Kingsolver, Barbara. 2007. *Animal, Vegetable, Miracle.* New York: HarperCollins.

Autobiographical telling of a family's year living—as much as possible—off the land, and the reasons why we all should consume closer to home.

Lyons, Dana, and John Seed. [1990] 2004. *At Night They Howl at the Moon: Environmental Songs for Kids*. Audio CD. Reigning Records.

Catchy tunes with eco-friendly messages.

Physics

Feynman, Richard. 1999. *The Pleasure of Finding Things Out.* New York: Perseus Publishing.

Interviews, articles, and speeches by the brilliant scientist himself.

Hakim, Joy. 2004. *The Story of Science.* 3 vols. Washington, DC: Smithsonian Books.

By the renowned author of *A History of Us*, these three books written for adolescent readers survey the history of physical sciences in intriguing detail with wonderful graphics.

Space Science

Hakim, Joy. 2004. *The Story of Science.* 3 vols. Washington, DC: Smithsonian Books. (described above.)

Sis, Peter. 1997. *Starry Messenger.* New York: Farrar, Straus & Giroux.
Gloriously illustrated biography of Galileo Galilei.

Some Sources for Science Current Events and High-Interest Texts About Science

National Public Radio: "Science Friday."
www.sciencefriday.com/

Podcasts and videos of current science news. May be more appropriate for teacher consumption, depending on your students.

The New Scientist
www.newscientist.com/home.ns

Weekly journal available online or in print. Cornucopia of current science discoveries and events in brief, readable articles.

New York Times: "Science" Section
www.nytimes.com/pages/science

Current events in science in well-written prose.

Science Daily
www.sciencedaily.com/

Another wonderful source for up-to-the-minute research about current science issues.

References

Allen, Patrick. 2009. *Conferring Keystones.* Portland, ME: Stenhouse.

American Association for the Advancement of Science. 1990. *Science for All Americans.* New York: Oxford University Press.

Barton, Angela Calabrese. 2003. *Teaching Science for Social Justice.* New York: Teachers' College Press.

Bennett, Samantha. 2008. *That Workshop Book.* Portsmouth, NH: Heinemann.

Berger, Ron. 1996. *A Culture of Quality: A Reflection on Practice*. Providence, RI: Annenberg Institute of School Reform.

Braund, Martin, and Michael Reiss. 2006. "Towards a More Authentic Science Curriculum." *International Journal of Science Education* 28 (12): 1373–88.

Brinkerhoff, Richard F. 1992. *One Minute Readings: Issues in Science, Technology, and Society.* New York: Addison-Wesley.

Bybee, Rodger W., C. Edward Buchwald, Sally Crissman, David Heil, Paul. J. Kuerbis, Carolee Matsumoto, and Joseph D. McInerney. 1990. *Science and Technology Education for the Middle Years: Frameworks for Curriculum and Instruction.* Washington, DC: National Center for Improving Science Education.

California Science Curriculum Framework and Criteria Committee. 1990. *Science Framework for California Public Schools.* Sacramento: California Department of Education.

Cameron, Lisa, and Margaret Thorsborne. 2001. "Restorative Justice and School Discipline." In *Restorative Justice and Civil Society*, eds. H. Strang and J. Braithwaite, 27–34. New York: Cambridge University Press.

Colorado Department of Education. 2007. "Colorado Model Content Standards." www.cde.state.co.us/coloradoscience/Science_Standards_July_2007.pdf

Daniels, Harvey, and Steven Zemelman. 2004. *Subjects Matter*. Portsmouth, NH: Heinemann.

Donovan, Suzanne, and John D. Brandsford, eds. 2005. *How Students Learn Science in the Classroom*. Washington, DC: National Academies Press.

Graves, Donald. 1983. *Writing: Teachers and Children at Work*. Portsmouth, NH: Heinemann.

Greene, Brian. 2008. "Put a Little Science in Your Life." *New York Times*, June 1. www.nytimes.com/2008/06/01/opinion/01greene.html

Harvard–Smithsonian Center for Astrophysics. 1987. *A Private Universe*. VHS. S. Burlington, VT: Annenberg/CPB. Merrill Education Products.

Healy, Jane M. 1990. *Endangered Minds: Why Our Children Don't Think and What We Can Do About It*. New York: Simon and Schuster.

Hill, Jane D., and Kathleen M. Flynn. 2006. *Classroom Instruction That Works for English Language Learners*. Alexandria, VA: Association for Supervision and Curriculum Development.

Hoffman, Lee, and Jennifer Sable. 2006. *Public Elementary and Secondary Students, Staff, Schools and School Districts: School Year 2003–2004*. Washington, DC: National Center for Educational Statistics.

Ibarra, Hector. 2006. "Teach Them to Fish." In *Exemplary Science in Grades 5–8: Standards-Based Success Stories*, 69–84. Arlington, VA: National Science Teachers' Association Press.

Keene, Ellin O., and Susan Zimmermann. 2007. *Mosaic of Thought: The Power of Comprehension Strategy Instruction*, 2d ed. Portsmouth, NH: Heinemann.

Marzano, Robert J. 2005. "What Works in Schools" [PowerPoint presentation]. www.maranoandassociates.com/pdf/Shortversion.pdf

Marzano, Robert J., Debra Pickering, and Jane E. Pollack. 2001. *Classroom Instruction That Works: Research-Based Strategies for Increasing Student Achievement*. Alexandria, VA: Association for Supervision and Curriculum Development.

Matthews, Christine M. 2007. *Foreign Science and Engineering Presence in U.S. Institutions and the Labor Force*. Washington, DC: Congressional Research Service.

McDonald, Joseph P., Nancy Mohr, Alan Dichter, and Elizabeth C. McDonald. 2003. *The Power of Protocols: An Educator's Guide to Better Practice*. New York: Teachers College Press.

McTighe, Jay, and Grant Wiggins. 2000. *Understanding by Design*. Alexandria, VA: Association for Supervision and Curriculum Development.

National Center for Educational Statistics. 2008. *Highlights from PISA: Performance of U.S. 15-Year-Old Students in Science and Mathematics Literacy*. Washington, DC: U.S. Department of Education.

National Research Council. 1996. *National Science Education Standards*. Washington, DC: National Academy Press.

———. 2000. *Inquiry and the National Science Education Standards*. Washington, DC: National Academy Press.

———. 2004. *How People Learn*. Washington, DC: National Academy Press.

———. 2005. *How Students Learn Science in the Classroom.* Washington, DC: National Academy Press.

Obama, Barack. 2007. "Our Kids, Our Future." Remarks from a speech given in Manchester, NH, on November 20. Available at www.barackobama.com/2007/11/20/remarks_of_senator_barack_obam_34.php.

Pearson, David, and M. C. Gallagher. 1983. "The Instruction of Reading Comprehension." *Contemporary Educational Psychology* 8: 317–44.

Perkins, David. 1998. "What Is Understanding?" In *Teaching for Understanding,* ed. Martha Stone Wiske, 39–57. San Francisco: Jossey-Bass.

Reardon, Jeanne. 2004. "Readers Are Scientists: A Reflective Exploration of the Reasoning of Young Scientists, Readers, Writers, and Discussants." In *Crossing Borders in Literacy and Science Instruction,* ed. Wendy Saul, 209–24. Arlington, VA: National Science Teachers' Association Press.

Sapon-Shevin, Mara. 1999. *Because We Can Change the World.* Boston: Allyn Bacon.

Seager, Joni, Clark Reed, and Peter Stottt. 2004. *The New State of the Earth Atlas: A Concise Survey of the Environment Through Full-Color International Maps.* New York: Touchstone Books/Simon & Schuster.

Stiggins, Richard J. 1997. *Student-Centered Classroom Assessment,* 2d ed. Columbus, OH: Merrill.

Tomlinson, Carol Ann, and Susan Demirsky Allan. 2000. *Leadership for Differentiating Schools & Classrooms.* Alexandria, VA: Association for Supervision and Curriculum Development.

Tomlinson, Carol Ann, and Jay McTighe. 2006. *Integrating Differentiated Instruction and Understanding by Design.* Alexandria, VA: Association for Supervision and Curriculum Development.

Tovani, Cris. 2004. *Do I Really Have to Teach Reading? Content Comprehension, Grades 6–12.* Portland, ME: Stenhouse.

Wiggins, Grant, and Jay McTighe. 2005. *Understanding by Design: The Expanded Second Edition.* Alexandria, VA: Association for Supervision and Curriculum Development.

Williams, Jack. 1992. "93% of Adults Are Illiterate Scientifically." *San Diego Union-Tribune,* September 2, C-1.

Wood, D., J. Bruner, and G. Ross. 1976. "The Role of Tutoring in Problem Solving." *Journal of Child Psychology and Psychiatry* 17: 89–100.

Wormeli, Rick. 2006. *Fair Isn't Always Equal.* Portland, ME: Stenhouse.

Yero, Judith Lloyd. 2002. *Teaching in Mind: How Teacher Thinking Shapes Education.* Hamilton, MT: Mindflight.

Zemelman, Steven, Harvey Daniels, and Arthur Hyde. 2005. *Best Practice: New Standards for Teaching and Learning in American Schools,* 3d ed. Portsmouth, NH: Heinemann.

Index